The Rise of Intelligence and Culture

Life in the Universe Series

The Rise of Intelligence and Culture

SETI Academy Planet Project

SETI INSTITUTE

1995

TEACHER IDEAS PRESS
A Division of
Libraries Unlimited, Inc.
Englewood, Colorado

TEACHER IDEAS PRESS
A Division of Libraries Unlimited, Inc.
P.O. Box 6633
Englewood, CO 80155-6633
1-800-237-6124

Series Production Editor: Kevin W. Perizzolo
Series Copy Editor: Jason Cook
Series Proofreader: Ann Marie Damian
Series Typesetting and Interior Design: Judy Gay Matthews

Library of Congress Cataloging-in-Publication Data

The rise of intelligence and culture : SETI academy planet project /
SETI Institute.
    xxvii, 277p. 22x28 cm. -- (Life in the universe series)
    Includes bibliographical references.
    ISBN 1-56308-326-4
    1. Life on other planets--Study and teaching (Elementary).
2. Life on other planets--Study and teaching (Elementary)--Activity
programs. 3. Civilization--Extraterrestrial influences--Study and
teaching (Elementary) I. SETI Institute. II. Series.
QB54.R48   1995
372.3'5--dc20   95-6871
                                                              CIP

Contents

Scope and Sequence
Life in the Universe Curriculum

This scope and sequence is designed to describe the topics presented and the skills practiced in the Life in the Universe series curriculum as they relate to factors in the Drake Equation: $N = R_* \bullet f_p \bullet n_e \bullet f_l \bullet f_i \bullet f_c \bullet L$. In this equation, N is an estimate of the number of detectable civilizations in the Milky Way Galaxy that have developed the ability to communicate over interstellar distances. If a civilization has such an ability, it most probably arose from the *desire* to communicate. It follows that such a civilization is probably trying to communicate, just as we are trying. This was the rationale for formulating the Drake Equation, and this is the rationale for the search for extraterrestrial life.

Factors in the Drake Equation	Related Topics
R_* = the number of new stars suitable for the origin and evolution of intelligent life that are formed in the Milky Way Galaxy each year	*Astronomy, Chemistry, Mathematics*
f_p = the fraction of these stars that are formed with planetary systems	*Astronomy, Mathematics, Physics*
n_e = the average number of planets in each such system that can sustain life	*Astronomy, Biology, Chemistry, Ecology, Physics*
f_l = the fraction of such planets on which life actually begins	*Astronomy, Biology, Chemistry, Ecology, Geology, Meteorology*
f_i = the fraction of life-sustaining planets on which intelligent life evolves	*Anthropology, Biology, Geology, Meteorology, Paleontology*
f_c = the fraction of systems of intelligent creatures that develop the technological means and the will to communicate over interstellar distances	*Language Arts, Mathematics, Physics, Social Sciences*
L = the average lifetime of such civilizations in a detectable state	*Astronomy, History, Mathematics, Paleontology, Social Sciences*

Life in the Universe Series	Topics	Skills
Grades 3-4 *The Science Detectives*	• Art • Astronomy • Chemistry • Language Arts • Mathematics • Physics	• Attribute Recognition • Cooperative Learning • Mapping • Measurement • Problem Solving • Scientific Process
Grades 5-6 *The Evolution of a Planetary System*	• Art • Astronomy • Biology • Ecology • Geography • Geology • Language Arts • Mathematics • Meteorology • Social Sciences	• Problem Solving • Cooperative Learning • Scientific Process • Mapping • Measurement • Inductive Reasoning • Graphing
Grades 5-6 *How Might Life Evolve on Other Worlds?*	• Art • Biology • Chemistry • Ecology • Language Arts • Mathematics • Paleontology • Social Sciences	• Classification • Inductive Reasoning • Laboratory Technique • Mapping • Microscope Use • Scientific Process • Cooperative Learning
Grades 5-6 *The Rise of Intelligence and Culture*	• Anthropology • Art • Biology • Ecology • Geography • Geology • Language Arts • Mathematics • Social Sciences • Zoology	• Creative Writing • Graphing • Laboratory Technique • Mapping • Problem Solving • Cooperative Learning
Grades 7-8 *Life: Here? There? Elsewhere? The Search for Life on Venus and Mars*	• Art • Astronomy • Biology • Chemistry • Comparative Planetology • Ecology • Engineering • Language Arts • Mathematics • Physics • Zoology	• Cooperative Learning • Design • Graphing • Inductive Reasoning • Laboratory Technique • Microscope Use • Problem Solving • Scientific Process
Grades 8-9 *Project Haystack: The Search for Life in the Galaxy*	• Anthropology • Art • Astronomy • Biology • Chemistry • Ecology • Geometry • Language Arts • Mathematics • Physics • Trigonometry • Zoology	• Cooperative Learning • Design • Graphing • Inductive Reasoning • Laboratory Technique • Microscope Use • Problem Solving • Scientific Process

Foreword

Carl Sagan, Cornell University

The possibility of life on other worlds is one of enormous fascination—and properly so. The fact that it's such a persistent and popular theme in books, television, motion pictures, and computer programs must tell us something. But extraterrestrial life has not yet been found—not in the real world, anyway. Through spacecraft to other planets and large radio telescopes to see if anyone is sending us a message, the human species is just beginning a serious search.

To understand the prospects, you need to understand something about the evolution of stars, the number and distribution of stars, whether other stars have planets, what planetary environments are like and which ones are congenial for life. Also required are an understanding of the chemistry of organic matter—the stuff of life, at least on this world; laboratory simulations of how organic molecules were made in the early history of Earth and on other worlds; and the chemistry of life on Earth and what it can tell us about the origins of life. Include as well the fossil record and the evolutionary process; how humans first evolved; and the events that led to our present technological civilization—without which we'd have no chance at all of understanding and little chance of detecting extraterrestrial life. Every time I make such a list, I'm impressed about how many different sciences are relevant to the search for extraterrestrial life.

All of this implies that extraterrestrial life is an excellent way of teaching science. There's a built-in interest, encouraged by the vast engine of the media, and there's a way to use the subject to approach virtually any scientific topic, especially many of the most fundamental ones. In 1966, the Soviet astrophysicist I. S. Shklovskii and I published a book called *Intelligent Life in the Universe,* which we thought of as an introduction to the subject for a general audience. What surprised me was how many college courses in science found the book useful. Since then, there have been many books on the subject, but none really designed for school curricula.

These course guides on life in the universe fill that need. I wish my children were being taught this curriculum in school. I enthusiastically recommend them.

Preface

Are we alone in the Milky Way Galaxy? Many people think of science fiction stories or tabloid reports about UFO abductions when they hear about the search for intelligent life on other planets. The reality is that many scientists take seriously the possibility of life on other worlds, and some have undertaken the difficult task of finding out if we are the only intelligent beings in our galaxy. Astronomer Frank Drake proposed an equation to estimate the number of civilizations in our galaxy that produce radio waves. We might be able to detect such civilizations with our radio telescopes. The Drake Equation estimates this number using the answers to the following sequence of questions:

1. How many stars are formed in the Milky Way Galaxy each year?

2. What fraction of stars are similar to our Sun?

3. What fraction of stars are formed with a planetary system?

4. What is the average number of planets in such a system?

5. What fraction of planets are like Earth, capable of sustaining life?

6. On what fraction of these planets does life actually begin?

7. On what fraction of life-sustaining planets does life evolve into intelligent civilizations?

8. What fraction of intelligent civilizations develop radio technology?

9. What is the average lifetime of a radio-transmitting civilization?

Scientists pursuing these questions work in many fields, including astronomy, geology, biology, anthropology, and the history of science. Several projects to "listen" for radio signals produced by civilizations on distant planets have been conducted. The most ambitious of these has been undertaken by the research staff at the SETI Institute (Search for Extraterrestrial Intelligence), at first in cooperation with NASA and later using privately donated funds. The SETI team is listening for intelligent signals. The interdisciplinary makeup and highly motivational nature of the search for intelligent life prompted the NSF (National Science Foundation) to support the development of the Life in the Universe Curriculum Project. Designed by curriculum developers working with teachers and NASA and SETI scientists, this program reflects the real-life methods of science: making observations, performing experiments, building models, conducting simulations, changing previous ideas on the basis of new data, and using imagination. It brings into the classroom the excitement of searching for life beyond Earth. This search is a unifying theme that can unleash the imagination of students through integrated lessons in the physical, life, space, and social sciences.

The *SETI Academy Planet Project* consists of three books, each of which is a teacher's guide for grades 5-6. *The Evolution of a Planetary System* examines an important aspect of the search for intelligent life: the evolution of stars and planets. Students visualize how our Sun and its family of nine planets have formed and evolved into the solar system we know today. By applying what they have learned about the evolution of Earth, students imagine how planets might have formed around other stars, how individual planets might have evolved through similar processes, and what such planets might look like today. They explore how Earth has changed over time, how tectonic forces deep inside our planet brought about these changes, and how geographic locations and geologic landforms influence climate. Students use the results of their research to design planetary systems that contain habitable planets, "evolve" individual planets into life-sustaining worlds, and create continental and climate maps of their planets.

How Might Life Evolve on Other Worlds? focuses on the vast expanses of time during which plant and animal life evolved on Earth. Students participate in a series of multidisciplinary activities to analyze the origin and evolution of life on Earth. Students discover that life evolved through interaction with the environment and that some life evolved from simple to complex forms. By applying what they have learned about the evolution of life-forms on Earth, students imagine realistic scenarios for how life might evolve on another planet.

The Rise of Intelligence and Culture emphasizes how intelligence and culture helped humans to form a civilization that now has the technology to detect and communicate with possible extraterrestrial civilizations. Students learn about indications and characteristics of intelligence, about the evolutionary increase in the size of the human brain, about survival needs, and about the stages of human culture. They examine the possibility of sending messages through space and the social issues related to the search for extraterrestrial intelligence. By applying what they have learned, students contemplate how an extraterrestrial civilization might have evolved.

The *SETI Academy Planet Project* provides an exciting, informative, and creative series of activities for elementary students, grades 5-6. In these activities, each student plays the role of a cadet at the SETI Academy, a fictitious institution. Each book of the *SETI Academy Planet Project* is designed to be a complete unit in itself as well as a subunit of a three-unit course. The use of these guides rests with each teacher.

Curriculum Development Team

Principal Investigator:	Dr. Jill Tarter, SETI Institute, Mountain View, CA
Project Director:	Dr. David Milne, Evergreen State College, Olympia, WA
Project Evaluator:	Dr. Kathleen A. O'Sullivan, San Francisco State University
Curriculum Development Manager:	Cara Stoneburner, SETI Institute
Editor:	Emily Theobald, SETI Institute
	Victoria Johnson, SETI Institute, San Jose State University, CA
Contributing Authors:	Kevin Beals, Lawrence Hall of Science, Berkeley, CA Mary Chafe-Powles, Woodside Elementary School, Concord, CA Lisa Dettloff, Lawrence Hall of Science Alan Hewitt, Lawrence Hall of Science Victoria Johnson, SETI Institute Betty Merritt, Longfellow Intermediate School, Berkeley, CA Dr. David Milne, Evergreen State College Dr. Cary Sneider, Lawrence Hall of Science Cara Stoneburner, SETI Institute Emily Theobald, SETI Institute Lisa Walenceus, Lawrence Hall of Science
AV Consultants:	Jon Lomberg, Honaunau, HI Dr. Seth Shostak, SETI Institute
Research Assistants:	Winslow Burleson, SETI Institute Amy Barr, student at Palo Alto High School, CA Lisa Chen, student at Palo Alto High School, CA Ladan Malek, San Lorenzo High School, CA
Evaluator:	Jennifer Harris, Educational Consultant, Redwood Valley, CA
Artist:	Stuart Timmons, Los Angeles
Poster:	Jon Lomberg, Honaunau, HI
Advisory Board:	Tom Pierson, SETI Institute Dr. Peter Backus, SETI Institute Edna K. DeVore, SETI Institute Dr. Gilbert Yanow, Jet Propulsion Laboratory, Pasadena, CA

Acknowledgments

Development and publication of the Life in the Universe series was made possible by grants from the National Science Foundation (grant #MDR-9510120) and the National Aeronautics and Space Administration. This support does not imply responsibility for statements or views expressed in this publication.

Field Test Teachers

Teacher	School
Marsha Barden	Seminary Hill School, West Lebanon, NH
Helen Campos-Sanchez	Carroll Bell Elementary School, San Antonio, TX
Kathy Chinn Chock	Lunalilo Elementary School, Honolulu, HI
Fred Donaldson	Carroll Bell Elementary School, San Antonio, TX
Carol Gison	Walker Elementary School, San Diego, CA
Rene Kimura	Hongwanji Mission School, Honolulu, HI
Henry Klein	Suisun Valley School, Suisun City, CA
Karen F. Madsen	Monterey Hills School, South Pasadena, CA
Fran Marshack	Foothill Elementary School, Pittsburg, CA
Christine M. Olfelt	Blessed Sacrament School, St. Paul, MN
Ruth M. Ruud	Walnut Creek Middle School, Fairview, PA
Angela Shane	Juarez-Lincoln Elementary School, San Diego, CA
Cynthia Wilkie	Seminary Hill School, West Lebanon, NH
Jim Zimmerman	Thomas Paine School, Urbana, IL

Science Reviewers

Content Reviewed	Science Reviewer Affiliation
Mission 1: The Rise of Human Intelligence	None (no science content)
Mission 2: Human Physical Traits and Behaviors	Dr. Lori Marino—Emory University, Atlanta, GA
Mission 3: Physical Traits and Behaviors of Earth Animals	Dr. Lori Marino—Emory University, Atlanta, GA
Mission 4: Cranial Changes	Dr. Lori Marino—Emory University, Atlanta, GA
Mission 5: Early Earth Cultures	Dr. Robert Wharton—Desert Research Institute, Reno, NV
Mission 6: Meet Planet Z	Dr. Robert Wharton—Desert Research Institute
Mission 7: Intelligent Life on Planet Z	Dr. Dean Falk—State University of New York, Albany
Mission 8: Cultures Evolve on Planet Z	Dr. Dean Falk—State University of New York, Albany
Mission 9: Extraterrestrial Communication	Dr. Mike Klein—Jet Propulsion Laboratory, Pasadena, CA
Mission 10: Decoding an Extraterrestrial Message	Dr. Frank Drake—SETI Institute, Mountain View, CA
Mission 11: What Do We Say, and How Do We Say It?	Jon Lomberg—Honaunau, HI; Dr. Frank Drake—SETI Institute
Mission 12: Detection	Bob Arnold—Ames Research Center, Moffett Field, CA
Mission 13: Mission Completed!	None (no science content)

Special Acknowledgments

The SETI Institute Life in the Universe team thanks the following people for their help, inspiration, insights, support, and ideas contributed over the three-year period during which this project was conducted.

Bob Arnold	Pam Bacon	Bernadine Barr	John Billingham
Linda Billings	Dave Brocker	Vera Buescher	Dawn Charles
David Chen	Tom Clausen	Gary Coulter	Kent Cullers
Seth DeLackner	Edna DeVore	Laurence Doyle	Frank Drake
Alice Foster	Friedmann Freund	Tom Gates	Janel Griewing
Sam Gulkis	Bud Hill	Wendy Horton	Garth Hull
Don Humphreys	Mike Klein	Carol Langbort	Steve Levin
Ivo Lindauer	Kathleen Marzano	Michelle Murray	Chris Neller
Barney Oliver	Ed Olsen	Frank Owens	Ray Reams
Don Reynolds	Hal Roey	Carol Stadum	

Introduction

Learning Objectives

Concepts

Through the activities in this book, students will learn about and be able to apply concepts in the following areas:

- Humans have many characteristics that help define them as intelligent beings.

- Human intelligence allowed us to develop many different cultures, which vary in their use of technology.

- SETI means the Search for Extraterrestrial Intelligence. The SETI Institute in Mountain View, California, is one place that is organizing this search. SETI technology looks for radio waves, so it would only detect a culture that uses radio technology.

- Certain characteristics indicate some organisms are intelligent.

- Some animals have physical behaviors that are similar to the traits that early humans used to develop cultures. These traits include: stereoscopic vision, varied diet, upright mobility, grasping appendage, a high brain to body ratio, communication, learning, building shelters, adapting to changing situations, social group skills, and tool use.

- The size of the hominid brain has increased over the past several million years; the size of an organism's braincase indicates a general level of intelligence.

- Humans have used natural resources to survive in most terrestrial habitats on Earth; some habitats are more hospitable than others.

- All species evolve physical traits that are adaptations to their specific habitat. This is physical or biologic evolution.

- Biomes are large geographic areas that share a type of climate, with average temperatures and rainfall, so they provide similar habitats.

- Cultures may be classified in "phases" according to the amount of technology they have developed; cultures do not all develop in the same way, at the same rate. An extraterrestrial culture might develop in many possible ways.

- Physically traveling to another solar system in a spacecraft would not be practical, since it would take many human lifetimes using currently available technology, but an ET may send a message by radio. This message might contain information based upon the laws of mathematics and the laws of physics, which will be the same for us and for any extraterrestrial cultures.

- Announcement by SETI scientists regarding the reception of an intelligent extraterrestrial radio signal will undoubtedly affect all the cultures on Earth.

Skills

The activities are also designed to help students develop the following abilities:

- Working in teams and alone.

- Critical thinking.

- Visualizing.

- Drawing.

- Comparing and contrasting.

- Identifying and discussing characteristics.

- Analyzing characteristics of intelligence.

- Analyzing traits and abilities.

- Analyzing habitats for resources.

- Determining human survival needs.

- Distinguishing biologic evolution from cultural evolution.

- Analyzing characteristics of culture.

- Analyzing fictional life-forms for traits that may indicate intelligence, and therefore their potential for technology.

- Reading and analyzing maps.

- Using a globe to identify biomes.

- Making decisions.

- Building models.

- Applying mathematics to real life.

- Using the metric system.

- Graphing.

- Using fractions.

- Using simple ratios.

- Understanding large numbers: million, billion.

- Recognizing prime numbers.

- Compiling and using a matrix.

- Recognizing patterns.

- Decoding messages.

- Comparing and contrasting messages.

- Interpreting and sending messages.

Timeline and Planning Guide

The following time estimates are based on feedback from teachers during trial tests. They do not include time required to read this guide or shop for materials. Actual times will depend on the particular group of students and the time spent extending these activities. Some missions will need to be taught over several class periods, and some may take longer the first time they are presented. Each mission subdivision is designed to take one class period. Teachers may want to take two or even three class periods with some mission subdivisions.

Mission 1: The Rise of Human Intelligence

Mission 1.1: Students write and draw what they already know about intelligence, culture, and interstellar communication.

Mission 1.2: Students answer questions to investigate how they developed their own traits and behaviors.

Mission 2: Human Physical Traits and Behaviors

Mission 2.1: Students study their stereoscopic vision, their opposable thumbs, and their ability to cooperate through simple lab activities.

Mission 3: Physical Traits and Behaviors of Earth Animals

Mission 3.1: Students work as a class, with the teacher's direction, to compile a matrix about physical attributes and behaviors that might indicate intelligence.

Mission 3.2: Students fill in the matrix for an assortment of Earth animals and then select the one animal that is the most intelligent—and therefore "Most Likely to Succeed" in the future. They discuss and define *intelligence* as it relates to Earth animals.

Mission 4: Cranial Changes

Mission 4.1: Students compare and contrast pictures of four skulls, from different time periods in hominid evolution, and measure the area of each skull cross section.

Mission 4.2: Students graph their data and then use these graphs to project approximate skull sizes for hominids of other periods, assuming a gradual, linear increase. Finally, they consider the ratios of brain weight to body weight for these fossil hominids.

Mission 5: Early Earth Cultures

Mission 5.1: Students determine areas on Earth where people have lived and then compile a list of human survival needs.

Mission 5.2: Students view transparencies about early Earth cultures and examine how those cultures survived in their specific environments.

Mission 5.3: Students review the transparencies or black-line masters to see how both biologic evolution and cultural evolution allowed early humans to adapt to their specific habitats.

Mission 6: Meet Planet Z

Mission 6.1: Students investigate biomes on a globe of Earth and then observe Planet Z to identify several alien environments that might support intelligent life. Students color biomes on Planet Z landmasses and arrange them on a global map.

Mission 6.2: Students color habitat pictures and find their proper Planet Z biomes.

Mission 7: Intelligent Life on Planet Z

Mission 7.1: Students analyze some fictional extraterrestrial life-forms for their habitats and biomes.

Mission 7.2: Students use a matrix to identify the physical traits and behaviors that might be indicative of intelligence.

Mission 7.3: The extraterrestrial life-form found to have the most traits and behaviors of intelligence is artificially developed by student teams to make it more capable of producing cultures specific to its habitat or habitats.

Mission 8: Cultures Evolve on Planet Z

Mission 8.1: Students create intelligent cultures on Planet Z and observe how these cultures change or do not change over time. Students work in teams to create eight fictional cultures for Planet Z using specified guidelines.

Mission 8.2: Planet Z's cultures evolve on separate landmasses in different climates, along lines similar to cultural evolution on Earth, as students play a game to simulate the cultural evolution of each fictional culture.

Mission 8.3: Students continue to simulate cultural evolution, observing how ocean trade affects the development of culture.

Mission 8.4: Students finish their simulation and analyze the development of culture.

Mission 9: Extraterrestrial Communication

Mission 9.1: Students consider different methods of communication on Earth and in space. They discuss and analyze different methods of communicating in space.

Mission 9.2: Students build a model that represents two methods of interstellar communication and then decide which method is the most practical for communicating with extraterrestrial life-forms.

Mission 10: Decoding an Extraterrestrial Message

Mission 10.1: Students hear a sample message and discuss codes.

Mission 10.2: Students have a chance to decode a complex "practice" extraterrestrial message made by a SETI scientist.

Mission 11: What Do We Say, and How Do We Say It?

Mission 11.1: Students compare and contrast the "practice" extraterrestrial message with three actual messages sent into space by scientists from Earth.

Mission 11.2: Students decide what information about their Planet Z cultures would be appropriate to send into space, and prepare messages from Planet Z. Students form Planet Z culture teams and send their messages to other teams in the classroom. The messages are interpreted and responses are sent.

Mission 12: Detection: What Could Happen?

Mission 12.1: Students consider and discuss what should be done in the event that we do detect or make contact with an extraterrestrial civilization. Students write about what it would mean to Earthlings.

Mission 13: Mission Completed!

Mission 13.1: Students write and draw what they learned about the evolution of intelligence and culture, as well as what they learned about interstellar communication.

Preparation

SETI Institute and "SETI Academy"

The SETI Institute is a real scientific organization, but the SETI Academy is pure *fiction*. It is a device to increase student involvement in this material. The people who are listed in each mission as members of the "SETI Academy Team" are real scientists and science educators, but most of them have never met one another!

Assessment

The projects in this book are designed to help teachers assess students' learning and understanding. The planet maps that students create, along with their responses on worksheets, will reflect their grasp of concepts and skills presented in the lessons, experiments, and projects. Teachers can use student logbooks and the projects themselves to make portfolio-based assessments, and use evaluations of student participation to assign grades and provide appropriate feedback.

Planning

Classroom trials show that the activities in this book require about four weeks, if science is taught every day. Time spent on the *SETI Academy Planet Project* can be counted for credit in language arts and mathematics, because skills in these areas are emphasized alongside science skills.

In *The Rise of Intelligence and Culture*, students endow a given life-form with intelligent capabilities and evolve cultures for that life-form.

Each book of the *SETI Academy Planet Project* is based on the detailed study of life as it has evolved on Earth and on the scientific observation of our neighborhood in space. Each book contains an exciting, informative, and creative series of integrated science activities for upper elementary students.

Expanding or Compressing the Unit

If time is available, create a variety of activities to add richness to this unit, such as "star parties" and performing analyses of moon rocks, or activities that expand on concepts presented in each mission. There are ideas in the "Going Further" section at the end of each mission.

If short on time, consider cutting some of the activities considered less crucial to your class because of their background or previous experience.

SETI Academy Cadet Logbooks

Masters for "mission briefings," student worksheets, and student handouts, all of which should be included in student logbooks, are provided following the details of each mission. A master for the logbook cover is provided in mission 1, "The Rise of Human Intelligence." Also make a copy of the glossary (found at the end of this book) for each student logbook. Paper is a limited resource both environmentally and at some school sites, so the following options for reproducing the masters are included.

Option One

Ideally, it is best to make copies of each master and assemble them into packets, one for each student. This option really motivates students by allowing each their own SETI Academy Cadet Logbook. To do so involves reproducing about 50 pages.

The reproduction can be done using a two-sided copier, but note that some of the student logbook pages are consumable, so be sure to copy those particular pages one-sided. When reproducing pages for student logbooks, use three-hole-punched paper so students can keep their logbook papers in binders alongside other papers. Papers may be collated and handed out as complete logbooks or kept in folders to be handed out one or two sheets at a time as students are ready for new missions.

Option Two

Save on materials costs by producing one copy of the student logbook for every group of two or three students.

Option Three

For those schools that have a limited supply of paper, teachers might try making transparencies of the mission briefing masters and using them on an overhead projector. Save the transparencies and reuse them each year. Have students copy and answer the pre-activity "What Do You Think?" questions and the post-activity "What Do You Think, Now?" questions onto their own binder paper, which should be placed in their logbooks. Reproduce student worksheets and handouts from each mission and distribute them as needed.

Helpful Procedures

In a typical mission, a teacher will

- conduct a mission briefing and ask students to answer pre-activity "What Do You Think?" questions;

- conduct a lab experiment or simulation that gives students more information on the topic of discussion;

- help students use the results of the experiment or simulation to further consider the possibilities of extraterrestrial intelligence; and

- conduct a mission closure and ask students to answer post-activity "What Do You Think, Now?" questions.

Prerequisite Skills

To complete the activities in this guide, students will need to be able to do the following:

1. Follow written directions for a series of lab experiment steps after they have been demonstrated.

2. Begin to grasp "big" numbers: million, billion.

3. Compare models and simulations to real objects and processes.

4. Make measurements using meter sticks.

5. Place data on a graph that has been set up for them.

6. Follow a flowchart for a dice game. (Example: If you roll a 1, 2, or 3, go to section A; if you roll a 4, 5, or 6, go to section B.)

7. Label a diagram.

8. Most importantly, students must be able to *apply* what they learn about the evolution of culture on Earth to create a realistic imaginary extraterrestrial culture.

Cooperative Learning

The *SETI Academy Planet Project* is well suited to the use of cooperative learning teams. Each team can have a materials monitor, a recorder, a speaker, and so forth. Successful cooperative learning teams should have a mix of learning styles and be balanced in sex and ethnicity. It is best if teams last at least several class periods so students have a chance to work together long enough to get comfortable. If two or all three of the *Project* books will be taught, new teams can be formed for each unit so that students have opportunities to work with different peers.

Preparation of Special Materials

Transparencies

A set of beautiful color transparencies by artist Stuart Timmons may be purchased to accompany this program. Black-line masters are supplied in the appendix.

Bulletin Board

Student teams will produce colorful, creative materials throughout this unit. Teachers will want to display their work in the classroom. If possible, set aside one entire wall of the classroom for this purpose.

Mission 1

The Rise of Human Intelligence
Welcome Aboard!

Overview

What has allowed the human species to form civilizations? Humans have physical traits and behaviors that are adaptations to our unique niche on Earth. Students already have an intuitive sense about some of these traits and behaviors.

In mission 1.1, students write and draw what they already know about intelligence, culture, and interstellar communication. In mission 13, students will answer the same questions again. Compare their answers to assess how much they have learned. In mission 1.2, students answer questions to investigate how they developed their own traits and behaviors.

Concepts

- Humans have many characteristics that help define them as intelligent beings.

- Human intelligence allowed us to develop social behavior.

- Once social behavior evolves, a culture may develop.

- There are many different cultures on Earth.

- Cultures vary in their use of technology.

- Some cultures have developed the use of radio technology.

- SETI means the Search for Extraterrestrial Intelligence.

- Most SETI search projects look for radio waves, so they can only detect extraterrestrial cultures that use radio technology.

Skills

- Critical thinking.

- Drawing.

- Analyzing characteristics of intelligence.

Mission 1.1

Materials

For Each Student

- 2 sheets of blank paper

- (optional) Crayons, markers, and other drawing materials

- SETI Academy Cadet Logbook

- Pencil

Getting Ready

One or More Days Before Class

1. Review the "Teacher Background Information" for this mission in the appendixes.

2. Prepare student logbooks. (See "SETI Academy Cadet Logbooks," on page 7.)

Classroom Action

1. **Introduction.** Tell students about the SETI Academy Planet Project and their place in human history.

> "We all live on one planet, the Earth, which revolves around a star that we call the Sun. The Sun is only one of a half-trillion stars in a *very* large galaxy that we call the Milky Way. Our planet formed over 4.5 billion years ago. Scientific evidence suggests that simple life evolved about 3.8 billion years ago and human ancestors just 3 million years ago! Since then humans have evolved into the creatures (*Homo sapien*) we see all over the world today. Humans exhibit a variety of physical qualities and cultural adaptations."

> You may want to talk about large numbers: what do million and billion really mean?

You may want to do a brief mathematical exercise or game to show this.

2. Project **Briefing**. Have the class refer to the "Project Briefing" from Chief Scientist Jill Tarter in their student logbooks while one student reads it aloud.

3. **Discussion**. Allow time for students to express their thoughts about the "Project Briefing."

4. **Mission Briefing**. Have the class refer to the "Mission Briefing" for mission 1 in their student logbooks while one student reads it aloud.

5. **What Do You Think?** Have students answer the pre-activity questions on the "Mission Briefing." They will each need two blank sheets of paper.

6. **Discussion**. Invite students to share their drawings, ideas, and answers in a class discussion. Do not judge students' ideas as right or wrong at this point. They will be learning much more about these concepts and may even change their ideas several times by the end of this series of missions. Tell students that it is okay to change their ideas as they learn more; after all, that is what scientists do all the time.

Teacher's Note: *Students will tend to view the world from their own perspective. Introduce the concept that their way of life is one of many ways of life, that their culture is one of many cultures. Refer to any cultural awareness activities in your school or community.*

7. **Preview**. As homework, assign the logbook sheet "Some Qualities of Human Intelligence." Check for comprehension. This sheet should be completed before beginning mission 1.2.

Mission 1.2

Materials

For Each Student

- SETI Academy Cadet Logbook

- Pencil

Getting Ready

No preparation is necessary.

Classroom Action

1. **Introduction**. Explain to students that studying some of their own qualities of human intelligence is the first step to imagining how intelligent life might arise on other planets. During this part of the mission, students will be challenged to explain how their traits and behaviors are important to the formation of a civilization.

2. **Lecture**. On the chalkboard or on butcher paper, write definitions for *civilization, culture*, and *intelligence*. Tell students that these terms are very hard to define, and that they will be refining their concepts of these terms throughout the following missions. If butcher paper is used, hang it on a classroom wall so that the following definitions may be added to or changed throughout the missions.

    Intelligence: The ability to learn, to solve problems, and to adapt to changing situations, as opposed to instinct. Instinct is inflexible behavior caused by genetics. Instinct does not adapt to new situations—learning can.

    Culture: The customs, techniques, ideas, beliefs, language, equipment, skills, and arts of a given group of people in a given period.

    Civilization: The culture of a people, at a time when that people is considered to have reached a high level of social or technological development.

3. **Discussion**. Have the class discuss the "Follow-Up to Some Qualities of Human Intelligence" sheet in their student logbooks. Encourage opinions from all.

4. **Activity**. Have students complete the "Follow-Up to Some Qualities of Human Intelligence" sheet.

5. **Discussion**. Ask students how each of the the traits or behaviors listed on the "Follow-Up to Some Qualities of Human Intelligence" sheet might be achieved in an alternative way. For example, ask how two or more individuals could communicate with one another if they could not speak. What are alternative ways of achieving the same goal of communication among individuals?

Teacher's Note: *It is easy to see how prejudices can enter into these definitions. For instance, the Spanish invaders of Mexico called the local peoples "uncivilized" despite their complex cultures. This topic alone is worthy of a class discussion.*

Closure

1. **What Do You Think, Now?** Have students answer the post-activity questions on the logbook sheet "What Do You Think, Now?" Each student will need two sheets of blank paper. Invite students to share their responses and their drawings. Ask them how their opinions have been changed by this mission.

Going Further

Research/Literature: Civilizations on Other Worlds

Have students research extraterrestrials in popular culture, especially the way that they and their cultures are portrayed. Have students read and analyze popular science fiction books.

Activity: Cultural Heritage

Have students bring in food, clothes, and so forth from their individual cultural backgrounds. Have them share songs, stories, dances, or drama unique to their heritages.

Research: Anthropology

Have students research native peoples (such as the native peoples of Brazil's rain forests). Have students compare today's cultures with those of the past.

Activity: Timeline

Have students create a timeline based on the events they indicated as being historically important (on their logbook sheets "Mission Briefing" and "What Do You Think, Now?").

Activity: Play Charades!

Have students act out the traits and behaviors of intelligence from the logbook sheet "Some Qualities of Human Intelligence."

Activity: Younger Siblings

Have students observe younger children, toddlers, and babies. Have them pick one trait, such as manipulation of objects, and then observe that trait in people of different ages.

The SETI Academy Planet Project

Book Three
The Rise of Intelligence and Culture

Cadet Logbook

Name _____

Date _____

Mission 1

Planet Project Briefing

Name:

Date:

Dr. Jill Tarter, Chief Project Scientist of the SETI Academy

Welcome to SETI Academy. I invite you to work with me and other scientists on the Search for Extraterrestrial Intelligence (SETI). Our job is to search for signs of intelligent life in our galaxy. Our home base is in Mountain View, California, where we work closely with scientists from the National Aeronautics and Space Administration (NASA) at Ames Research Center, and with scientists from all over the world.

Your task is to consider how intelligent life might have arisen on other planets, and how we might communicate with that life. You will start by learning about the rise of intelligence and culture on Earth, which is the only planet we know of where intelligent life evolved. Then you will apply what you learn to invent an intelligent species for another planet, create a culture for it, and finally imagine what information they might send in a communication to Earth. Good luck!

Mission 1

The Rise of Human Intelligence
Mission Briefing

Name:

Date:

Tom Pierson, Executive Director of the SETI Academy

As a cadet at the SETI Academy, we'd like to know more about you and what you already know about intelligence and culture. Please answer the questions below and then draw an intelligent Earth life-form and an intelligent extraterrestrial life-form on the next two pages.

What Do You Think?

1. What do you think are the most important events in human history? List these events in the order in which they occurred.

2. What is *culture*? Is modern technology necessary to culture?

3. What enables humans to create culture?

4. What is the best way of detecting an extraterrestrial civilization? Explain why you think so.

Mission 1

The Rise of Human Intelligence

Draw planet Earth's most intelligent life-form. Label the things that make it exceptional.

Mission 1

The Rise of Human Intelligence

Draw an intelligent life-form from a fictional planet. Label the things that make it exceptional.

Mission 1

The Rise of Human Intelligence

Some Qualities of Human Intelligence

Name:

Date:

Members of your species, *Homo sapiens*, have physical traits and behaviors that enabled them to form a civilization. Consider when *you* first developed these traits and behaviors by having your parents help you answer the following questions:

How old were you when you

1. began manipulating objects with accuracy?

2. took your first steps without holding onto something?

3. recognized family members?

4. said your first words?

5. appeared to cooperate with others?

6. learned to read?

7. learned to write?

Mission 1

The Rise of Human Intelligence

Follow-Up to Some Qualities of Human Intelligence

Name:

Date:

For each of the traits or behaviors listed below, explain its importance to the formation of a civilization.

Manipulating objects:

Walking upright:

Recognizing members of one's group, or family:

Communicating with spoken language:

Cooperating with others:

Communicating with written language:

Mission 1

The Rise of Human Intelligence
What Do You Think, Now?

Name:

Date:

After you have completed this mission, please answer the following questions:

1. What do you think are the most important events in human history? Number these events in order of their occurrence, from first to last.

2. What is *culture?* Is modern technology necessary to culture?

3. What enabled humans to create culture?

4. What is the best way of detecting an extraterrestrial civilization? Explain why you think so.

Mission 2

Human Physical Traits and Behaviors
How Do They Contribute to Intelligence?

Overview

In mission 2, students explore other traits that humans share with certain other intelligent life-forms, traits that may be similarly important in the evolution of intelligent *extraterrestrial* beings. In mission 2.1, students study their stereoscopic vision, their opposable thumbs, and their ability to cooperate through simple lab activities.

Concepts

- Opposable thumbs and stereoscopic vision are examples of physical traits that allow primates, including humans, to perform complex tasks.

- The ability to cooperate has contributed to the development of civilization.

Skills

- Comparing and contrasting.

- Analyzing traits and abilities.

Mission 2.1

Materials

For the Stereoscopic Vision Center

- 4 copies of the logbook sheet "Stereoscopic Vision Center Directions"

- 4 thumb tacks

- 8 marking pens in two different colors

For the Opposable Thumbs Center

- 4 copies of the logbook sheet "Opposable Thumb Center Directions"

Notes

In mission 1, students answered questions to examine their physical traits and behaviors, and discussed the role these same attributes played in the development of human civilizations.

15

- 4 cups or small containers

- Mixture of 40 small, flat objects (coins, paper clips, washers, plastic chips, etc.), 10 for each cup

- 1 roll of masking tape for each table at a Center

- 4 stopwatches (or clocks/watches with second hands)

For the Cooperation Center

- 4 copies of the logbook sheet "Cooperation Center Directions"

- Large bag of peanuts (about 1 pound, 4 peanuts for each pair of students)

- 4 stopwatches (or clocks/watches with second hands)

- Trash can

For Each Student

- SETI Academy Cadet Logbook

- Pencil

Getting Ready

One or More Days Before Class

1. Review the "Teacher Background Information" for this mission in the appendixes.

2. Make four copies of each Center directions (there are three Centers). Collect all the supplies needed for the Centers.

3. Try each Center activity yourself to become familiar with its results.

Just Before the Lesson

1. Set up the Centers. Set up each of the three centers so that four pairs of students can work simultaneously. Each center should consist of a large table or four desks clustered together, and have four sets of center supplies each with its own set of directions.

2. Divide the class into pairs.

Teacher's Note: *You may need to arrange a "filler" activity, such as quiet reading, writing, or research, for student pairs that find themselves waiting for a Center or who finished early.*

Classroom Action

1. **Mission Briefing.** Have the class refer to the "Mission Briefing" for mission 2 in their student logbooks as one student reads it aloud.

2. **What Do You Think?** Read aloud and discuss the pre-activity questions on the "Mission Briefing." Ask students to discuss the value of having opposable thumbs and stereoscopic vision. Be sure students understand these terms. Have students answer the questions in their logbooks. Invite them to share their answers in a class discussion.

3. **Demonstration.** Briefly demonstrate the activities at each Center. Explain when and how to participate in the "filler" activity (if you have set one up). Show students where to find the "Physical Traits and Behaviors Recording Sheet" in their logbooks.

4. **Activity.** Divide the class into three teams of student pairs and assign each team to a Center. Instruct students to remain at a Center until all teams are ready to rotate. Allow approximately 30 minutes total, 10 minutes per Center.

5. **Discussion.** Review the Center activities. Ask students to share their results. Discuss the value of having opposable thumbs and stereoscopic vision as physical traits. Ask students how their opinions have been changed by the Center activities. Answers will vary for the Stereoscopic Vision, Opposable Thumb, and Cooperation Centers, but you should expect improvement in all areas by almost all students. Be aware that some students may not have stereoscopic vision.

Closure

1. **What Do You Think, Now?** Have students answer the post-activity questions on the logbook sheet "What Do You Think, Now?" Invite students to share their responses and their drawings. Ask them how their opinions have been changed by this mission.

2. **Discussion.** Review the traits and behaviors studied so far. Ask students if people can adapt to changing conditions using these traits and behaviors. Assign the following writing assignment about adaptability, or discuss the ideas in class.

   - All life-forms have some ability to adapt to change.

   - Usually, the more intelligent a life-form is, the faster it adapts to change.

   - Environment, food supply, and climate all change, sometimes dramatically.

   - The more extreme the change, the greater the challenge to the life-form's adaptability.

   - *You* adapt all the time. You adapted to opening peanuts with a partner and to picking up objects with no thumb. Because humans are very intelligent, you probably improved your cooperative and thumbless-grasping abilities rapidly. Think of a situation where your environment changed, or where you were physically challenged in some way. Write a description of the change and how you adapted to it.

Going Further

Homework Assignment: Adaptability

Have students write a paragraph or two about what civilization might be like if humans did not have one or more of the adaptations explored at the Centers (stereoscopic vision, opposable thumbs, or cooperation).

Activity: At the Zoo

Have students watch animals eat and manipulate objects. Have students try and determine which animals have stereoscopic vision and how good their stereoscopic vision is. How can they tell? Which animals have opposable thumbs? Which animals cooperate?

Creative Writing: In Our Image

On *Star Trek*, almost every alien is very human in appearance. This is a limitation imposed by what make-up artists and costume makers can do to transform a human actor. But it is also true that we have a bias that civilization requires our "image"—stereoscopic vision, opposable thumbs, and so on! Write about an alien civilization that is not in our image.

Mission 2

Human Physical Traits and Behaviors
Mission Briefing

Name:

Date:

Lori Marino, Biologist on the SETI Academy Team

There are many traits and behaviors that might enable a life-form to develop a civilization. Please explore three of them—stereoscopic vision, opposable thumbs, and cooperation. These are traits and behaviors that humans might have in common with other intelligent creatures. These may also be important to the evolution of intelligent *extraterrestrial* beings.

What Do You Think?

1. How has stereoscopic vision helped us in forming civilization?

2. How would civilization be different if we did not have opposable thumbs?

3. How has our ability to cooperate helped us in forming civilization?

Mission 2

Human Physical Traits and Behaviors

Stereoscopic Vision Center Directions

For this Center, you and your partner will need

> a thumb tack
> "Physical Traits and Behaviors Recording Sheet"
> two markers (different colors)

Please read all of the following directions before beginning.

1. Find the section titled "Stereoscopic Vision" on your recording sheet. It looks like a target. Poke the thumb tack up through the center of the target from the backside of the page, so it looks like this:

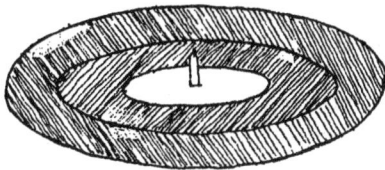

2. Put your chin on the table and place your target an arm's length away. Pick up a colored marker and cover one eye. Hold the marker with the tip down. Move the marker until you think that it is directly over the thumb tack. Lower it to the paper and mark an *X*. Do this three times, keeping the same eye covered.

3. On your recording sheet, keep track of how many points you score. For the example below, the final score is $1 + 5 + 5 = 11$.

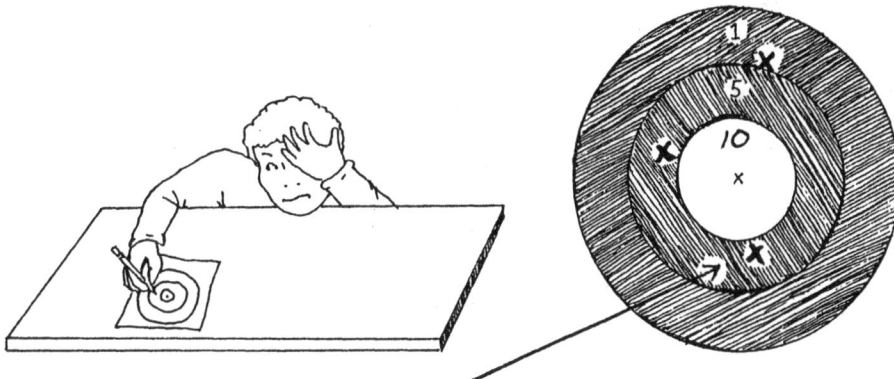

4. Now choose the other color of marker and repeat the test using *both* eyes. Record your score again.

5. Repeat the entire Center for your partner.

From *The Rise of Intelligence and Culture.* © 1995. Teacher Ideas Press. (800) 237-6124.

Mission 2

Human Physical Traits and Behaviors

Opposable Thumbs Center Directions

For this Center, you and your partner will need

10 small, flat objects (coins, paper clips, washers, plastic chips, etc.)
8 pieces of masking tape, each 4 inches long
"Physical Traits and Behaviors Recording Sheet"
a stopwatch or clock with second hand
pencil
a cup or small container

Please read all of the following directions before beginning.

1. Put the 10 small objects and the cup on the table in front of you. Using *only* your dominant hand (the one you write with), pick up the objects one at a time and put them into the cup. Have your partner time you.

2. Find the section on your recording sheet titled "Opposable Thumb." Record the time in minutes and seconds that it took to pick up the 10 objects.

Record Your Data	Time to Pick Up 10 Objects with Thumb	minutes 5 3 seconds
	Time to Pick Up 10 Objects Without Thumb	2 minutes 4 5 seconds

3. Take the objects out of the cup. Have your partner gently tape down the thumb of your dominant hand as shown below. The tape should prevent you from using your thumb but not cut off circulation.

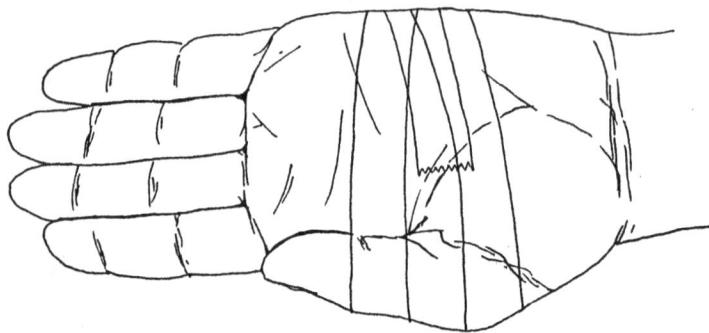

4. Now have your partner time you again while you pick up the same 10 objects, one at a time, and put them into the cup. Use *only* your dominant hand, this time without the help of your thumb.

5. Record your time again and repeat the entire Center for your partner.

6. Answer the questions on the "Opposable Thumbs" section of your recording page.

From *The Rise of Intelligence and Culture.* © 1995. Teacher Ideas Press. (800) 237-6124.

Mission 2

Human Physical Traits and Behaviors
Cooperation Center Directions

For this Center, you and your partner will need

> 4 peanuts
> "Physical Traits and Behaviors Recording Sheet"
> a stopwatch

Please read all of the following directions before beginning.

1. Sit close to your partner. Each of you should use only one hand—the hand you *don't* use for writing. Work together to crack open and eat your first peanut. Time yourselves.

2. Record the time in minutes and seconds on the section of your recording sheet titled "Cooperation."

3. Try to improve your time as you open the next three peanuts. Record all of your times and complete the graph on your recording sheet. An example is shown below.

Cooperation

Time to Open
First Test: 3 min 12 sec

Second Test: 1 min 55 sec

Third Test: 2 min 4 sec

Fourth Test: 1 min 30 sec

Make a Graph Showing Your Improvement

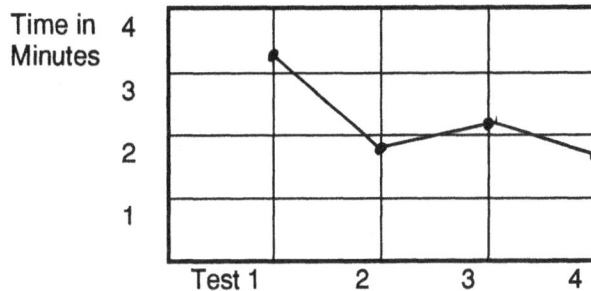

What Can You Conclude About the Value of Cooperation?

4. Clean up this center before you go to the next one.

5. Write your conclusions about the value of cooperation on your recording sheet.

From *The Rise of Intelligence and Culture.* © 1995. Teacher Ideas Press. (800) 237-6124.

Mission 2

Human Physical Traits and Behaviors
Physical Traits and Behaviors Recording Sheet

Name:

Date:

Stereoscopic Vision

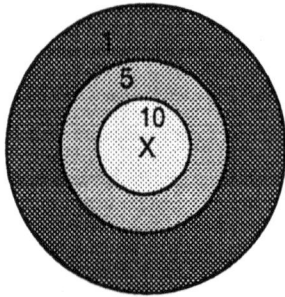

Total Score for One Eye: _____

Total Score for Both Eyes: _____

Did You Score Higher with One Eye or Two?

Opposable Thumbs

Record Your Data	Time to Pick Up 10 Objects with Thumb	minutes seconds
	Time to Pick Up 10 Objects Without Thumb	minutes seconds

Which was easier, using your thumb or not using your thumb? Explain why.

Cooperation

Make a Graph Showing Your Improvement

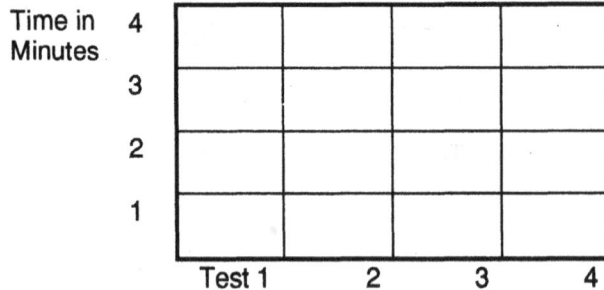

Time to Open

First Test: _____

Second Test: _____

Third Test: _____

Fourth Test: _____

Time in Minutes

4

3

2

1

Test 1   2   3   4

What Can You Conclude About the Value of Cooperation?

Mission 2

Human Physical Traits and Behaviors

What Do You Think, Now?

Name:

Date:

After you have completed this mission, please answer the following questions:

1. How has stereoscopic vision helped us in forming civilization?

2. How would civilization be different if we did not have opposable thumbs?

3. How has our ability to cooperate helped us in forming civilization?

Mission 3

Physical Traits and Behaviors of Earth Animals
What Species Might Develop Culture?

Overview

In mission 3, students consider an assortment of Earth animals and draw conclusions about their intelligence. They will then consider whether continued evolution of these animals might permit them to develop culture and eventually build and use radio technology.

The emphasis in this mission is discussion and debate. In mission 3.1, students work as a class, with the teacher's direction, to compile a matrix about physical traits and behaviors that might indicate intelligence. In mission 3.2, students fill in the matrix for an assortment of Earth animals and then select the one animal that is the most intelligent—and therefore "Most Likely to Succeed" in the future. Students discuss and define *intelligence* as it relates to Earth animals.

Concepts

- Some animals have physical traits that are similar to the physical traits that early humans used to develop culture.

- We assume that certain physical traits are prerequisites for intelligence, as we know it, to develop.

- Physical traits of an animal that indicate intelligence include stereoscopic vision, varied diet, upright mobility, and a grasping appendage.

- Some animals have behaviors that are similar to the behaviors that early humans used to develop culture.

- We assume that certain behaviors are prerequisites for intelligence, as we know it, to develop.

Notes

In mission 2, students explored four traits and behaviors that humans have in common with certain other life-forms on Earth, traits and behaviors that were important in the evolution of human technological abilities.

27

- Behaviors of an animal that indicate intelligence include communicating with others of its species, learning from others, building shelters, adapting to changing situations, living in organized groups, making or using tools, and protecting its group and coordinating group efforts.

Skills

- Comparing and contrasting.

- Identifying and discussing characteristics.

- Compiling and using a matrix.

Mission 3.1

Materials

For the Class

- 3 pieces of butcher paper or poster paper

- Marking pens

For Each Student

- SETI Academy Cadet Logbook

- Pencil

Getting Ready

One or More Days Before Class

1. Review the "Teacher Background Information" for this mission in the appendixes.

2. Label the first sheet of butcher paper "Earth Animals" and make a vertical list of the Earth animals shown in figure 3.1; leave space at the bottom for additions. Label the second piece of paper "Useful Physical Traits and Behaviors." Label the third "Top 10 Useful Physical Traits and Behaviors" and number from 1 to 10 down the left side.

Just Before the Lesson

1. Hang the "Earth Animals," the "Useful Physical Traits and Behaviors," and the "Top 10 Useful Physical Traits and Behaviors" papers side by side on a wall at the front of the classroom as shown in figure 3.1.

Figure 3.1—Butcher Paper Lists.

Earth Animals	Useful Physical Traits and Behaviors	Top 10 Useful Physical Traits and Behaviors
Pig Gorilla Human Elephant Leaf-Cutter Ant Horse Dolphin Snake Kangaroo Monkey Parrot Mole Cat Dog		1. 2. 3. 4. 5. 6. 7. 8. 9. 10.

Classroom Action

1. **Mission Briefing.** Have the class refer to the "Mission Briefing" for mission 3 in their student logbooks while one student reads it aloud.

2. **What Do You Think?** Have students answer the pre-activity questions on the "Mission Briefing." Invite them to share their answers in a class discussion.

3. **Discussion.** Ask students to name animals that are smart and animals that are not very smart. Ask students if there are characteristics that indicate the intelligence of an animal. What if we were to explore an alien planet? How would we know whether or not an alien species was intelligent?

   Brainstorm a list of physical traits and behaviors of Earth animals that the class believes to be intelligent. Make sure students understand the difference between physical traits and physical behaviors. Use examples to illustrate the difference.

   The following is a *partial* list of physical traits and behaviors that indicate intelligence; this list is by no means exhaustive.

Physical Traits of Intelligence

    a. Stereoscopic vision.
    b. Varied diet.
    c. Upright mobility.
    d. A grasping appendage.

Physical Behaviors of Intelligence

    a. Communicates with others of its species.
    b. Learns from others.
    c. Builds shelters.
    d. Adapts to changing situations.
    e. Lives in organized groups.
    f. Makes or uses tools.
    g. Protects its group and coordinates group efforts.

Once the brainstorming has ended, the class should reach a consensus on the 10 most important physical traits and behaviors. Record these traits and behaviors on the "Top 10" list. This list will be the key to their matrix. Save this "Top 10" list for mission 7.

4. **Activity.** Have students copy the "Top 10" list into their logbooks on the sheet of the same name.

5. **Discussion.** Review with students the list of Earth animals. Are there any other important animals that should be added? Are there other animals that have many of the listed traits and behaviors? Allow students to suggest additions.

Next, have students analyze the list of Earth animals and discuss which of the "Top 10" traits and behaviors each animal has. This can be done in a class discussion or discussed by teams of students in class, or as a homework assignment (a thinking exercise only—the writing will be done in mission 3.2).

There is no consensus among *all* biologists as to what constitutes intelligence, or as to which animals are most intelligent.

Teacher's Note: *Keep in mind that the younger the student, the more he or she will tend to attribute human form and personality to these animals.*

Record students' ideas on the "Useful Physical Traits and Behaviors" list. Encourage students to go beyond the traits and behaviors listed here. For example, they might add: has vocal cords that can make many sounds, can learn new skills, recognizes individuals, has an ability to reason abstractly, has curiosity, has a long memory, can control its environment, and so forth.

Mission 3.2

Materials

For Each Student

- SETI Academy Cadet Logbook

- Pencil

Getting Ready

1. Hang the "Earth Animals," "Useful Physical Traits and Behaviors," and the "Top 10 Useful Physical Traits and Behaviors" lists side by side on a wall at the front of the classroom as shown in mission 3.1.

Classroom Action

1. **Discussion.** Analyze each Earth animal for the "Top 10" traits and behaviors. For each animal, list next to it the numbers that correspond to the "Top 10" traits and behaviors it exhibits.

2. **Activity.** Have students record their findings on the logbook sheet "Physical Traits and Behaviors Matrix" as shown in figure 3.2.

Figure 3.2—Example of Useful Physical Traits and Behaviors Matrix.

Animal	1	2	3	4	5	6	7	8	9	10	Total	Rank
Pig	✓							✓			2	
Gorilla		✓		✓	✓		✓				4	
Human	✓		✓	✓	✓		✓		✓	✓	7	
Elephant						✓					1	

For each animal, have students check the numbers that correspond to the traits or abilities that they believe the animal has.

Have students add up the check marks in each row and enter the numbers into the "Total" column. This information is used to find the relative rank of each animal. The animal that has the most "Useful Physical Traits and Behaviors" (the most check marks) receives a rank of "1"; the animal with the next largest total number of traits and behaviors receives a rank of "2"; and so on. Have students complete the "Rank" column.

Closure

1. **Review.** Ask students to recall the mission briefing. SETI scientists are ultimately interested in the physical traits and behaviors that might enable intelligent animals to build and use radio technology! Ask students to consider what would happen if humans became extinct. What other species might evolve to "take our place" as a technological civilization?

2. **What Do You Think, Now?** Have students answer the post-activity questions on the logbook sheet "What Do You Think, Now?" Invite students to share their responses. Ask them how their opinions have been changed by this mission.

Teacher's Note: *You will discover that the "Top 10 Useful Physical Traits and Behaviors" students select is biased toward traits and behaviors that humans exhibit. It is very difficult to imagine what we cannot experience—the abilities of other animals. The American Heritage Dictionary defines intelligence as "the capacity to acquire and apply knowledge." This means that all animals have intelligence, but that it is specific to the success each has in its habitat.*

Going Further

Experiment: A Maze Run

Challenge students to build a small maze in which to test the intelligence of crawling insects, or a class or family pet. Even a planarian flatworm can learn a two-choice, Y-shaped maze to get food. (Planarian flatworms are studied in *How Might Life Evolve on Other Worlds?*—book 2 of the *SETI Academy Planet Project*.)

Teacher's Note: *Using animals with backbones for experimental purposes in the classroom requires certain permits. Consult with your principal for specific requirements.*

Research/Activity: Sign Language

Are humans the only animals that can master a language? No! Chimpanzees have been taught ASL—American Sign Language. And Koko the gorilla also learned to sign. Have students read about and report on these primates. Have students learn to use ASL as a "secret code"! How fast can the class learn 10 signs?

Mission 3

Physical Traits and Behaviors of Earth Animals

Mission Briefing

Name:

Date:

Ann Warner, Zoologist on the SETI Academy Team

SETI's business is to search for extraterrestrial intelligence; the most common way of doing that is to use radio telescopes to see (hear) if they are sending any signals. In this mission, you should consider all the possible physical traits and behaviors that are characteristics of intelligent life-forms, traits and behaviors that might enable extraterrestrial life-forms to send the type of message that we could receive.

What Do You Think?

1. Which four Earth animals do you think have the most useful physical traits and behaviors?

2. How do you define *intelligence*?

3. How could you test the intelligence of an animal?

Mission 3

Physical Traits and Behaviors of Earth Animals

Top 10 Useful Physical Traits and Behaviors

Name: _____

Date: _____

1. _____

2. _____

3. _____

4. _____

5. _____

6. _____

7. _____

8. _____

9. _____

10. _____

Mission 3

Physical Traits and Behaviors of Earth Animals

Physical Traits and Behaviors Matrix

Name:

Date:

1. For each animal, check the numbers that correspond to the traits or behaviors (use your "Top 10" list) that you think the animal has.

2. Add up the check marks for each animal and record that number into the "Total" column.

3. Rank the animals according to the number of useful traits and behaviors they have ("1" = the animal with the most, "2" = the animal with the next largest total, and so on).

Table 3.1—Useful Physical Traits and Behaviors Matrix.

Animal	1	2	3	4	5	6	7	8	9	10	Total	Rank
Pig												
Gorilla												
Human												
Elephant												
Leaf-Cutter Ant												
Horse												
Dolphin												
Snake												
Kangaroo												
Monkey												
Parrot												
Mole												
Cat												
Dog												

Mission 3

Physical Traits and Behaviors of Earth Animals

What Do You Think, Now?

Name:

Date:

After you have completed this mission, please answer the following questions:

1. Which four Earth animals did you find to have the most useful physical traits and behaviors?

2. How do you define *intelligence?*

3. How could you test the intelligence of an animal?

Mission 4

Cranial Changes
Measuring Hominid Skulls

Overview

In mission 4, students examine the skulls of human ancestors and draw conclusions about human evolution. Some anthropologists believe that the size of an animal's braincase—the interior of the skull that encloses the brain—can indicate a level of intelligence (relative to humans). Generally speaking, for a given body weight, the bigger the brain, the smarter the animal. We can judge how smart a living organism is by how capable it is of completing complex and sophisticated tasks. Scientists can get a good idea of the relative intelligence of ancient hominids by measuring their braincases.

In mission 4.1, students compare and contrast pictures of four skulls, from different time periods in hominid evolution, and measure the area of each skull cross section. In mission 4.2, students graph their data and then use these graphs to project approximate skull sizes for hominids of other periods, assuming a gradual, linear increase.

Concepts

- The size of a fossil skull indicates the size of the brain that was present while the animal was living.

- Hominids are fossil human ancestors.

- The size of the hominid brain has increased over the past several million years.

- The size of an animal's braincase generally indicates its level of intelligence.

- As hominid brains got bigger, more complex behaviors emerged, such as tool use.

Notes

In missions 2 and 3, students explored traits and behaviors that helped humans develop a culture and civilization that could build and use radio technology.

- A graph can be used to project data in the future, or estimate data that is not available, if assumptions are made.

Skills

- Graphing.

- Using fractions.

- Visualizing.

Mission 4.1

Materials

For the Class

- Transparency of "Skull Worksheet 1"

- Overhead projector

For Each Student

- SETI Academy Cadet Logbook

- Pencil

Getting Ready

One or More Days Before Class

1. Review the "Teacher Background Information" for this mission in the appendixes to develop a good understanding of the hominid family (which hominid appeared when and the duration of each).

2. Make a transparency of "Skull Worksheet 1."

Just Before the Lesson

1. Set up the overhead projector.

Classroom Action

1. **Mission Briefing.** Have the class refer to the "Mission Briefing" for mission 4 in their student logbooks as one student reads it aloud.

2. **What Do You Think?** Read aloud and discuss the pre-activity questions on the "Mission Briefing." Have students answer the questions

in their logbooks. Invite them to share their answers in a class discussion.

3. **Lecture.** Discuss student ideas from the "What do you think" questions and introduce the idea of cranial changes over time. Explain that a large brain contains more brain cells and has more neural connections than a smaller brain, and therefore more information can be processed. Encourage students through discussion to discover how the brain size of an animal can indicate that animal's ability to function on more sophisticated levels.

A network of telephones is an analogy that can be used to illustrate this difficult concept. Each telephone represents a brain cell and the telephone lines represent the connections between the cells. If there are only two telephones, only two people can be talking—to each other— at any given time. But as more telephones are added, the number of possible connections increases and with it the number of possible conversations.

A snake's brain is very small, but it is large enough to do everything that a snake needs to do. It enables a snake to see moving light and dark shapes, sense vibrations and heat, and regulate its temperature by moving about. Humans, however, have a relatively large brain that enables them to invent and use language, to move and balance, to see with stereoscopic vision, to use tools, to think symbolically, and to remember and recall vast amounts of information. Both humans and snakes are well adapted to their individual lifestyles. Scientific evidence suggests that the larger the brain, in comparison to body size, the more the animal can do, both physically and mentally.

Teacher's Note: *The relative brain size issue does not necessarily apply to comparisons within a species. It is a gross measure that applies best to changes across millions of years in a specific lineage, such as the hominid line examined in this lesson.*

4. **Demonstration.** Explain to students that they will be examining the outlines of skulls from three hominids (all possible ancestors of *Homo sapiens*). They will measure a side view of the skull area that contains the brain to find the approximate brain size of each hominid. Then they will compare all four.

Make a sketch of figure 4.1 on the chalk-board. Explain how the brain fits inside the skull.

Figure 4.1.

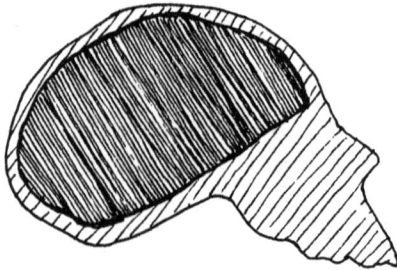

Put the transparency of "Skull Worksheet 1" on the overhead projector. Ask students to look at the same page in their logbooks. Have students follow along and record the data into their logbooks as you do so on the transparency. Suggest to students that they should record right on the grid the fraction of each square that is darkened, as shown in figure 4.2.

Figure 4.2.

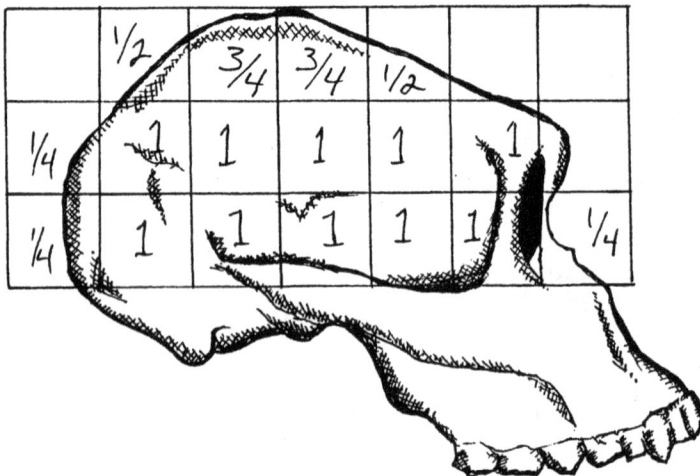

- There are two ways to calculate the total area of the cross section. Students can 1) use the equation in the data box to convert the numbers to decimals and then use a calculator to find the total area of the side view, as shown in table 4.1; or 2) add the fractions as shown in figure 4.3.

Table 4.1—Using the Equation.

Record Your Data Here			
	Count	**Convert**	**Area**
Whole Squares		x 1.0	cm^2
One-Half Squares		x 0.5	cm^2
Three-Quarter Squares		x 0.75	cm^2
One-Quarter Squares		x 0.25	cm^2
			Total Area = cm^2

Table 4.2—Skull-Size Answer Key.

Answer Range	
Skull 1 (example)	13-15 cm^2
Skull 2	12-14 cm^2
Skull 3	17.5-19.5 cm^2
Skull 4	22-23.5 cm^2

Figure 4.3.

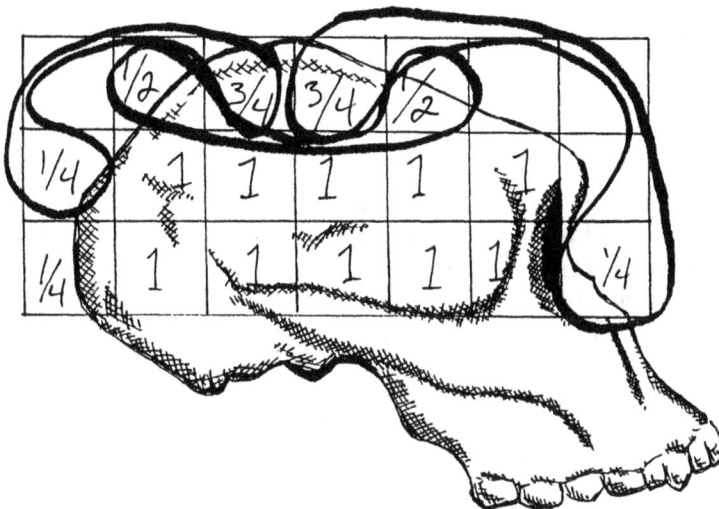

In either case, the total is the cross-sectional area of the brain, in square centimeters.

5. **Activity.** Have students turn to the "Skull Worksheets" 2, 3, and 4 in their logbooks. Check students' understanding about what is to be done. Monitor students progress to be sure they are proceeding correctly.

Teacher's Note: *For students who haven't learned to convert decimals to fractions, use overhead pens on the "Skull Worksheet 1" transparency to demonstrate grouping first and then adding fractions, as shown in figure 4.3.*

6. **Discussion.** After students finish, they should compare data. If the answers vary from student to student by more than 1 or 2 centimeters, discuss why there are differences and how students could measure more accurately. Point out that skull *volume* would need a third axis (a cross section of the front or back of the skull). Volume would be a closer indication of the true brain size than cross-sectional area.

Mission 4.2

Materials

For Each Team or Pair

- Blank graph paper

- (optional) Calculator

For Each Student

- SETI Academy Cadet Logbook

- Pencil

Getting Ready

One or More Days Before Class

1. (optional) Locate calculators.

Classroom Action

1. **Lecture.** Ask students to hypothesize (or guess) which hominid skull is oldest, next oldest, and so forth. They should have a sense that the smaller-brained hominids are older, and that brain size increased over time. On the chalkboard or on an overhead projector, write the ages of the fossil hominids from table 4.3 below.

Teacher's Note: *There are species overlaps, that is, two hominids living at the same time, one of which is bigger-brained. Explain to students that evolution is a tree, not a ladder, and that some branches become extinct while others evolve (see figure 4.4).*

Table 4.3—Skull-Age Answer Key.

Answer Range	
Skull 1 (example)	2.5-1.5 mya
Skull 2	3.5-2.0 mya
Skull 3	1.5-0.5 mya
Skull 4	0.5-Present

Figure 4.4—Evolution Is a *Tree*.

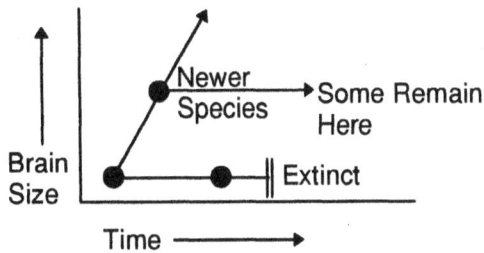

2. **Activity.** Have students turn to the "Graphing Cranial Changes" worksheet in their logbooks. Direct students to complete the table on the worksheet by adding the age ranges and sizes for the four skulls.

3. **Lecture.** Explain to students how you want them to graph the four skulls. (Students can create their graphs from scratch on blank graph paper or use their "Cranial Graph" logbook sheet.)

4. **Demonstration.** Show students how they can use their graphs to estimate brain sizes for hominids from other ages, by drawing a straight line across the points in their graph, as shown in figure 4.5.

Teacher's Note: *In student graphs, logic must prevail! Obviously, human brain size cannot continue to increase forever. In fact, it will always be limited to the size of the mother's pelvis and birth canal.*

Figure 4.5—Estimating Brain Sizes.

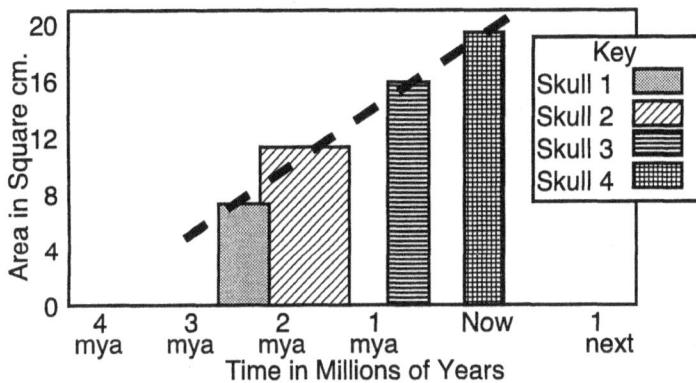

5. **Activity.** Have students make their graphs, and have them answer the questions at the bottom of the "Graphing Cranial Changes" logbook sheet.

6. **Discussion.** Have students share their graphs and discuss how they made their projections.

Closure

1. **Discussion.** Ask students what conclusions they now can draw about brain size, intelligence, and human evolution.

   Animals with larger bodies tend to have larger brains because a very important part of a brain's function is to control the body. Does this necessarily mean that big people will be automatically smarter than small ones? Of course not! Make sure students understand this.

2. **What Do You Think, Now?** Have students answer the post-activity questions on the logbook sheet "What Do You Think, Now?" Invite students to share their responses and their drawings. Ask them how their opinions have been changed by this mission.

Teacher's Note: *Discuss with students some of the characteristics of each hominid so that they can see when certain skills and capacities emerged, such as tool use, cave painting, organized camps, and so forth. There is evidence in the fossil record that as brain size increased, technology too increased: first crude stone tools, then advanced stone tools, later clothing, burials, cities, and so on.*

Going Further

Creative Writing: How Big Will the Human Brain Become?

Have students write a story about how they think a larger brain size might affect humans of the future.

Math Activity: Take a Survey

Have students take a survey in other classes about what students think will happen to the size of the human brain.

Timelines: Human Evolution

Have students create physical (biologic) timelines of evolution. Have them use the skull pictures from this mission or draw their own pictures of fossil hominids. Have them mark brain sizes on their timelines.

Have students create cultural timelines of evolution for fossil hominids.

Drama: Meet *The Flintstones*

Have students play the roles of cave people being interviewed by a skeptical scientist (the teacher): "What species are you, anyway?" "Did you know that dinosaurs became extinct 65 million years ago and that people 'began' about 4 million years ago?"

Mission 4

Cranial Changes
Mission Briefing

Name:

Date:

Dr. Jim Funaro, Anthropologist on the SETI Academy Team

Our efforts to understand how intelligence might have evolved elsewhere in the universe have led us to investigate the way human brains evolved on Earth. In this mission, we would like you to examine the skulls of human ancestors and think about what you find. What could your discoveries mean as they relate to the future of human evolution?

What Do You Think?

1. How has the human brain size changed over time?

2. How do you think brain size is related to intelligence and the development of culture?

Mission 4

Cranial Changes

Skull Worksheet 1 (example)

Name:

Date:

Figure 4.6.

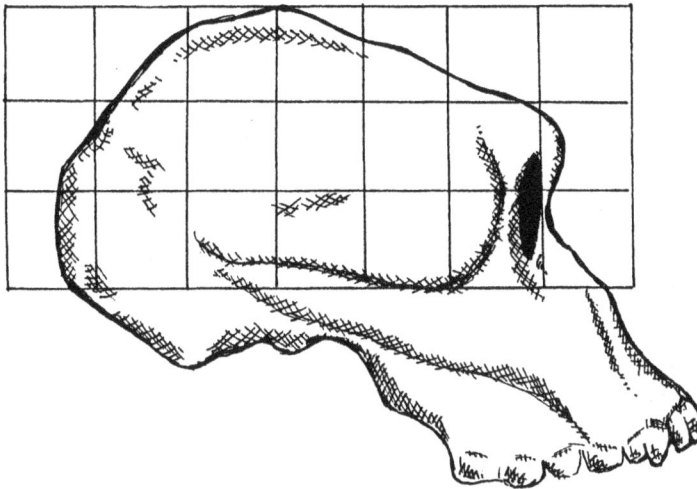

Key to counting the squares (when in doubt, make your best guess):

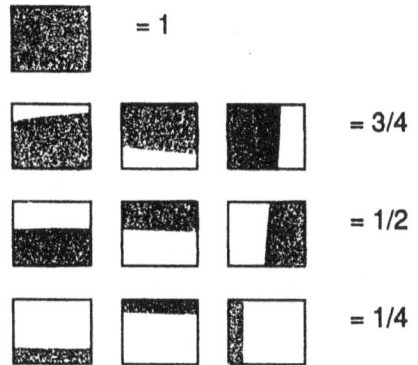

Record Your Data Here			
	Count	Convert	Area
Whole Squares		x 1.0	cm²
One-Half Squares		x 0.5	cm²
Three-Quarter Squares		x 0.75	cm²
One-Quarter Squares		x 0.25	cm²
		Total Area =	cm²

Mission 4

Cranial Changes

Skull Worksheet 2

Name:

Date:

Figure 4.7.

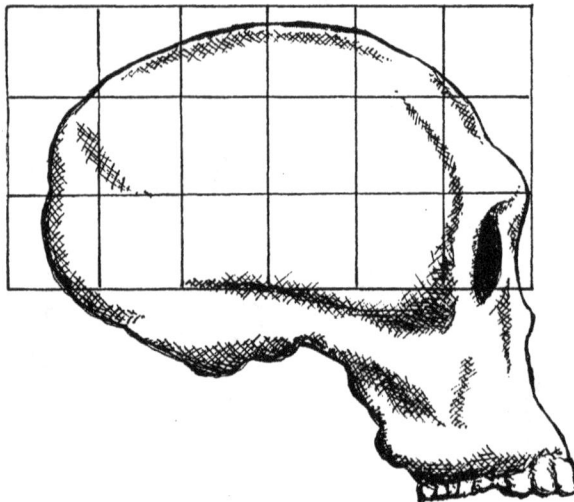

Key to counting the squares (when in doubt, make your best guess):

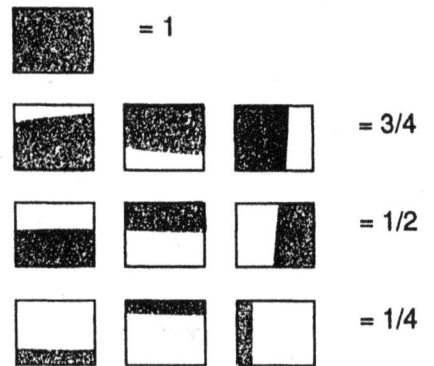

= 1

= 3/4

= 1/2

= 1/4

Record Your Data Here			
	Count	**Convert**	**Area**
Whole Squares		x 1.0	cm²
One-Half Squares		x 0.5	cm²
Three-Quarter Squares		x 0.75	cm²
One-Quarter Squares		x 0.25	cm²
		Total Area =	cm²

Mission 4

Cranial Changes

Skull Worksheet 3

Name:

Date:

Figure 4.8.

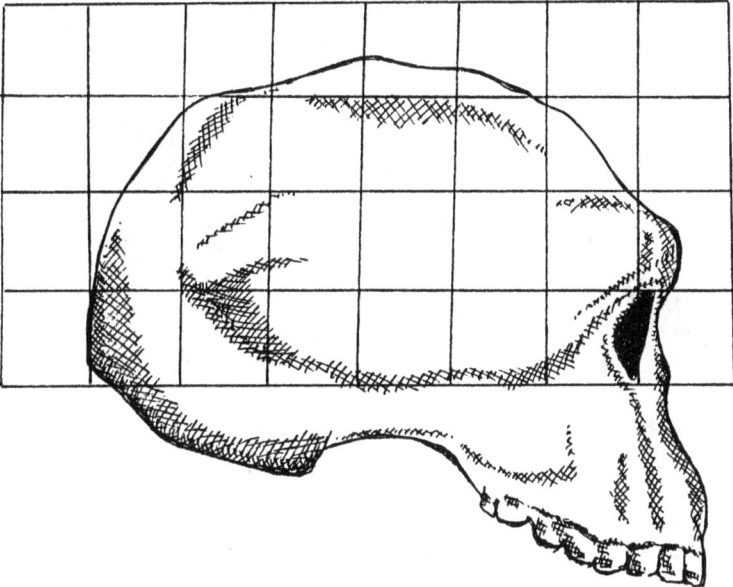

Key to counting the squares (when in doubt, make your best guess):

= 1

= 3/4

= 1/2

= 1/4

Record Your Data Here			
	Count	**Convert**	**Area**
Whole Squares		x 1.0	cm²
One-Half Squares		x 0.5	cm²
Three-Quarter Squares		x 0.75	cm²
One-Quarter Squares		x 0.25	cm²
			Total Area = cm²

Mission 4

Cranial Changes

Skull Worksheet 4

Name:

Date:

Figure 4.9.

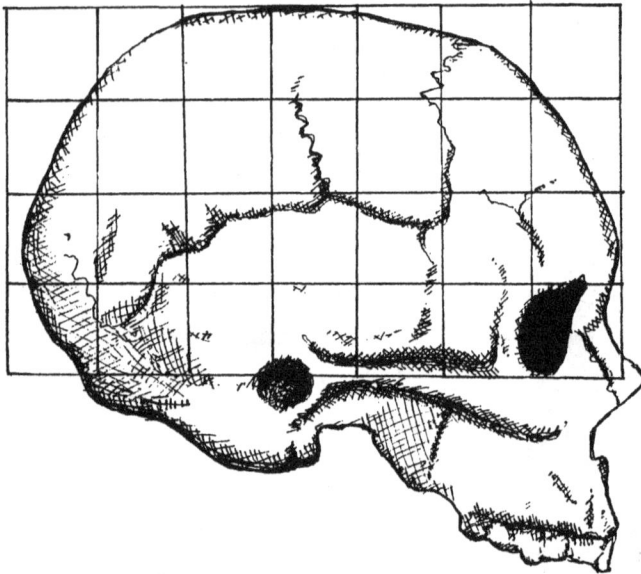

Key to counting the squares (when in doubt, make your best guess):

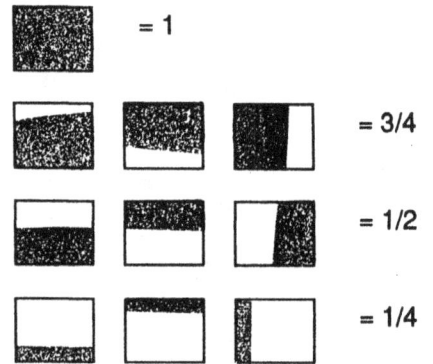

	Record Your Data Here		
	Count	**Convert**	**Area**
Whole Squares		x 1.0	cm^2
One-Half Squares		x 0.5	cm^2
Three-Quarter Squares		x 0.75	cm^2
One-Quarter Squares		x 0.25	cm^2
		Total Area =	cm^2

Mission 4

Cranial Changes

Graphing Cranial Changes

Name:

Date:

1. Enter the age and size for each of the four skulls into the table below.

Skull Number	Age Range (in millions of years) From Your Teacher	Size (in square centimeters) From Your Data
Skull 1 (example)		
Skull 2		
Skull 3		
Skull 4		

2. Create a graph that shows the difference in cranial sizes of the four skulls. (Hints: Use a ruler, include a title, include a key, and be sure that you present the information clearly.)

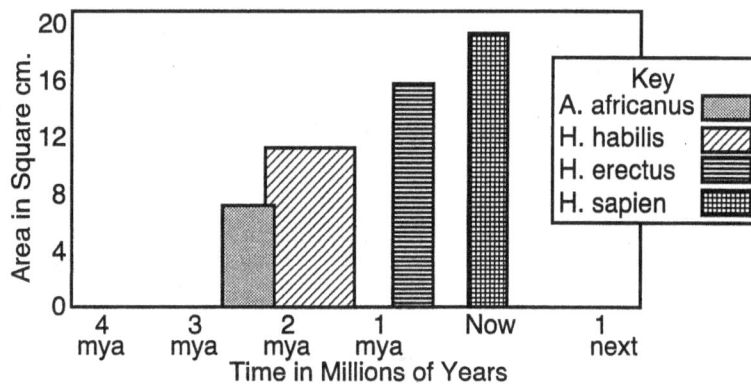

3. Use your graph to estimate the brain size (in square centimeters) for a hominid that may have lived 4.5 million years ago. What is your estimate?

4. Use your graph to project the brain size (in square centimeters) for a hominid that might live 1 million years in the future. What is your projection?

5. How did you make your estimate and your projection?

From The Rise of Intelligence and Culture. © 1995. Teacher Ideas Press. (800) 237-6124.

Mission 4

Cranial Changes

Cranial Graph

Figure 4.10—Cranial Graph Paper.

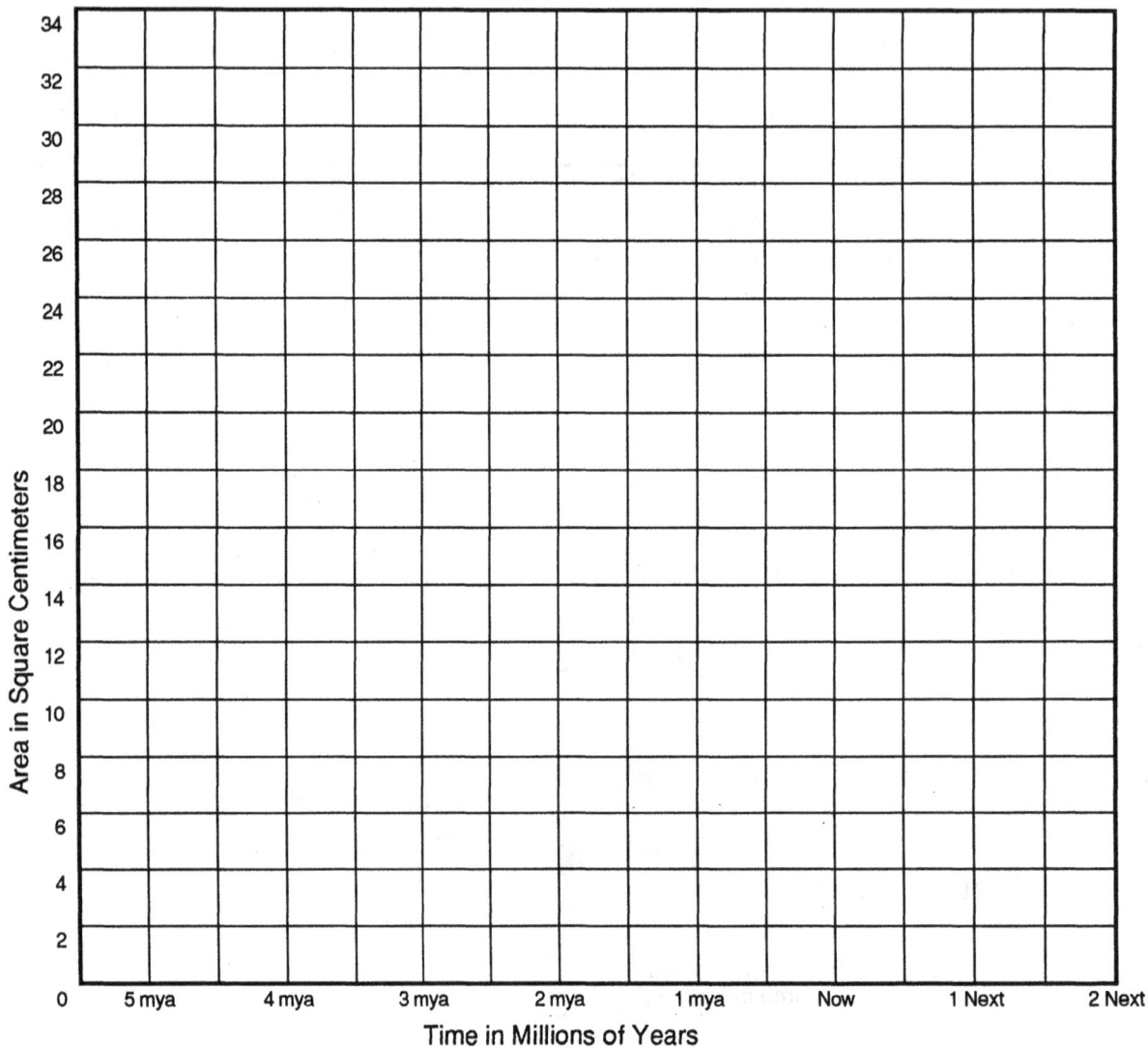

Mission 4

Cranial Changes

What Do You Think, Now?

Name:

Date:

After you have completed this mission, please answer the following questions:

1. How has the human brain size changed over time?

2. How do you think brain size is related to intelligence and the development of culture?

From *The Rise of Intelligence and Culture.* © 1995. Teacher Ideas Press. (800) 237-6124.

Mission 5

Early Earth Cultures
Biological and Cultural Adaptations of Humans

Overview

In mission 5, students go back in time and investigate several early cultures of Earth. In mission 5.1, students determine areas on Earth where people have lived and then compile a list of human survival needs. In mission 5.2, students view transparencies about early Earth cultures and examine how those cultures survived in their specific environments. In mission 5.3, students review the transparencies to see how both biologic evolution and cultural evolution allowed early humans to adapt to their specific habitats.

Concepts

- Humans have basic survival needs.

- Natural resources enabled early human cultures to survive.

- Humans can and have survived in most terrestrial habitats on Earth; some habitats are more hospitable than others.

- All species evolve physical traits and behaviors that are adaptations to their specific habitat. This is called *biologic evolution*.

- Some physical traits and behaviors make the species more intelligent, and can lead to *cultural evolution*.

- Cultural evolution involves learning, memory, and the transmission of cultural values and concepts from parents to offspring.

- Any species that evolves as humans did, to use their brains to develop tools and to change their environments, is likely to develop technology.

Notes

In missions 1-4, students examined useful physical traits and behaviors that led to the evolution of human intelligence, culture, civilization, and today's technology.

55

- Once technology begins to develop, it is possible that radio technology will be developed.

Skills

- Analyzing habitats for resources.

- Determining human survival needs.

- Distinguishing biologic evolution from cultural evolution.

Mission 5.1

Materials

For the Class

- Cardboard Earth globe

- 20 map pins

For Each Student

- SETI Academy Cadet Logbook

- Pencil

Getting Ready

One or More Days Before Class

1. Review the "Teacher Background Information" for this mission in the appendixes.

Just Before the Lesson

1. Put a globe of Earth where it can be seen by everyone.

Classroom Action

1. **Mission Briefing.** Have the class refer to the "Mission Briefing" for mission 5 in their student logbooks while one student reads it aloud.

2. **What Do You Think?** Have students answer the pre-activity questions on the "Mission Briefing." Invite them to share their answers in a class discussion.

3. **Discussion.** Ask students what people *must* have to survive. Divide the class into teams and have each team elect a secretary to record their ideas on paper. Ask groups to narrow down their lists to four things that are absolutely essential for human survival. Have teams share their lists with the rest of the class. Write the ideas on the chalkboard as they are shared. Discuss the chalkboard list and help the class narrow it down and come to a final agreement on the four basic human survival needs: food, water, shelter, and warmth.

4. **Activity.** Ask the class where on Earth early people found these four things that they needed to survive. Have student teams brainstorm and record (each student) their ideas on the logbook sheet "Habitats." Have teams share their ideas with the class.

   Ask for volunteers to insert map pins into the Earth globe at locations where they determined that early humans could survive. The entire class should be in agreement that survival needs for early humans could be met at each location before each map pin is added to the Earth globe. Do this for 20 locations. Leave the pins in the globe for mission 5.2.

Mission 5.2

Materials

For the Class

- Overhead projector

- "Early Human Cultures" transparencies or black-line masters (8)

- Earth globe

- 8 map pins

- (optional) Labels for the map pins

For Each Student

- SETI Academy Cadet Logbook

- Pencil

Getting Ready

Just Before the Lesson

1. Set up the overhead projector.

2. Put a globe of Earth where it can be seen by everyone.

Classroom Action

1. **Activity.** Review with students the four basic survival needs (food, water, shelter, and warmth). Tell students that they will now view transparencies that feature representations of actual cultures that existed on Earth thousands of years ago. Some of these cultures have changed, and no longer exist. Others still survive.

   Show the "Early Human Cultures" transparencies and read or paraphrase the scripts provided below. Instruct students to look for clues in each picture that show how each culture met its survival needs. Encourage the class to point out specific things that *show* how survival needs were met for each culture. Also included below for each transparency is a list of survival resources.

Script for Transparency 1

In this transparency you see a representation of early Egyptian culture. Look carefully to identify this culture's habitat, and find the resources that these people used to meet their survival needs.

Table 5.1—Early Egyptian Resources.

Food	Domestic crops of wheat, barley, fruiting vines, fruit and nut trees, and vegetables. Waterfowl and fish from the Nile River. Sheep, cattle, and goats for milk and meat.
Water	Nile River and rainfall.
Shelter	Wealthy people lived in houses built from wood and clay. Peasants lived in huts made of mud and reeds.
Warmth	Linen garments were worn by upper classes. Cotton garments were worn by lower classes. Ornaments were worn by upper classes.

Script for Transparency 2

In this transparency you see a representation of an early Asian culture. Look carefully to identify this culture's habitat, and find the resources that these people used to meet their survival needs.

Table 5.2—Early Asian Resources.

Food	Rice, millet, and sugar cane. Fish, domestic birds. Bananas, oranges, pomegranates, and other tropical fruit.
Water	Lakes, rivers, creeks, and rainfall.
Shelter	Bamboo and palm fronds. Huts raised on stilts.
Warmth	Cotton frocks for the lower class. Silk robes for the upper class and for royalty.

Script for Transparency 3

In this transparency you see a representation of an early Pygmy culture. Look carefully to identify this culture's habitat, and find the resources that these people used to meet their survival needs.

Table 5.3—Early Pygmy Resources.

Food	Elephant and other game. Fish, crab, larvae, and insects. Mushrooms, edible roots, fruit, and other wild plant foods.
Water	Rivers, streams, and rainfall.
Shelter	Huts made from sapling frames stuck in the ground and woven at the ends to make a dome shape. They were then covered with very large leaves from nearby trees to create a waterproof roof. Women could make a hut in two hours.
Warmth	Pygmies did not need to cover their bodies for warmth, but men and women wore loincloths made of fig-tree bark. Women painted designs on their bodies with pigments made from forest plants mixed with water.

Script for Transparency 4

In this transparency you see a representation of an early Plains Indian culture. Look carefully to identify this culture's habitat, and find the resources that these people used to meet their survival needs.

Table 5.4—Early Plains Indian Resources.

Food	Buffalo, squash, beans, corn, and sunflowers.
Water	Creeks, steams, and rivers.
Shelter	Earth-covered lodges and later tipis covered with bison hides.
Warmth	Animal skins adorned with quills and beads.

Script for Transparency 5

In this transparency you see a representation of early Inca culture. Look carefully to identify this culture's habitat, and find the resources that these people used to meet their survival needs.

Table 5.5—Early Inca Resources.

Food	Domestic crops: potatoes, corn. Llamas, alpacas, and wild turkeys.
Water	Lakes, streams, and rainfall.
Shelter	Stone blocks from mountains.
Warmth	Gold and clay ornaments for upper class. Wool from alpaca and llama. Cotton from crops.

Script for Transparency 6

In this transparency you see a representation of early Greek culture. Look carefully to identify this culture's habitat, and find the resources that these people used to meet their survival needs.

Table 5.6—Early Greek Resources.

Food	Grapes, olives, and other vegetables. Food sheep, and goats. Goat milk for drinking and making cheese.
Water	Rainfall, streams, and creeks.
Shelter	Craftsmen built houses from stone and wood.
Warmth	Wool tunics worn by men and women.

Script for Transparency 7

In this transparency you see a representation of early Eskimo culture. Look carefully to identify this culture's habitat, and find the resources that these people used to meet their survival needs.

Table 5.7—Early Eskimo Resources.

Food	Fish, whale, walrus, polar bear, caribou, fox, geese, birds, eggs, and berries.
Water	From snow and ice.
Shelter	Igloos built from stone and earth. Tents made of animal skins. Temporary igloos made of ice blocks.
Warmth	Clothing made from caribou and other animal skins.

Script for Transparency 8

In this transparency you see a representation of early aborigine culture. Look carefully to identify this culture's habitat, and find the resources that these people used to meet their survival needs.

Table 5.8—Early Aborigine Resources.

Food	Edible meat and plants including fish, waterfowl, grubs, lizards, roots, bulbs, wild fruits, and nuts.
Water	Rivers, creeks, and roots rich in water.
Shelter	Absence of shelter reflects a desert-like habitat as well as a nomadic lifestyle. Occasionally used caves for religious purposes and in extreme rain.
Warmth	No clothing worn by either sex in summer. During cooler weather, men and women wore animal-skin loin cloths.

---

2. **Discussion.** After viewing the transparencies, discuss how cultures in different habitats were able to meet the same basic survival needs in various ways.

3. **Activity.** Have students insert map pins into the Earth globe as they locate the habitats of these eight early cultures. They may flag or label each pin with the name of the culture. Ask students to notice whether or not these pins are near the pins from mission 5.1. Are any in unexpected places? Why?

Mission 5.3

Materials

For the Class

- Overhead projector

- "Early Human Cultures" transparencies or black-line masters (8)

For Each Student

- SETI Academy Cadet Logbook

- Pencil

Getting Ready

Just Before the Lesson

1. Set up the overhead projector.

Classroom Action

1. **Discussion.** Tell students that they will see again the transparencies from mission 5.2. Remind students that the last time they saw these pictures, they were observing how early people met the same survival needs in different habitats. Today they will look for physical (biologic) and cultural adaptations to these habitats.

   First, they will analyze each transparency for information as to how humans have *physically* adapted to their habitats. These are physical, or biologic, traits that have evolved through *natural selection*. Discuss with students the principles of natural selection. Ask students for ideas about what might happen, in general, to any life-form that was *not* born with traits helpful to survival. Is it possible that they might weaken and die before reproducing? Ask students what happens over thousands of generations to those that are born *with* traits helpful to survival. Is it possible that entire populations who live in a particular habitat will evolve to have a particular set of characteristics in common? Make sure students understand that this is natural selection, the mechanism of biologic evolution. In biologic evolution, people cannot decide what traits they want; they inherit them from their parents.

Human Physical Adaptations to Habitats

Sunny, hot climates

- Dark-colored skin to protect against damage from UV (ultraviolet) light.

- Tall and/or thin bodies to shed heat easily, because they have a large ratio of surface area to volume.

Cloudy, cool climates

- Light-colored skin to absorb enough sunlight to make vitamin D internally.

- Thick hair to insulate the head.

Cloudy, cold climates

- Stocky build and a layer of fat to insulate against extreme cold, because bodies have a small ratio of surface area to volume.

- Narrowed eyelids with a fat deposit to shade the eyes from direct and reflected sunlight and to keep the eyes warm.

- Thick, dark hair to warm and insulate the head.

Second, students will analyze each transparency for information as to how humans have *culturally* adapted to their habitats. Cultural adaptations are behaviors, skills, knowledge, ideas, inventions, and so forth that have been originated by some individuals and then taught to others. In cultural evolution, people can decide what traits or behaviors they want to keep, what they want to eliminate, and what new traits or behaviors they want to develop.

Human Cultural Adaptations to Habitat

Sunny, hot climates

- Few clothes to keep cool.

- Nomadic lifestyle to follow food sources.

- Fragile, easily built houses to keep cool.

- Agriculture, where irrigation is possible.

Teacher's Note: *Following is a list of human physical (biologic) adaptations that can be inferred from the transparencies. Prompt students before or during the show, or wait and discuss these after the show.*

Teacher's Note: *Following is a list of human cultural adaptations that can be inferred from the transparencies. Prompt students before or during the show, or wait and discuss these after the show.*

Cloudy, cool climates

- Warm clothing.

- Sturdy, well-insulated houses to keep warm.

- Agriculture; they grew crops that could withstand freezing.

Cloudy, cold climates

- Warm leather and fur clothing.

- Nomadic lifestyle to follow food sources.

- Sturdy, well-insulated houses to keep warm.

2. **Activity.** As students view the "Early Earth Cultures" transparencies again, ask them to look for examples of physical (biologic) and cultural adaptations of each culture to its habitat. Have students share and discuss their examples. Write ideas on the chalkboard before, during, or after the show, and have students write down their ideas on their logbook sheet "Adaptations" after the show.

Closure

1. **Discussion.** Ask students if they were surprised that each of the early cultures could meet its survival needs in its specific habitat. Ask students what they can conclude about the adaptability of humans. How much of this adaptability is due to our biologic evolution (opposable thumbs, stereoscopic vision), and how much is due to our cultural evolution (writing, weaving)? Would students consider all of these cultures to be composed of intelligent people? Which of these cultures could have been detected by an extraterrestrial culture that used radio telescopes to search for intelligent life-forms? Did any of these cultures later develop radio technology? The Greek and Asian cultures mixed with European culture and developed "Western" radio technology.

2. **What Do You Think, Now?** Have students answer the post-activity questions on the logbook sheet "What Do You Think, Now?" Invite students to share their responses and their drawings. Ask them how their opinions have been changed by this mission.

Going Further

Activity: Draw a Culture

Ask students to think of themselves as members of a newly discovered culture. Have them make a drawing in black and white that shows how their survival needs are met today in that culture. Make a transparency of one or more of these to add to the set of "Early Earth Cultures" transparencies.

Research: More Cultures

Have students do additional research about aspects of the "Early Earth Cultures" transparencies that interested them. Have them research cultures that were not shown. Have students illustrate these cultures, or write and act out plays based on them.

Activity: Where on Earth?

Have students insert flagged pins into locations to show where their families' ancestors came from.

Mission 5

Early Earth Cultures
Mission Briefing

Name:

Date:

Gay Franklin, Cultural Anthropologist on the SETI Academy Team

During this mission, you will compile a list of basic human survival needs. Then you will view a series of transparencies about early Earth cultures to gather information about how early humans satisfied their survival needs in various habitats. We want you to look for examples of both physical (or biologic) evolution and cultural evolution that are adaptations of each group of people and their culture to their specific habitat.

What Do You Think?

1. What do intelligent life-forms need to survive?

2. What would an intelligent life-form do to survive in a desert habitat?

3. Will all cultures eventually develop "modern" technology? Why or why not?

From *The Rise of Intelligence and Culture.* © 1995. Teacher Ideas Press. (800) 237-6124.

Mission 5

Early Earth Cultures

Habitats

Name:

Date:

Look at the continents on the Earth globe. In which areas do you think early hominids lived? In which areas do you think early *Homo sapiens* lived? List the places on Earth where people can live in the "Habitats" column and the resources available in each habitat in the "Survival Needs" column.

Table 5.9—Habitats Worksheet.

Habitats (Places on Earth where people can live)	Survival Needs (Reources available in a habitat)
1.	1.
2.	2.
3.	3.
4.	4.
5.	5.
6.	6.
7.	7.
8.	8.

Mission 5

Early Earth Cultures

Adaptations

Name:

Date:

Think about the transparencies of early Earth cultures. In which habitats did these people live? How were these people adapted to their habitats? List the physical adaptations to several habitats in the "Biologic Evolution" column and the cultural adaptations to several habitats in the "Cultural Evolution" column.

Table 5.10—Adaptation Worksheet

Biologic Evolution (Physical adaptations to a habitat)	Cultural Evolution (Cultural adaptations to a habitat)

From *The Rise of Intelligence and Culture.* © 1995. Teacher Ideas Press. (800) 237-6124.

Mission 5

Early Earth Cultures

What Do You Think, Now?

Name:

Date:

After you have completed this mission, please answer the following questions:

1. What do intelligent life-forms need to survive?

2. What would an intelligent life-form do to survive in a desert habitat?

3. Will all cultures eventually develop "modern" technology? Why or why not?

Mission 6

Meet Planet Z
Biomes and Habitats on an Alien World

Overview

In missions 6-8, students investigate a fictional planet, Planet Z, where they apply concepts learned when studying Earth, to identify habitats, to find an intelligent life-form, and to observe the rise of culture.

In mission 6.1, students investigate biomes on Earth continents, and then compare them to Planet Z. Students color biomes on pictures of Planet Z landmasses and arrange them on a global map. In mission 6.2, students color habitat pictures and locate their proper place on the map.

Concepts

- *Biomes* are large geographic areas that share a type of climate, with similar average temperatures and rainfall, such as rain forests or deserts.

- The rain forest biome is a large geographic area in which there is a lot of rainfall and a warm climate; on Earth it is found in a belt around the equator.

- The desert biome is a large geographic area in which there is little rainfall and great temperature variations.

- Habitats are specific places where organisms live.

Skills

- Using a globe to identify biomes.

- Analyze habitats for resources.

- Reading and analyzing maps.

Notes

In Mission 5, students determined the survival needs of human beings and the ways in which various early human cultures made use of their different environments to meet these needs. They saw that both biologic and cultural evolution helped humans adapt to specific habitats.

71

Mission 6.1

Materials

For the Class

- Chart paper

- Markers

- Large physical map of Earth

- Transparency of Teacher's Key for Planet Z maps

- Overhead projector pen or grease pencil

For Each Student

- SETI Academy Cadet Logbook

- Globe or map of Earth (try a social studies text)

- Set of Planet Z continents

- Crayons or markers

- Tape

- Glue or paste

Getting Ready

One or More Days Before Class

1. Locate a physical map of Earth.

2. Review or become familiar with how to use the biome key for this mission. Consult an atlas as needed.

3. Make transparencies of Teacher's Key for Planet Z maps (pages 79 and 80).

4. Organize students into six groups.

Just Before the Lesson

1. Display the world map and the chart paper where all the students can see them.

Classroom Action

1. **Mission Briefing.** Have the class refer to the "Mission Briefing" for mission 6 in their student logbooks while one student reads it aloud.

2. **What Do You Think?** Have students answer the pre-activity questions on the "Mission Briefing." Invite them to share their answers in a class discussion.

3. **Discussion.** Read and discuss the question on the briefing page: If you were an extraterrestrial looking at Earth, where would you expect to find intelligent life? Direct students' attention to the world map and have them briefly share ideas.

   Ask students what features the colors and symbols represent on the map. Help the students determine that colors on a physical map may represent elevation, land features, vegetation, and so forth. Determine how your map shows land features such as mountains, rivers, and deserts. Point out that, on a typical map, each color represents a biome. Ask the students: What is the difference between a "biome" and a "habitat"? A biome *is a general, large geographic area that shares a type of climate, with average temperatures and rainfall, such as "rain forest" or "desert."* A habitat *is the specific place in which an organism lives; this is the specific environment to which an organism is adapted.*

   For example, the general "desert" biome includes the Sonoran Desert habitat in Arizona and Mexico, the Mohave Desert habitat in California, the Sahara Desert habitat in Africa, and many other specific places. How are they all the same? *They all have little rain or water, and can get very hot or very cold.* How are they all unique? *Each has its own species of plants and animals.*

   Have them turn to the Earth maps in their student logbooks and introduce the Biome Key for this lesson, as shown in figure 6.1 (page 74).

Teacher's Note: *Reinforce the idea that intelligent life will not necessarily be present on a planet that has plant and animal life. We will assume that there is intelligent life on such a planet for the purpose of this lesson.*

Figure 6.1—Biome Key.

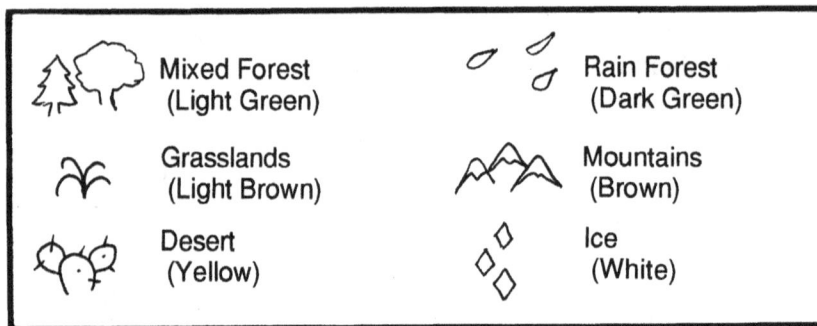

4. **Activity.** Instruct students to color in the Earth map in their logbooks according to the key. Ask them to look for patterns in biome distribution as they color. For instance, is there a general rule about where rain forests appear on the globe? Mountains? Deserts? Ice? Hand out crayons and markers and allow time for work.

5. **Discussion.** When most of the students have completed the coloring, ask them to tell you what they learned about biome distribution. Record their ideas on the chart paper.

   Mountains are represented by triangular symbols and/or brown or purple colors. Their location varies.

   Grasslands exist on Earth approximately 30-45 degrees above or below the equator, generally on the leeward side of a mountain range. Consult an atlas to become familiar with specific grassland locations.

   Desert exists on Earth approximately 30 degrees above or below the equator. Consult an atlas to become familiar with specific desert locations.

   Rain forest exists on Earth along the equator between the Tropic of Cancer and the Topic of Capricorn.

   Mixed forest includes deciduous and coniferous forests, and exists on Earth mostly 30-70 degrees above the equator.

   Ice, or polar regions, are areas of permanent ice or snow that exist on Earth at the top and bottom of its rotational axis.

Aquatic habitats on Earth are very diverse. They include freshwater rivers and lakes as well as saltwater oceans and seas.

6. **Activity.** Tell students that you have Planet Z continents for their blank maps. Instruct them to first color the continents according to the key, cut them out, then arrange them on the blank Planet Z maps using what they learned about biomes on Earth. Tell them to refer to the chart paper list and the Earth map for help. Once they feel like the continents are placed where they fit all the guidelines about biome location on Earth, they should gently tape their continents to the paper so that they can be moved later. Hand out continents and tape. Encourage students to check each other's work. Emphasize that they may need to relocate the continents at the end of the activity. This is a chance to experiment with possible continent locations and demonstrate what they learned about biomes.

7. **Discussion.** Choose several students to display their maps to the class. Have them explain briefly why they made the continent placement choices they did. Acknowledge their good thinking and explain that, since everyone will need to have the same map, you will give them one possible continent arrangement to copy. Put the first transparency of the Planet Z Teacher's Key on the overhead projector and give the students time to rearrange their continents. Repeat for the second transparency.

    Ask students to assume that survival needs for Planet Z life-forms are the same as for Earth life-forms. Have students determine up to eight places they would look to find intelligent organisms on Planet Z. Mark their choices on the transparencies of the Planet Z maps. Be sure students can defend why they think a particular biome on Planet Z would be a good candidate for intelligent life. The entire class should agree that survival needs for extraterrestrial life could be met at each location marked on the Planet Z map.

Teacher's Note: *As with patterns of evolution of intelligence and culture, we are assuming that Planet Z is very Earth-like. This is the only example we can use. You may want to point out that other planets may be very different from Earth.*

Mission 6.2

Materials

For the Teacher

- Planet Z Teacher Keys

For Each Student

- SETI Academy Cadet Logbook

- Pencil

For Each Team

- Crayons or markers

- Poster paper 2 feet by 3 feet or larger

- Set of Planet Z habitats

- Tape

- Glue

Getting Ready

One or More Days Before Class

1. Organize the class into teams of three or four.

2. Copy a set of Planet Z habitat pictures for each group.

3. Gather enough poster paper for each team to have a piece.

Classroom Action

1. **Lecture.** Review the differences between biome and habitat. Today, the student teams will receive pictures of Planet Z habitats. Explain that they will analyze each habitat picture to see which biome it belongs to. They will create a large map of Planet Z, tape the colored habitat pictures to it, and draw lines from each picture to the biomes that could contain it. See figure 6.2.

   As a class decide on a color for the Planet Z plants. Explain that on Earth plants are green because they have chlorophyll. However, photosynthetic pigments on other planets might be any color: purple, orange, cyan, and so forth. Choose *one* color for Planet Z plants to be.

Figure 6.2—Planet Z Maps with Habitats.

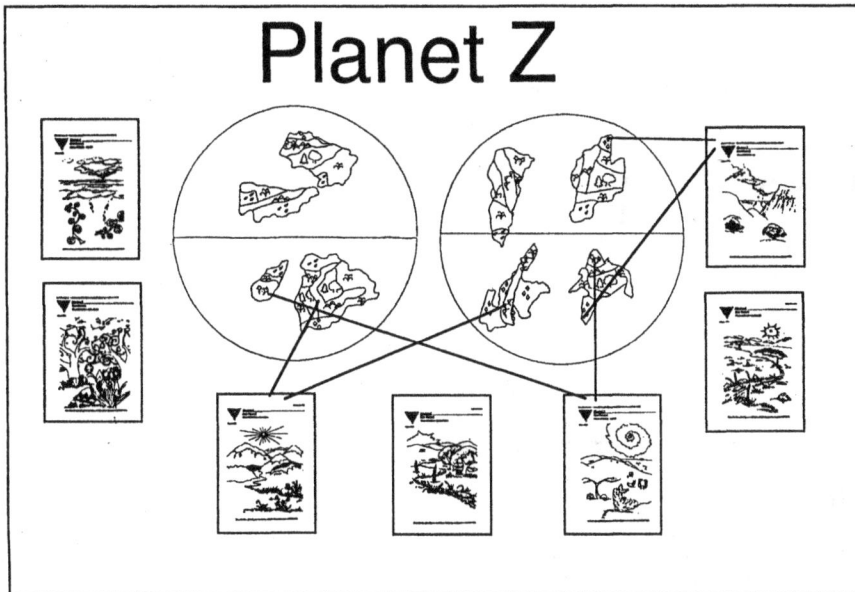

2. **Activity.** Hand out the habitat pictures. Give one set of habitat pictures and one piece of poster paper to each team. Let the teams color their habitat pictures and draw their maps using the completed Planet Z maps in their student logbooks. Remind them that all Planet Z plants will be the color they chose. They may add very minor things to the habitat pictures, such as another plant or a few clouds, but they may *not* add any animal life. (In the next mission, they will place extraterrestrial organisms into these habitats.) Once they have drawn the map and colored the habitat pictures, go on to the next step.

3. **Discussion.** Ask the students: Where on the Planet Z map could each of the habitats exist? You may post a class map, and have them put map pins where they think each habitat could exist. Or you may let them put star symbols on their own maps. Be sure students can defend why they think a particular habitat exists within a particular biome on Planet Z. Ask: What kind of alien creatures might live in these alien habitats? Tomorrow we will meet some!

Teacher's Note: *These habitat pictures must be saved for use in the next mission.*

Closure

1. **Lecture.** Review the types of biomes that exist on Earth and what types of biomes could exist on Planet Z. Tell students that they should begin thinking about *specific* places, or habitats, on Planet Z where extraterrestrials might live.

2. **What Do You Think, Now?** Have students answer the post-activity questions on the logbook sheet "What Do You Think, Now?" Invite students to share their responses. Ask them how their opinions have been changed by this mission.

Going Further

Discussion: Cartography

Have students collect different types of maps. Discuss the uses of and differences among the maps.

Research: The Solar System

Have students research maps of other planets in our solar system. What would a map of Mars or Venus show? Do these planets have Earth-type biomes? Which are they most like?

Art: High-Gravity Worlds

Ask students to imagine what life on a high-gravity world would look like. Would the biomes be different? The habitats?

Figure 6.3—Planet Z Teacher's Key.

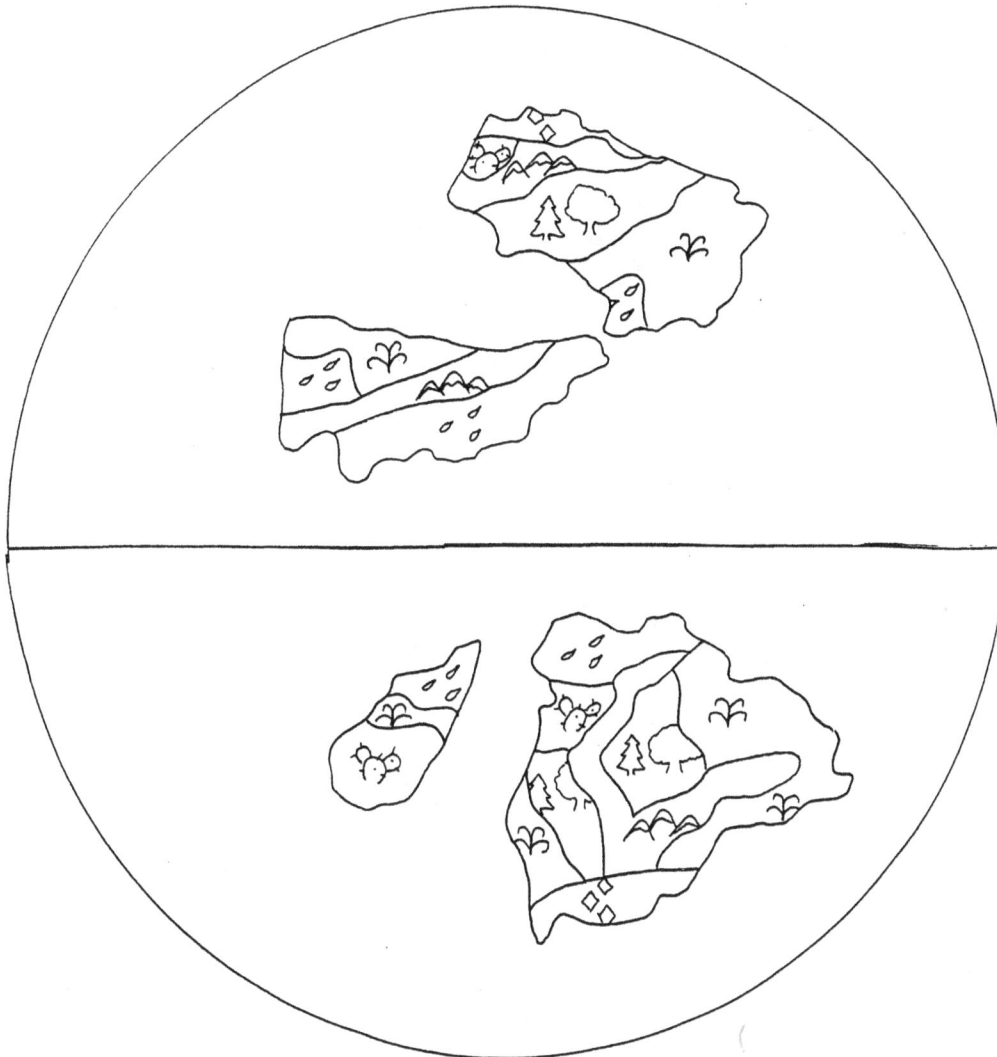

Figure 6.4—Biome Key.

Mixed Forest
(Light Green)

Rain Forest
(Dark Green)

Grasslands
(Light Brown)

Mountains
(Brown)

Desert
(Yellow)

Ice
(White)

Figure 6.5—Planet Z Teacher's Key.

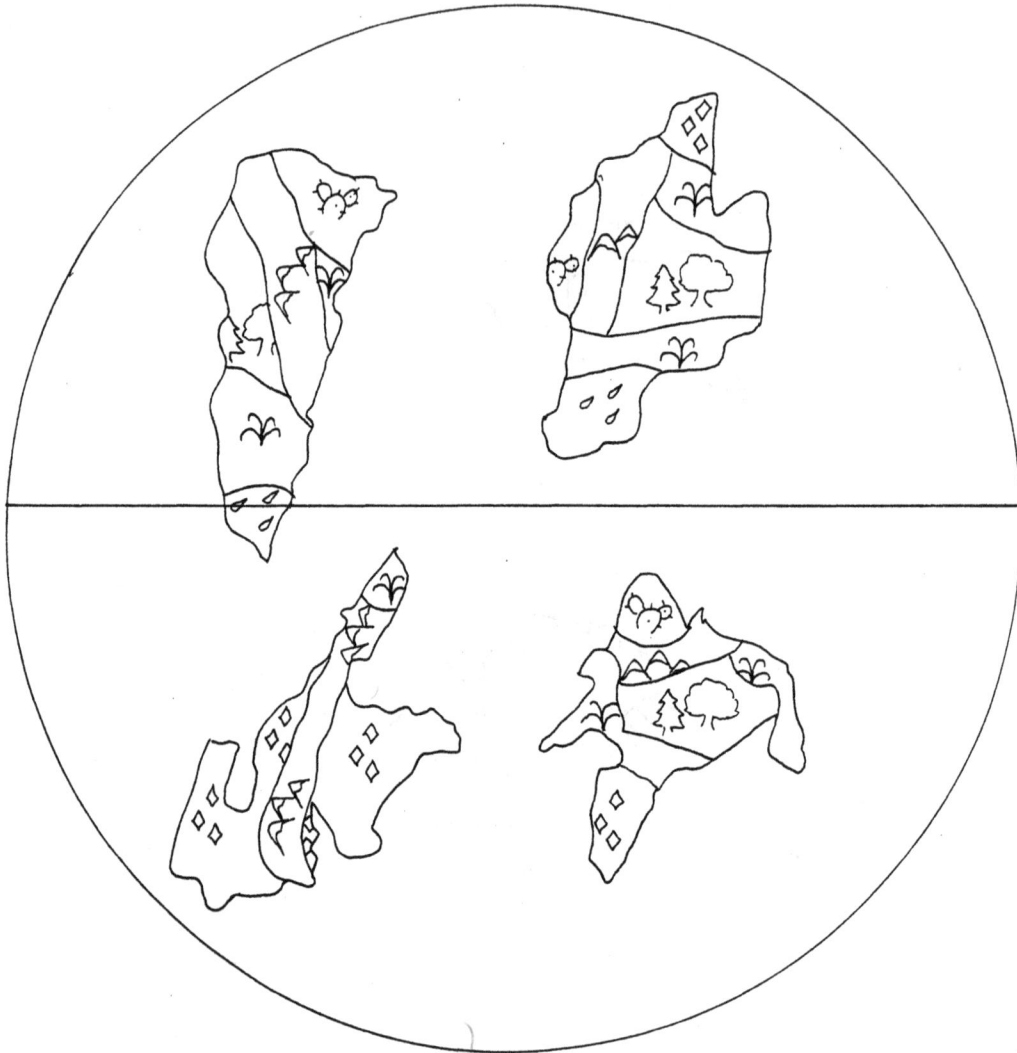

Figure 6.6—Biome Key.

Mixed Forest
(Light Green)

Rain Forest
(Dark Green)

Grasslands
(Light Brown)

Mountains
(Brown)

Desert
(Yellow)

Ice
(White)

Mission 6

Meet Planet Z
Mission Briefing

Name:

Date:

**Dr. Anthony Garcia,
Cultural Anthropologist
on the SETI Academy Team**

Where would you look for life on an alien world? During this mission you will examine a map of Earth to see the distribution of its *biomes*, which are large geographic areas such as deserts and rain forests. You will use this information to create an accurate biome map of Earth and of an Earth-like, habitable, fictional planet—Planet Z. Then you will examine pictures of several specific habitats on Planet Z and put them on the biome map.

What Do You Think?

1. If you were an extraterrestrial looking at Earth, where would you expect to find intelligent life-forms? Why?

Mission 6

Meet Planet Z

Earth Landmasses—Australia and Greenland

Figure 6.7.

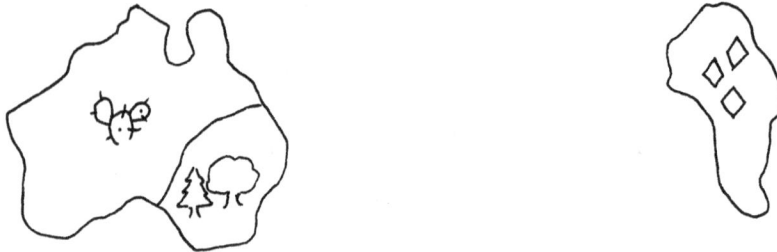

🌲🌳	Mixed Forest (Light Green)		Rain Forest (Dark Green)
🌱	Grasslands (Light Brown)		Mountains (Brown)
	Desert (Yellow)		Ice (White)

Mission 6

Meet Planet Z

Earth Landmasses—North America and South America

Figure 6.8.

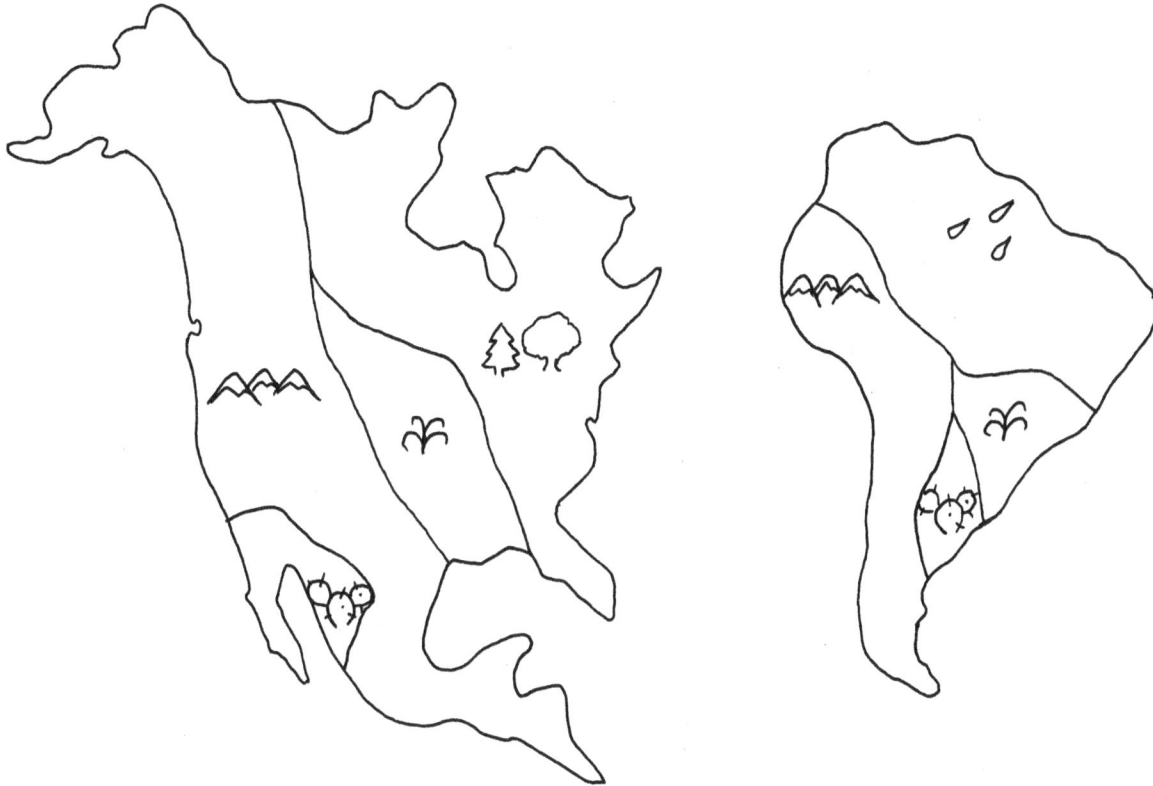

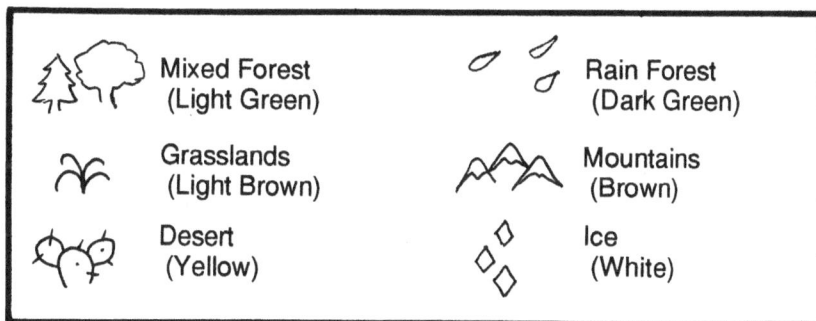

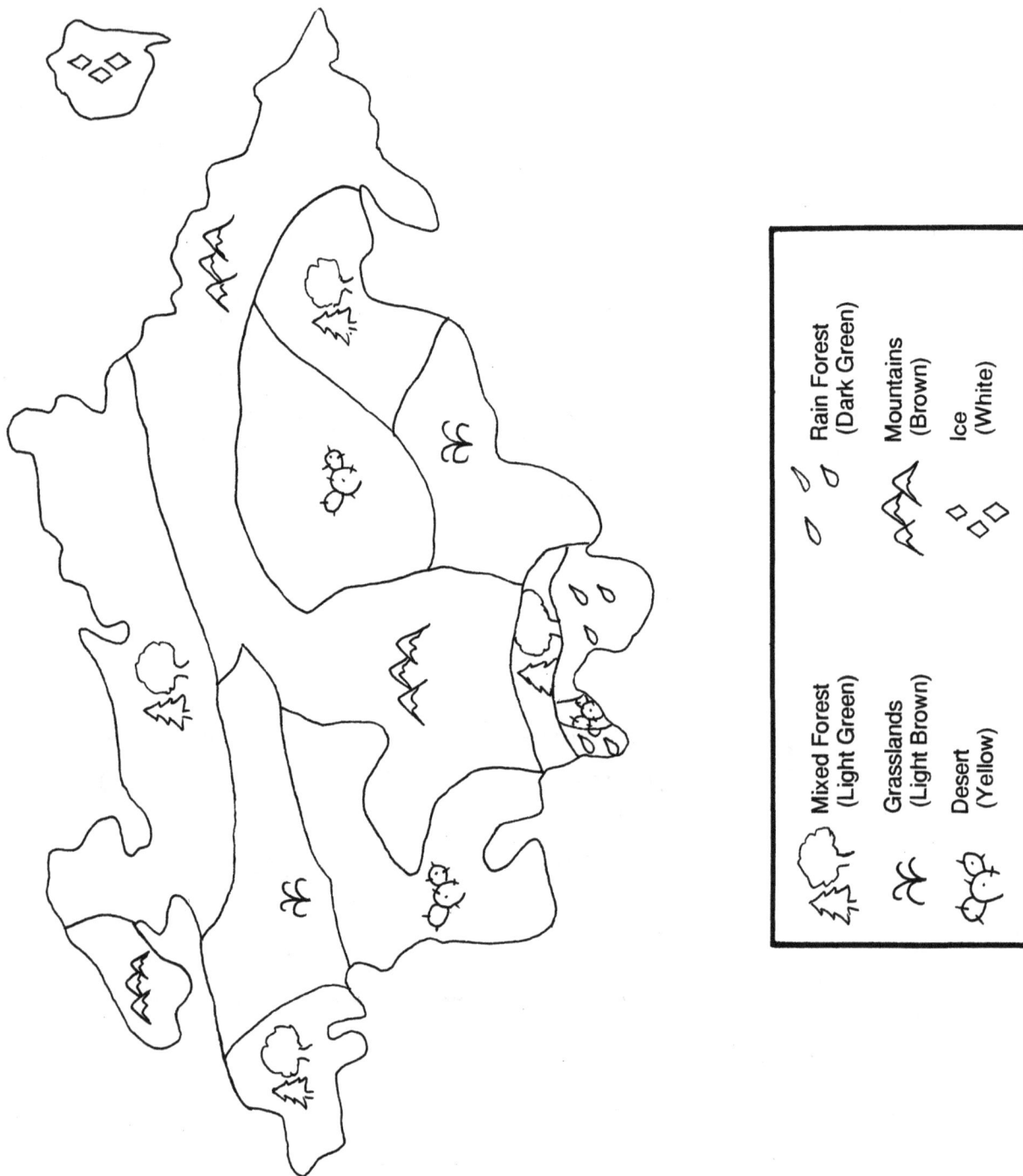

Mission 6

Meet Planet Z

Earth Landmasses—Eurasia and Arctic Ice (Floating)

Figure 6.9.

Rain Forest
(Dark Green)

Mountains
(Brown)

Ice
(White)

Mixed Forest
(Light Green)

Grasslands
(Light Brown)

Desert
(Yellow)

Mission 6

Meet Planet Z

Earth Landmasses—Africa and Antarctica

Figure 6.10.

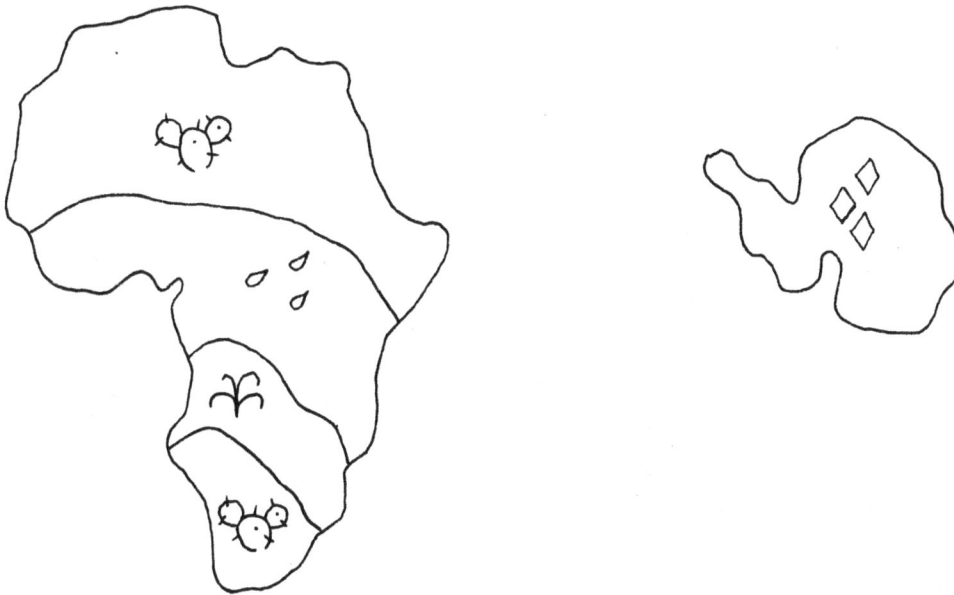

Mixed Forest (Light Green)		Rain Forest (Dark Green)	
Grasslands (Light Brown)		Mountains (Brown)	
Desert (Yellow)		Ice (White)	

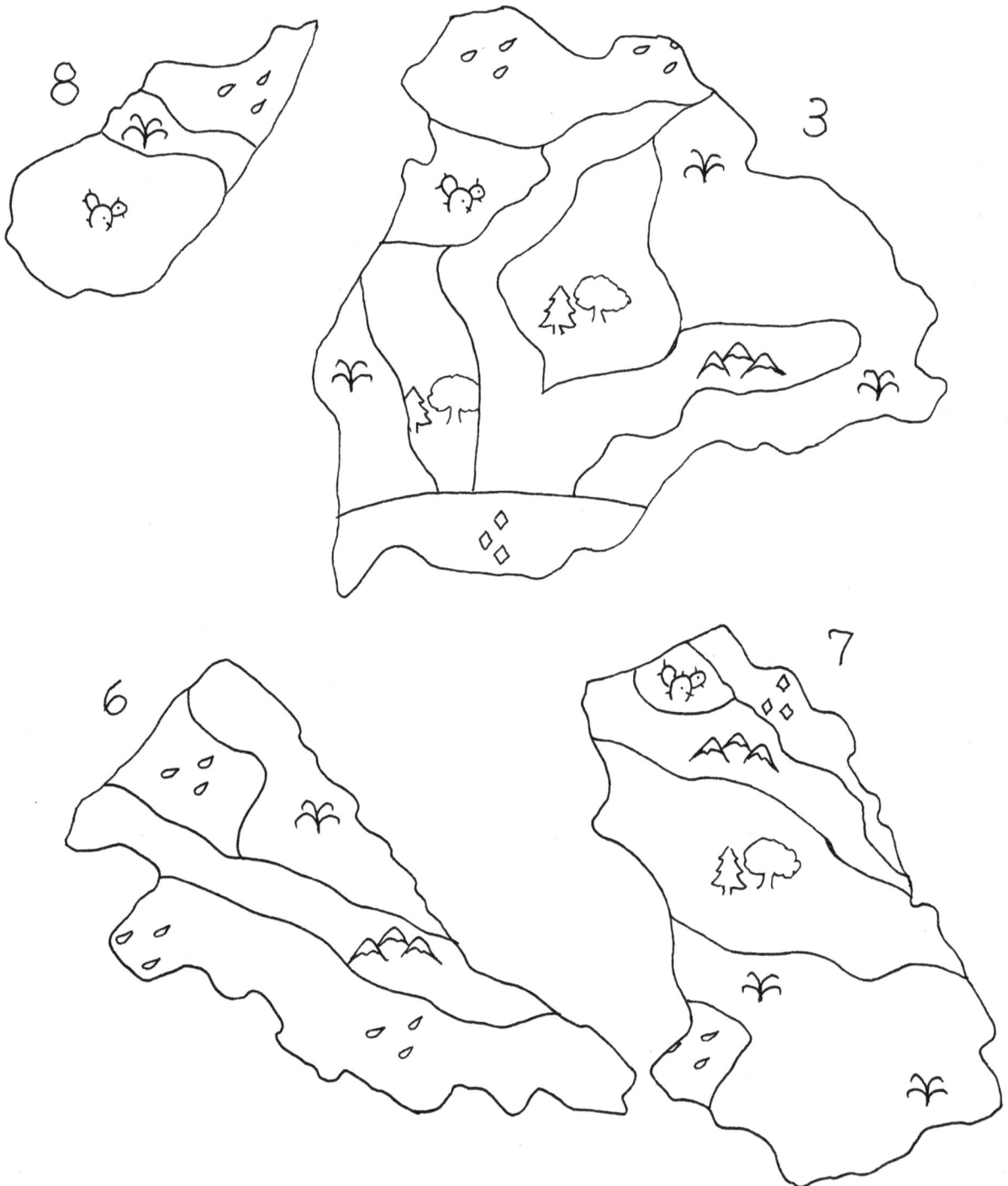

Mission 6

Meet Planet Z

Planet Z Landmasses, Page 1

Figure 6.11.

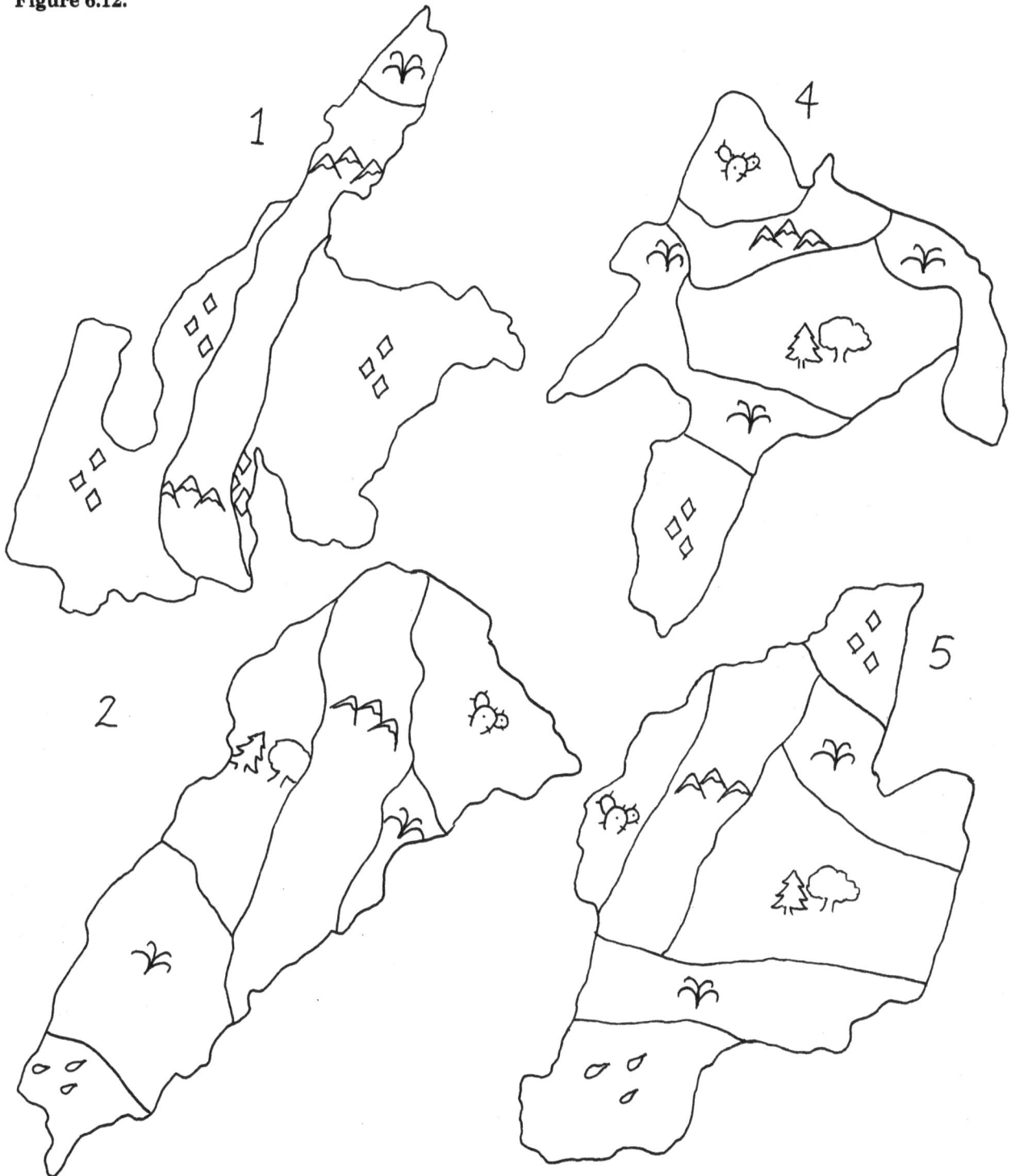

Mission 6

Meet Planet Z

Planet Z Landmasses, Page 2

Figure 6.12.

Mission 6

Meet Planet Z

Earth Map, Page 1

Figure 6.13.

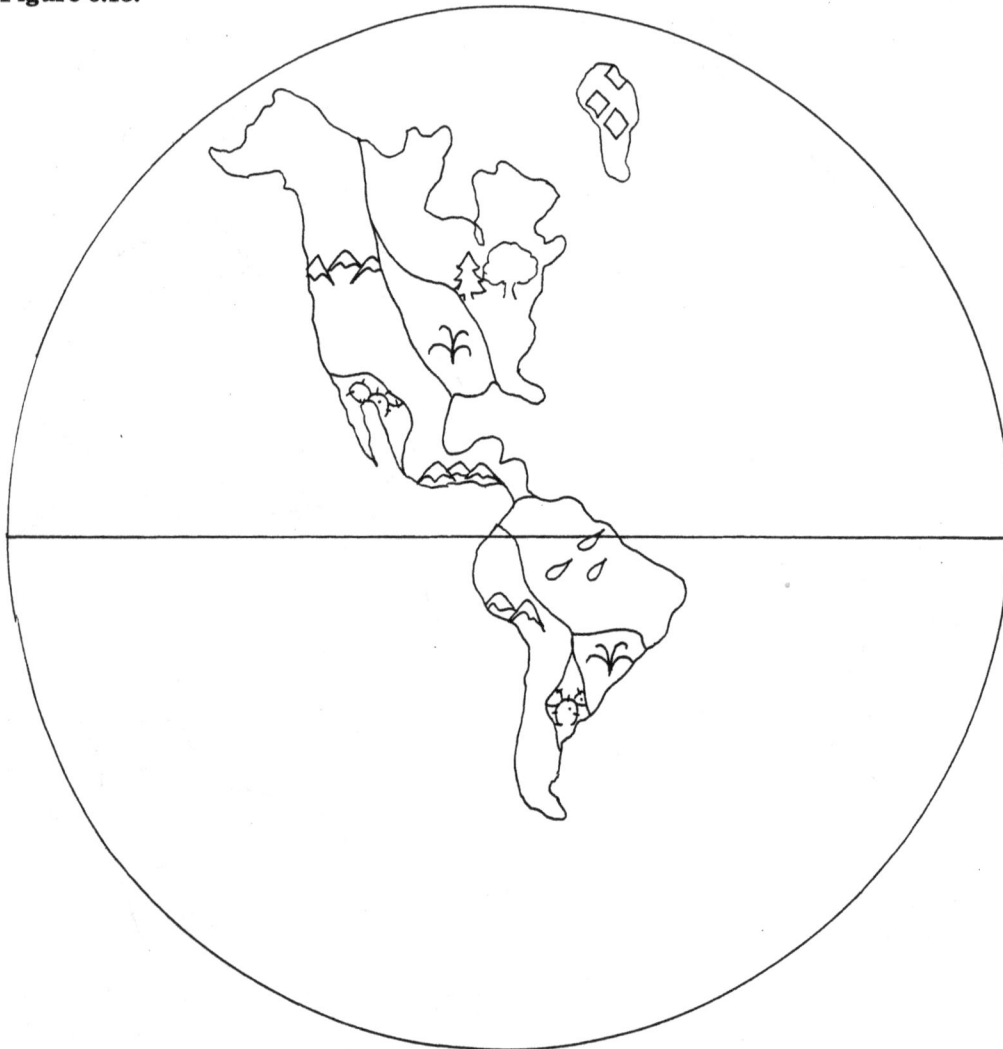

	Mixed Forest (Light Green)		Rain Forest (Dark Green)
	Grasslands (Light Brown)		Mountains (Brown)
	Desert (Yellow)		Ice (White)

From *The Rise of Intelligence and Culture.* © 1995. Teacher Ideas Press. (800) 237-6124.

Mission 6

Meet Planet Z

Earth Map, Page 2

Figure 6.14.

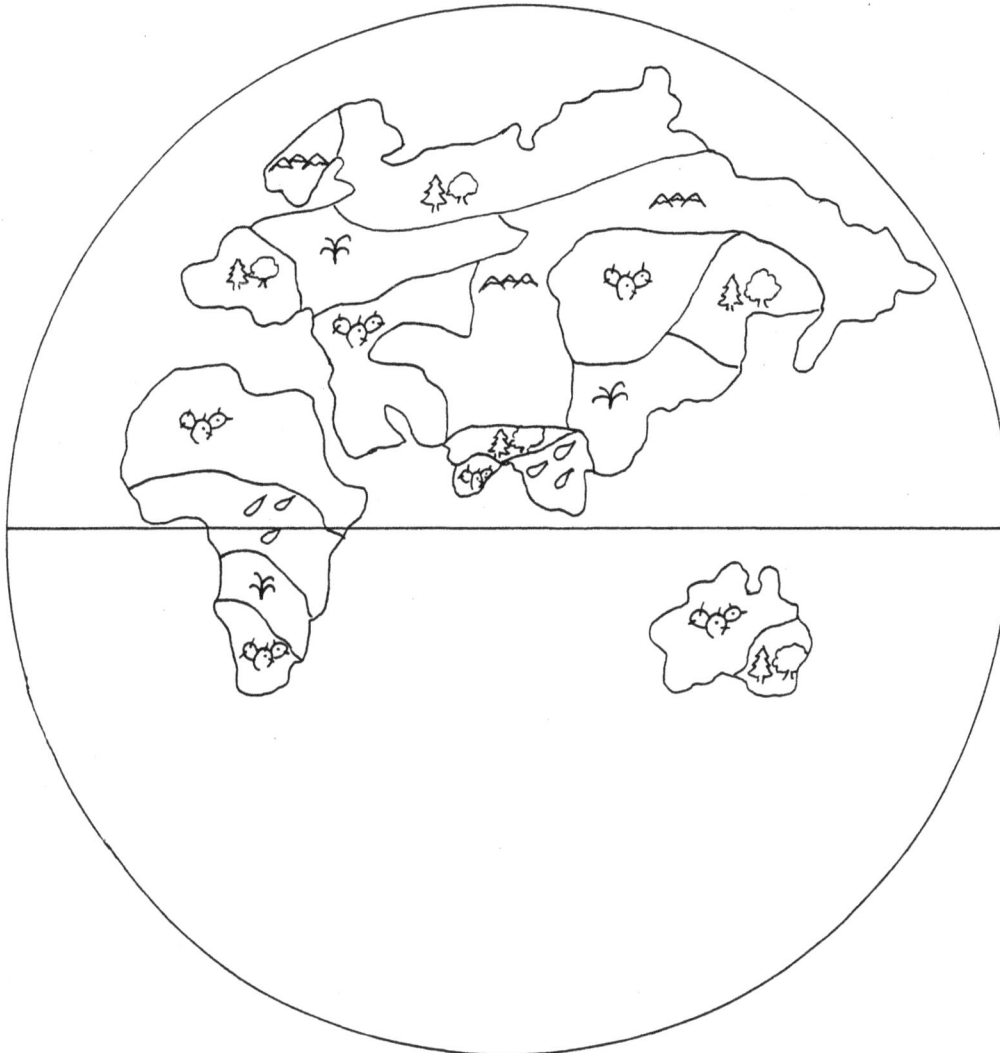

🌲🌳	Mixed Forest (Light Green)		Rain Forest (Dark Green)
	Grasslands (Light Brown)		Mountains (Brown)
	Desert (Yellow)		Ice (White)

Mission 6

Meet Planet Z

Planet Z Map, Page 1

Figure 6.15.

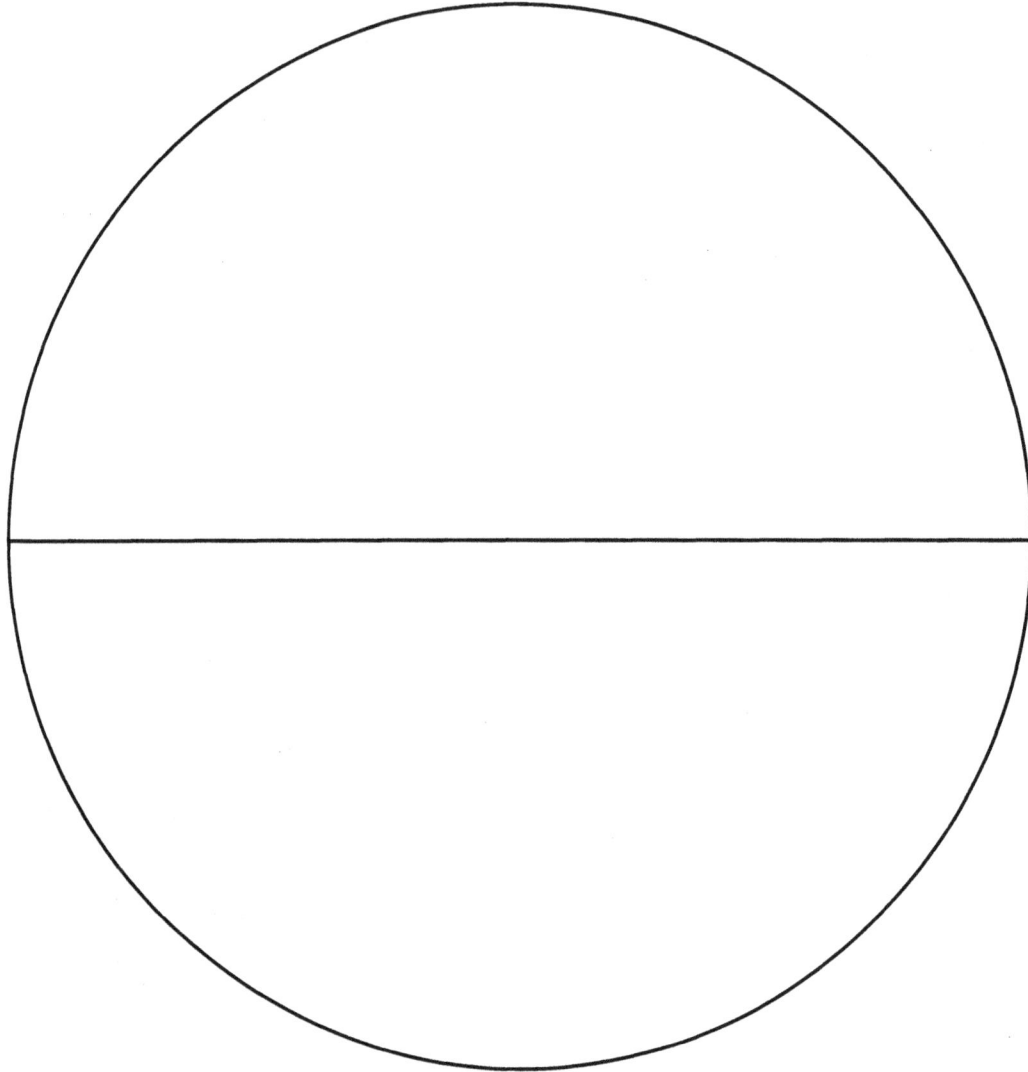

Mixed Forest (Light Green)		Rain Forest (Dark Green)	
Grasslands (Light Brown)		Mountains (Brown)	
Desert (Yellow)		Ice (White)	

Mission 6

Meet Planet Z

Planet Z Map, Page 2

Figure 6.16.

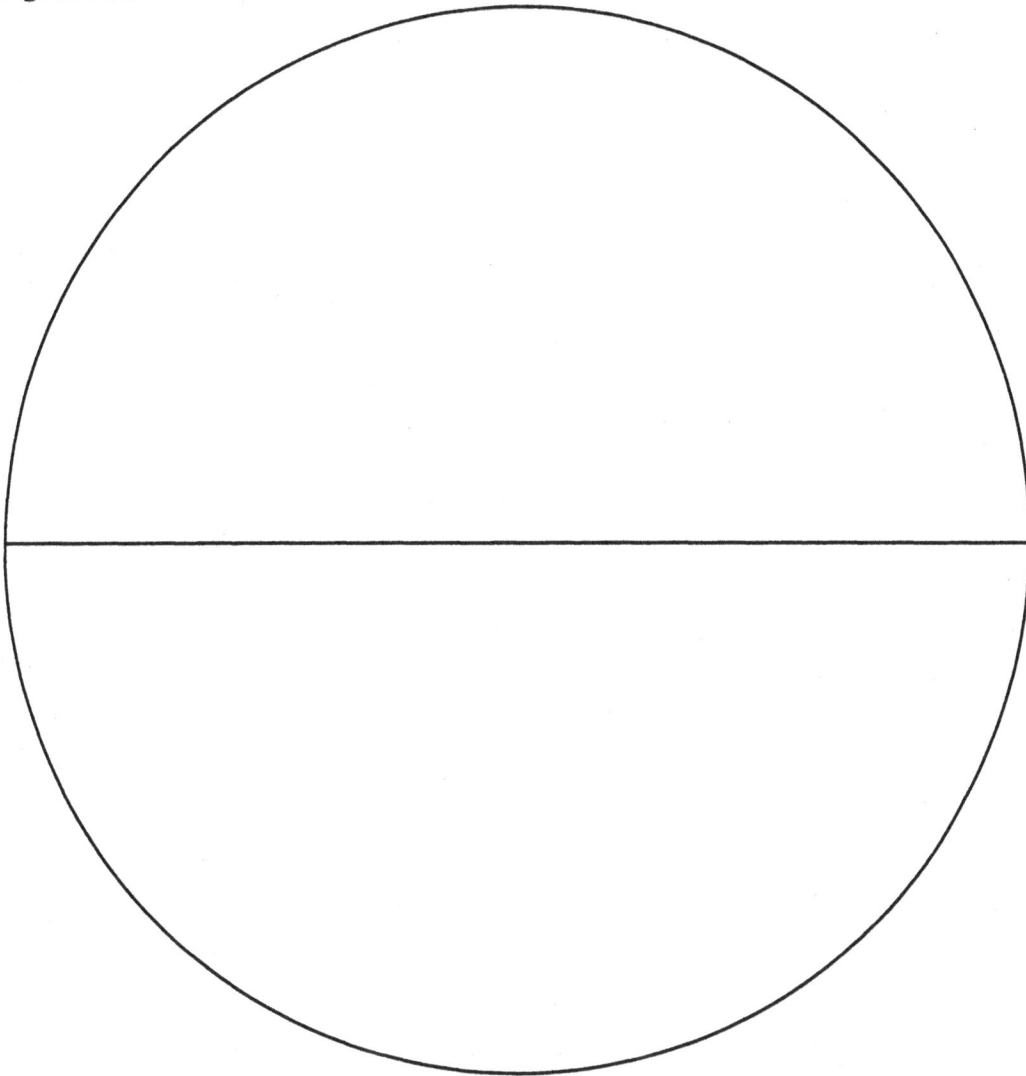

🌲 Mixed Forest (Light Green)		Rain Forest (Dark Green)	
Grasslands (Light Brown)		Mountains (Brown)	
Desert (Yellow)		Ice (White)	

From *The Rise of Intelligence and Culture.* © 1995. Teacher Ideas Press. (800) 237-6124.

Mission 6

Meet Planet Z

Planet Z Habitat—Rain Forest

Figure 6.17.

From *The Rise of Intelligence and Culture.* © 1995. Teacher Ideas Press. (800) 237-6124.

Mission 6

Meet Planet Z

Planet Z Habitat—Mountains

Figure 6.18.

Mission 6

Meet Planet Z

Planet Z Habitat—Desert

Figure 6.19.

Mission 6

Meet Planet Z

Planet Z Habitat—Grasslands

Figure 6.20.

From *The Rise of Intelligence and Culture.* © 1995. Teacher Ideas Press. (800) 237-6124.

Mission 6

Meet Planet Z

Planet Z Habitat—Ice

Figure 6.21.

Mission 6

Meet Planet Z

Planet Z Habitat—Mixed Forest

Figure 6.22.

Mission 6

Meet Planet Z

Planet Z Habitat—Aquatic

Figure 6.23.

Mission 6

Meet Planet Z

What Do You Think, Now?

Name:

Date:

After you have completed this mission, please answer the following question:

1. If you were an extraterrestrial looking at Earth, where would you expect to find intelligent life-forms? Why?

From *The Rise of Intelligence and Culture.* © 1995. Teacher Ideas Press. (800) 237-6124.

Mission 7

Intelligent Life on Planet Z
Could Beings from Planet Z
Develop Technology?

Overview

In mission 7, students are introduced to some fictional extraterrestrial life-forms that live on Planet Z, life-forms that have some biologic structures and traits and behaviors that are similar to various Earth animals.

In mission 7.1, students analyze the habitats of the extraterrestrial life-forms. In mission 7.2, students use a matrix to identify the physical traits and behaviors that might be indicative of intelligence, much as they did with Earth animals in mission 3. In mission 7.3, the extraterrestrial life-form found to have the most traits and behaviors indicative of intelligence is artificially developed by student groups to make it more capable of producing cultures specific to its habitat or habitats, cultures that might become civilizations with advanced technology.

Concepts

- A life-form that is an *ecological specialist* is highly adapted to one habitat and cannot live in other habitats.

- A life-form that is an *ecological generalist* can live in many habitats, although it evolved in one habitat and may be more adapted to that one habitat.

- All species evolve physical traits that are adaptations to their specific habitat. This is called *biologic evolution*.

- In biologic evolution, *nature* selects the traits that will survive.

- Some physical traits and behaviors make the life-form more intelligent, and can lead to *cultural evolution*.

In mission 6, students investigated biomes and habitats on Earth and on Planet Z.

101

- Cultural evolution involves learning, memory, and the transmission of cultural ideas from adults to young.

- In cultural evolution, the life-form itself selects the behaviors that will enable it to survive.

- Any species that evolves as humans did, to use their brains to develop tools and to change their environments, is likely to develop technology.

- Once technology begins to develop, it is possible that radio technology will be developed.

Skills

- Analyze fictional life-forms for traits that may indicate intelligence, and therefore their potential for technology.

- Constructing and using a matrix.

Mission 7.1

Materials

For the Class

- Overhead projector

- Transparencies of "Extraterrestrial Life-Forms" logbook sheets (see page 118)

For Each Team

- 1 life-form (see pages 118-130) and 1 blank attribute matrix (see page 110)

- Scissors

- Paste or tape

- Map and habitat pictures from previous mission

- (optional) Crayons or markers

For Each Student

- SETI Academy Cadet Logbook

- Pencil

Getting Ready

One Or More Days Before Class

1. Make transparencies of the seven "Extraterrestrial Life-Forms."

2. Copy one full set of "Extraterrestrial Life-Forms" and seven blank attribute forms.

Just Before the Lesson

1. Set up the overhead projector.

Classroom Action

1. **Mission Briefing.** Have the class refer to the "Mission Briefing" for mission 7 in their student logbooks while one student reads it aloud.

2. **What Do You Think?** Have students answer the pre-activity questions on the "Mission Briefing." Invite them to share their answers in a class discussion.

3. **Lecture.** Announce that to complete this mission students will be working in the same teams they were in for mission 6. Their first team task will be to analyze one of the seven extraterrestrial life-forms to determine in which of the habitats (they worked with in mission 6) it belongs. The seven habitats are: mountains, desert, grasslands, ice, rain forest, mixed forest, and aquatic.

   Some life-forms are ecological specialists, while others are ecological generalists. Ecological specialists are life-forms that are highly adapted to one specific habitat—the one they evolved in and never left. A polar bear is a specialist: It is very good at living in the ice habitat, but could not survive in a tropical rain forest or a desert! Ask students if they can think of other Earth animals that are ecological specialists. Ecological generalists are life-forms that can survive in several different habitats, although they originated in one habitat and may be better adapted to that habitat than any other. A bobcat is a generalist: It can survive in deserts, forests, and even grasslands. Ask students if they can think of other Earth animals that are ecological generalists.

Ask students if humans are specialists or generalists? *Generalists.* Ask students which they think would be more likely to be intelligent? *Evolution suggests that the generalist is more likely to be intelligent, because it is more flexible, and it is able to adapt to changing conditions. Besides, humans are generalists!*

4. **Activity.** Divide the class into seven groups. Give each group one of the seven life-forms and one blank attribute form. Allow students time to read about and discuss the life-forms assigned to their team. After they have read the descriptions, they should fill out the blank attribute form. They should decide upon a habitat or habitats for each life-form, based upon its characteristics as interpreted from reading the descriptions. Life-forms that appear to be specialists should be labeled with their one possible habitat. Life-forms that appear to be generalists should be labeled with their primary habitat and any other possible habitats.

5. **Discussion.** Gather the teams together. Put the first transparency of an extraterrestrial life-form on the overhead. Have the team that studied that life-form report their findings. Help the class come to agreement on the habitat or habitats for each life-form, and whether it is a generalist or a specialist. Record the information on the transparency. Repeat the process with the rest of Planet Z's life-forms. Encourage students to explain their reasons for each habitat they select. Tape the transparencies to the chalkboard side by side for future reference. Have the teams hand in their completed attribute forms and extraterrestrial life-form descriptions for use in mission 7.2.

Table 7.1—Teacher's Key to ETs in a Habitat.

Life-Form	Ecological Type	Habitat(s)
Aquatica	Specialist	Aquatic
Bat-Rat	Specialist	Rain Forest
Hawkroach	Generalist	All Terrestrial Habitats are Possible, Even Ice
Spheroid	Specialist	Desert
Segmenter	Specialist	Mixed Forest
Two-Header	Generalist	Grasslands, Mountains, Mixed Forest, and Desert
Monoid	Specialist	Ice

Explain to students that their teams will now work together to create dioramas for the seven life-forms that live on Planet Z. The first step is to have them draw or paste each life-form into the correct habitat picture, as shown in figure 7.1.

Figure 7.1—Sample Diorama.

6. **Activity.** Have the class break into their teams again. Have them turn to the tiny extraterrestrials pages in their logbook.

   Allow time for students to cut out their pictures and add them to the Planet Z map and habitat poster they made in mission 6. They may want to add a few imaginary creatures of their own directly into the habitat pictures.

Mission 7.2

Materials

For the Class

- Completed attribute forms from mission 6

- Life-form descriptions from mission 6

- Chart paper

- Markers

- Transparency of "Physical Traits and Behaviors Matrix"

- Overhead projector pens or grease pencil

For Each Team

- Blank paper

For Each Student

- SETI Academy Cadet Logbook

- Pencil

Getting Ready

1. Make a transparency of the "Physical Traits and Behaviors Matrix" (see page 137).

2. Have handy the completed attribute forms and life-form descriptions from mission 6.

3. Label the chart paper "New Top 10 Traits and Behaviors of Intelligence," and add the numbers 1 through 10 in a column down the left-hand side. Hang the chart where all students can see it.

4. Organize your class into seven new teams.

Classroom Action

1. **Discussion.** Have students turn to the Top 10 list from mission 3 in their logbooks. Ask them if they have any new ideas about what constitutes traits and behaviors of intelligence. Ask them to reach a new consensus about the top 10 traits and behaviors of intelligence. Record their answers on the chart paper.

2. **Activity.** Explain that each team will become specialists on one life-form. They will list all the traits and behaviors of intelligence they believe their life-form has, then share the information with the class by adding it to the transparency "Physical Traits and Behaviors Matrix." Redistribute the completed attribute forms and life-form descriptions from mission 6, one life-form per team. Allow the teams time to review and list the traits and behaviors of their life-form. When they have completed their list they can record their findings on the transparency.

3. **Discussion.** As a class, consider the completed matrix. Check the totals and settle any disagreements regarding the traits and behaviors allocated to each life-form. Reach a class consensus as to which life-form has the greatest potential for intelligence. It should be the Hawkroach, which has all five attributes. Ask students if the Hawkroach is capable of surviving in many of the seven habitats on Planet Z. Why might this be so? *It is a generalist, not a specialist.* Ask students what might happen next with such an intelligent life-form. Could it develop even more intelligence and perhaps develop a culture? Tell students that in mission 7.3 they will help the Hawkroach do just that!

Teacher's Note: *The Two-Header is also a likely candidate (with three of five attributes). Either the Hawkroach or the Two-Header will work well for later missions, but choose just one!*

Mission 7.3

Materials

For Each Student

- SETI Academy Cadet Logbook

- Pencil

Getting Ready

No preparation is necessary.

Classroom Action

1. **Discussion.** Once the class has reached a consensus as to which life-form should evolve greater intelligence (the one most likely to evolve other traits of intelligence or other social behaviors, because it already possesses some of these traits and behaviors), they should decide as a class which characteristics they want to change before they begin to work in their teams.

   The choices for traits that can be chosen to "evolve" (change) are listed on their logbook sheets (3) "Helping Your Life-Form Survive." Review these pages briefly and have the class agree on several traits or behaviors that could change.

2. (optional) **Lecture.** Review the "Early Earth Cultures" transparencies to give students clues on how to proceed with their life-form's evolution on Planet Z.

3. **Activity.** Have the teams reunite and work together to complete the three "Helping Your Life-Form Survive" logbook sheets. Assign each of the seven teams a different habitat. Have each team pick a Planet Z landmass (have them use their two "Planet Z Map" logbook sheets from mission 6) where their life-form will live, evolve, and develop a culture.

   Have each student circle their team's choices in their logbooks on the "Helping Your Life-Form Survive" page for reference. Each team should then decide changes that would make the life-form more intelligent. Check each team's changes before they draw their "evolved" life-form. This is a chance to determine if students

Teacher's Note: *The next step is to "evolve" one life-form toward its cultural capacity. This involves letting students make conscious choices as to what adaptations should occur in a species. This may give them a major misconception about evolution! You may wish to explain to students that, as far as scientists can tell, there is no conscious intelligence directing evolution in a specific path. Ask students if they think that natural selection and evolution really work this way. Explain that natural selection and evolution proceed by chance. The environment selects the best traits from among those already available. Students are selecting the traits here so that they can see how intelligence might evolve in a species.*

Teacher's Note: *Why limit students in what they can change? Evolution proceeds by "descent with modification." In other words, existing structures slowly change into newer structures; over geologic time, an arm might evolve into a wing, but a wing would not suddenly appear on a life-form's back.*

understand which adaptations will aid their life-form's survival and which will contribute to greater intelligence.

Closure

1. **Discussion.** Have each group report on how its life-form has adapted to biome conditions on Planet Z.

2. **What Do You Think, Now?** Have students answer the post-activity questions on the logbook sheet "What Do You Think, Now?" Invite students to share their responses. Ask them how their opinions have been changed by this mission.

Going Further

Activity: Back on Planet Y

If your students completed the missions in *How Might Life Evolve on Other Worlds?* (book 2 of the *SETI Academy Planet Project*) and created their own alien species, they might enjoy checking that species for its intelligence. Have students watch (and direct) its continued evolution toward greater intelligence, culture, and eventually radio technology.

Activity: A New Life-Form for Planet Z

Use a blank "Attribute Matrix" and have students fill in their ideas for each attribute, and then draw this new creature. Have students analyze and continue its evolution. Have the whole class work together to create one "Classy Creature"!

Activity: Talking About Evolution

Have students write a new description for one of the seven life-forms in this mission. It should describe how the life-form's adaptations help it to survive on Planet Z.

Table 7.2—Blank Attribute Matrix.

Attribute	Description of Your Planet Z Life-Form	✓
1. Kind of skin		
2. Ecological type		
3. Basic body shape		
4. Segments		
5. Appendages		
6. Hard parts		
7. Brain-body ratio		
8. Body size		
9. Social behavior		
10. Moving around		
11. Hearing		
12. Smell and taste		
13. Sight		
14. Eating		
15. Defense		
16. Reproduction		
17. Babies		
18.		
19.		
20.		
21.		
22.		

Table 7.3—Teacher's Key—Aquatica Attributes.

Note: Attributes that may indicate intelligence are in boldface. See page 118 for logbook sheet.

Attribute	Description of Your Planet Z Life-Form	✓
1. Kind of skin	Soft, slimy, mucus-covered skin	
2. Ecological type	Specialist for aquatic environment	
3. Basic body shape	Round	
4. Segments	One	
5. Appendages	Five stiff flippers; no grasping capability	
6. Hard parts	Internal skeleton	
7. Brain-body ratio	Low; brain about 1 kilogram	
8. Body size	1,100 to 2,200 kilograms	
9. Social behavior	Swims in small schools	✓
10. Moving around	Swims in water	
11. Hearing	Ear holes sense vibrations in water	
12. Smell and taste	Nostrils around mouth smell food	
13. Sight	Two large eyes at the end of its tube-like neck, one on each side	✓
14. Eating	Filters microscopic plant cells through baleen like a whale	
15. Defense	Swims into surf	
16. Reproduction	Male fertilizes female who gives birth eight months later	
17. Babies	Young accompany mother	
18.		
19.		
20.		
21.		
22.		

Table 7.4—Teacher's Key—Bat-Rat Attributes.

Note: Attributes that may indicate intelligence are in boldface. See page 120 for logbook sheet.

Attribute	Description of Your Planet Z Life-Form	✓
1. Kind of skin	Fur-covered, leathery skin, the color of soil	
2. Ecological type	Specialist for rain forest	
3. Basic body shape	Round	
4. Segments	Not segmented	
5. Appendages	Six forelegs, back legs, and wing flaps	
6. Hard parts	Internal skeleton, plus claws and teeth	
7. Brain-body ratio	Low	
8. Body size	Less than half a kilogram, mouse size	
9. Social behavior	None; they only meet to mate	
10. Moving around	Scurries on legs, hops and glides, digs underground in loose soil	
11. Hearing	Whiskers on head and face sense vibrations	
12. Smell and taste	Mouth senses what it eats, hands and feet sense what they touch	
13. Sight	Two eyes with good binocular, full-color vision	✓
14. Eating	Plant-eater. Drills into soft fruits and water-storing plants and sucks moisture and nutrients out.	
15. Defense	Camouflage—soil-colored. No poison. Runs and glides, burrows underground, hides in plants	
16. Reproduction	Sexual reproduction, organs are in tail. Two sexes, all indviduals have both sexes. Two organisms are needed to mate. Tail changes to green to indicate ability to mate.	
17. Babies	Babies develop in tail-like appendage, they crawl out when partly developed; they are taught how to feed	✓
18.		
19.		
20.		
21.		
22.		

Table 7.5—Teacher's Key—Hawkroach Attributes.

Note: Attributes that may indicate intelligence are in boldface. See page 122 for logbook sheet.

Attribute	Description of Your Planet Z Life-Form	✓
1. Kind of skin	Appendages are leathery; feathers on the joints	
2. Ecological type	Generalist; lives in most or even all the terrestrial habitats	✓
3. Basic body shape	Long	
4. Segments	Three: head, thorax, abdomen	
5. Appendages	Six: two legs and four arms with pincer-like grasping "hands"	✓
6. Hard parts	Hard outside parts: protein covering like an insect	
7. Brain-body ratio	High; brain weighs about 10 kilograms	✓
8. Body size	95 to 100 kilograms	
9. Social behavior	Fights and works with others of its species; hunts in packs	✓
10. Moving around	Walks on land	
11. Hearing	Ear holes and touch	
12. Smell and taste	Mouth and nose	
13. Sight	Two eyes on side of head, giving limited binocular black-and-white vision	✓
14. Eating	An omnivore; eats fruits and vegetables; as a meat-eater, hunts prey, tears at prey with beak, captures prey with grasping appendages	
15. Defense	Strong beak and claws; no poison	
16. Reproduction	Sexual; three sexes; mating call	
17. Babies	Lay eggs and take care of young	
18.		
19.		
20.		
21.		
22.		

Table 7.6—Teacher's Key—Spheroid Attributes.

Note: Attributes that may indicate intelligence are in boldface. See page 124 for logbook sheet.

Attribute	Description of Your Planet Z Life-Form	✓
1. Kind of skin	Hard shell	
2. Ecological type	Specialist for desert habitat	
3. Basic body shape	Round	
4. Segments	One	
5. Appendages	Twelve jointed legs, with flat clawless feet	
6. Hard parts	Hard shell; protein covering like an insect	
7. Brain-body ratio	Low; brain weighs about 1 kilogram	
8. Body size	90 to 95 kilograms	
9. Social behavior	None	
10. Moving around	Runs on land	
11. Hearing	Tiny hairs on legs sense vibrations	
12. Smell and taste	Smells through breathing ducts on either side of compound eye; shutter-type mouths	
13. Sight	One compound eye similar to an Earth fly	
14. Eating	Eats buds, tender young shoots, and branches of leafless plants	
15. Defense	Spines on body secrete poison from tips; runs away	
16. Reproduction	Sexual; requires two individuals to reproduce; female lays eggs that emit an odor that attracts males	
17. Babies	Lay eggs; don't care for babies	
18.		
19.		
20.		
21.		
22.		

Table 7.7—Teacher's Key—Segmenter Attributes.

Note: Attributes that may indicate intelligence are in boldface. See page 126 for logbook sheet.

Attribute	Description of Your Planet Z Life-Form	✓
1. Kind of skin	Leathery skin covers armored exoskeleton	
2. Ecological type	Specialist for mixed forest	
3. Basic body shape	Long	
4. Segments	Six	
5. Appendages	Two per segment, plus mouthparts	✓
6. Hard parts	Hard parts are skin covered during part of the year and exposed during molting and mating season	
7. Brain-body ratio	Low; brain weighs about 2 kilograms	
8. Body size	Approximately 3 meters in length, it weighs 200 to 220 kilograms	
9. Social behavior	None	
10. Moving around	Crawls on land, climbs trees, and drifts on water	
11. Hearing	Feels vibrations in the ground	
12. Smell and taste	Hundreds of tiny sensors on its abdomen	
13. Sight	One eye-spot	
14. Eating	Uses mouthparts to snip off plants and insert into oral cavity; grazes on grass and other low-growing plants	
15. Defense	Thick protective covering and horns for protection during season when covered with skin; no poison; rolls into a ball and freezes	
16. Reproduction	Sexual; lays soft eggs that harden and hatch after incubation; emits smell to attract a mate	
17. Babies	Lay many eggs but don't care for babies after hatching	
18.		
19.		
20.		
21.		
22.		

Table 7.8—Teacher's Key—Two-Header Attributes.

Note: Attributes that may indicate intelligence are in boldface. See page 128 for logbook sheet.

Attribute	Description of Your Planet Z Life-Form	✓
1. Kind of skin	Scaly skin	
2. Ecological type	Generalist; primarily adapted for grasslands, but can live in mountains, mixed forests, and even desert	✓
3. Basic body shape	Long	
4. Segments	One	
5. Appendages	Two strong hind legs; two small, short arms with small, weak fingers on almost useless hands	
6. Hard parts	Endoskeleton; spikes on tail	
7. Brain-body ratio	High; about 9 percent of its body size	✓
8. Body size	450 to 1,475 kilograms	
9. Social behavior	They do not cooperate or hunt in packs; no teaching of young	
10. Moving around	Hops like a kangaroo	
11. Hearing	Two large ears on one head for hearing	
12. Smell and taste	One large mouth on lower head for tasting; taller head sees, hears, and senses the presence of a mate	
13. Sight	Two eyes per head	✓
14. Eating	Meat-eater; hits prey with spiked tail	
15. Defense	Spiked tail; no poison; fights	
16. Reproduction	Sexual; requires two individuals to mate; male impregnates female; pregnancy lasts 24 months	
17. Babies	Young are born fully developed and able to care for themselves	
18.		
19.		
20.		
21.		
22.		

Table 7.9—Teacher's Key—Monoid Attributes.

Note: Attributes that may indicate intelligence are in boldface. See page 130 for logbook sheet.

Attribute	Description of Your Planet Z Life-Form	✓
1. Kind of skin	Covered with hair except for leathery plates	
2. Ecological type	Specialist for ice habitat	
3. Basic body shape	Long	
4. Segments	One	
5. Appendages	Four, with clawed, webbed feet	
6. Hard parts	Endoskeleton; bones hold up and fold plates	
7. Brain-body ratio	Medium; brain weighs one kilogram	✓
8. Body size	22 to 25 kilograms	
9. Social behavior	None	
10. Moving around	Burrows	
11. Hearing	Deaf	
12. Smell and taste	One large mouth on lower head for tasting; taller head sees and senses the presence of a mate	
13. Sight	One eye	
14. Eating	Primarily photosynthetic; can eat small prey if available	
15. Defense	Hides underground	
16. Reproduction	Hermaphroditic; requires two individuals to mate; mates once in its life; lays two to three eggs per year	
17. Babies	Young are born fully developed and able to care for themselves	
18.		
19.		
20.		
21.		
22.		

Mission 7

Intelligent Life on Planet Z

Extraterrestrial Life-Forms—Aquatica

Figure 7.2.

Mission 7

Intelligent Life on Planet Z

Extraterrestrial Life-Form Attributes—Aquatica

Aquatica. These air-breathing life-forms live in salt water. They paddle along in shallow water, and often wash ashore when they die. They appear to be an abundant source of food for land-dwelling, meat-eating life-forms along the coasts of all Planet Z landmasses.

The Aquatica has soft skin and an internal skeleton within a round body. It weighs between 2,000 and 2,200 kilograms and is the size of an Earth whale. It is cold-blooded and has one heart. Its brain is tiny, weighing only about 1 kilogram. The Aquatica has two large eyes at the end of its tube-like neck, one on each side. On its body are five appendages in the form of one dorsal, two pectoral, and two pelvic flippers. The flippers are stiff and are only used to steer the body as it swims. The Aquatica is a slow but powerful swimmer that seeks shelter in surf as a defense against predators.

The adult life-form feeds by way of a large, slit-like mouth filled with baleen, similar to that of some Earth whales. It feeds by sucking large quantities of water into its mouth, filtering out microscopic plants through the baleen, and expelling the water through gill slits in its neck. An Aquatica's ear holes sense vibrations in water; its nostrils, around the mouth, smell food.

These creatures have two sexes: males and females. Males fertilize the females, which give birth to young eight months later. The young accompany the mother. They have short necks and sharp teeth. They eat fish. As they grow, their necks get longer and their teeth fall out while the baleen develops, and then they begin eating plants.

From *The Rise of Intelligence and Culture*. © 1995. Teacher Ideas Press. (800) 237-6124.

Mission 7
Intelligent Life on Planet Z

Extraterrestrial Life-Forms—Bat-Rat

Figure 7.3.

Mission 7

Intelligent Life on Planet Z

Extraterrestrial Life-Form Attributes—Bat-Rat

Bat-Rat. At first glance, this life-form appears much like an Earth flying squirrel. It is small, about the size of an Earth mouse, weighing under half a kilogram. It has fur-covered, leathery skin, an internal skeleton, one heart, and is warm-blooded. The Bat-Rat has leathery flaps between its arms and legs that enable it to do an extended glide from trees. Its two eyes are placed near the front of its head, so that the Bat-Rat can sense depth while it glides or climbs trees. The sensitive hairs on its head enable this winged creature to sense when predators are nearby. Then it takes off gliding, escaping most predators, except for those that can fly.

Young Bat-Rats are immediately taught to feed themselves. They are herbivores that use their long noses with sharp teeth on the end to drill into fruits and succulents and suck out the flesh and moisture of the plant. These winged life-forms never drink water, receiving all the necessary liquid from the plants they graze upon. The trees in which they live have flowers inside large, hollow, hanging structures. The Bat-Rat burrows into these structures and feeds, fertilizing the flowers in the process.

The Bat-Rat is hermaphroditic, which means each individual has both sex organs, but needs another individual to mate. Bat-Rats know it is time to find a mate when their tails change color to a bright green. This is the only time that a Bat-Rat meets another Bat-Rat. During mating, each individual sperm is deposited through an opening in the tip of the tail of the other life-form, where it meets an egg. The fertilized egg grows into either two or four identical baby Bat-Rats. During the gestation (pregnancy) period, the babies stay inside the tails until they are mature enough to move about on their own. The babies demonstrate this by crawling out into the world through the opening in the tail.

Mission 7

Intelligent Life on Planet Z

Extraterrestrial Life-Forms—Hawkroach

Figure 7.4.

Mission 7

Intelligent Life on Planet Z

Extraterrestrial Life-Form Attributes—Hawkroach

Hawkroach. The Hawkroach has an exoskeleton of armor-like plates, which it molts every other year for 20 years during growth. The molted plates are used by the life-form to construct shelters. This life-form has some features like Earth birds: a beak and insulating feathers around its joints. The Hawkroach walks upright, using two bird-like, jointed legs. It has four arms covered with leathery skin. The end of each arm has a grasping pincer-like claw. A Hawkroach weighs between 95 and 100 kilograms; its brain weighs about 7 kilograms. It is about the size of an Earth deer. Hawkroaches eat ripe fruits and vegetables, which they smell from far away. They also hunt in small packs, killing and eating small life-forms, ripping their bodies apart with beaks and claws. Water appears to be a requirement for this species to reproduce. This life-form is highly adaptable in its behavior.

Hawkroaches have three different genders: males, females, and sterile, incubator Hawkroaches. Each is responsible for a different role in reproduction. The different sexes find each other by means of a song, or mating call. The Hawkroach mates for life. The female deposits jelly-like eggs into water. The male then fertilizes the eggs with a special chemical produced within its body that causes the eggs to become either male or female. Next, a sterile, incubator Hawkroach scoops the eggs out of the water with its spoon-shaped bill and carries them to a feather-lined nest. The sterile Hawkroach then lies down over the eggs and secretes a hardening chemical from openings on its stomach onto the jelly-like eggs and positions its body over the eggs to hatch them. The resulting offspring are either male or female Hawkroaches. The sterile third gender of Hawkroach is the result of the female's unfertilized eggs. Hatching occurs four months after the incubator Hawkroach begins to rest over the eggs. During the nesting phase of reproduction, the male and female must provide food for the incubator and the young Hawkroaches. The incubator feeds the offspring until they are able to catch and eat food on their own. The male and female care for the babies and the incubator until the babies grow to maturity, in about three years.

Mission 7

Intelligent Life on Planet Z

Extraterrestrial Life-Forms—Spheriod

Figure 7.5.

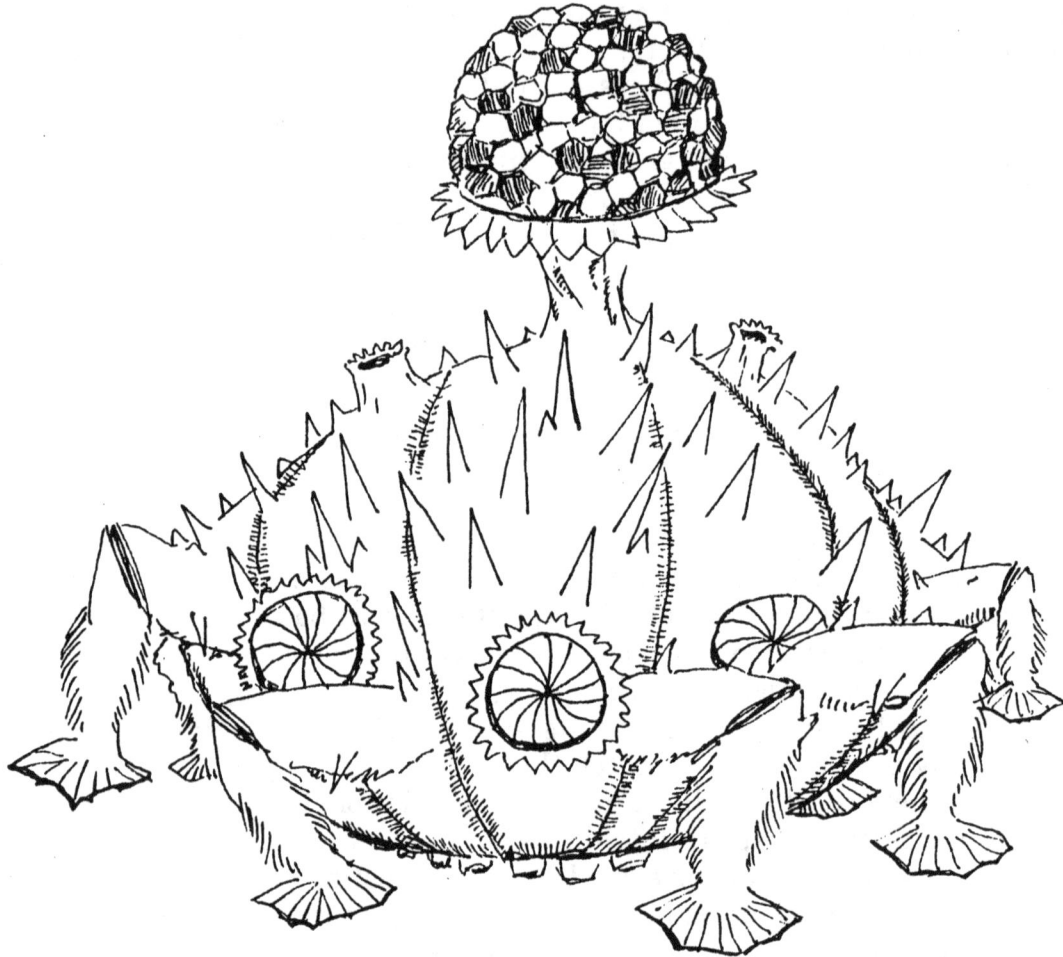

Mission 7

Intelligent Life on Planet Z

Extraterrestrial Life-Form Attributes—Spheroid

Spheroid. The Spheroid has a hard shell covering a round, almost ball-shaped body. This shell is a waterproof protein covering secreted through pores in the skin beneath it. The hard protein covering is shed in plates every year. A Spheroid weighs between 90 and 95 kilograms, about the size of an Earth deer. Its centrally located brain weighs about 1 kilogram. On the top of its body is one large, compound eye, similar to an eye on an Earth fly. It has 12 openings on its body. Two pipe-shaped openings on either side of its compound eye are used for breathing; four more duct-shaped openings on its bottom side are used for excreting waste and for laying and fertilizing eggs. It has six circular mouth openings with sharp teeth around its body. Its mouths open like the shutter of a camera. The Spheroid's 12 jointed legs end in flat, clawless feet.

This plant-eater eats flower buds or tender shoots of plants by opening its mouths over them and then snapping its teeth closed, shearing off each bite. Just below its mouths, around its body, are the Spheroid's 12 jointed legs, which give this creature a look similar to an Earth spider. It is very agile and can run in any direction. Tiny hairs on its legs sense vibrations in the air or from the ground. This life-form defends itself by running away and by means of sharp spines that are all over its body. The spines inject poison into anything that touches them. These spines look very much like the spines on certain varieties of Earth cactus. This enables the Spheroid to blend in with its habitat, another way of defending itself.

In order to reproduce, the female Spheroid lays a few dozen spine-covered eggs on sand, and then leaves. The eggs emit an odor that attracts a male of the species; the male then fertilizes the eggs and buries them in the sand. At this point, the eggs are on their own to hatch and survive without either parent caring for them.

Mission 7

Intelligent Life on Planet Z

Extraterrestrial Life-Forms—Segmenter

Figure 7.6.

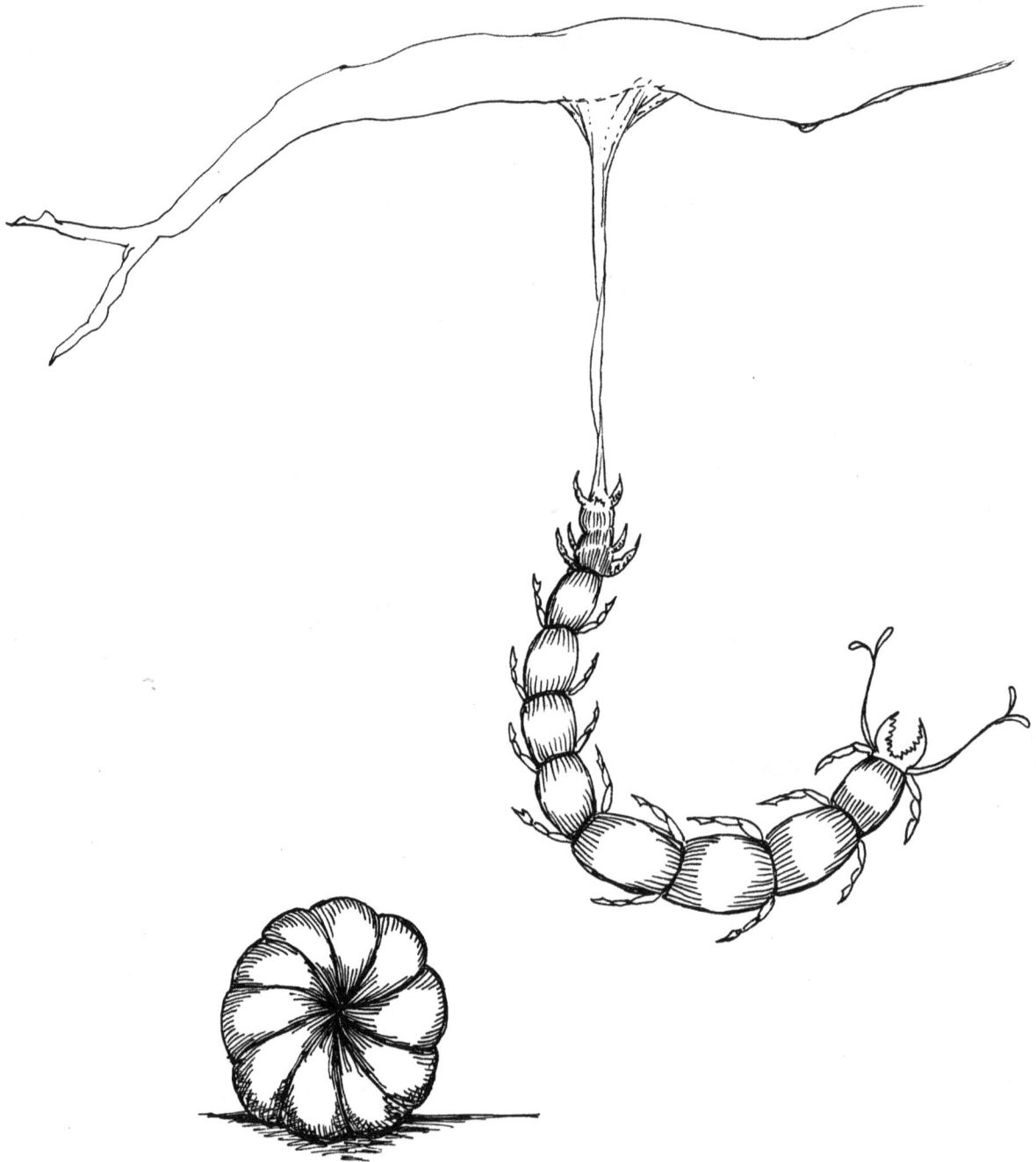

Mission 7

Intelligent Life on Planet Z

Extraterrestrial Life-Form Attributes—Segmenter

Segmenter. The Segmenter is a grazing life-form that resembles an Earth centipede in some ways. Its body consists of many identical segments, each with a pair of legs. Its mouthparts are limbs modified from some of the segments that evolved to form its head. They can grasp their food, rip it up, and transport it to the mouth. Unlike an Earth centipede, a Segmenter weighs between 200 to 220 kilograms and reaches a length of nearly 3 meters; its brain weighs about 2 kilograms. This life-form climbs trees to feed. When it feeds, it snips off pieces of plants with its mouthparts and inserts them into its mouth cavity. It seems to smell what to eat when it crawls among the branches: A Segmenter will pause for a moment and then back up and begin to eat. This is because it has chemical sensors on its abdomen that it uses to smell or taste. It eats the leaves of trees and the dense growth of plants that grow on the limbs of trees. Old adults sometimes spin a thread like an Earth spider and lower themselves from a tree into a river. A Segmenter is nearly blind, having only one light-sensing eye-spot that cannot form images located on the center of its head.

This life-form is covered with a tough, leathery skin, which it molts during Planet Z's fall, prior to mating and laying eggs. Segmenters mate while in hiding, in dense foliage during Planet Z's rainy season, and lay soft eggs that harden in shallow rows inside the heat-producing piles of rotting vegetation beneath fruit-bearing trees during Planet Z's spring and early summer.

Some Segmenters were discovered floating as rolled-up balls in the oceans. This was originally thought to be the way in which they died, but later they were found crawling out of the sea on different continents. It appears that this is their manner of migration: They close up their shells and roll into a ball shape to drift with ocean currents to different continents. It was later noticed that they also assume this closed-up ball position when a predator is near.

Mission 7

Intelligent Life on Planet Z

Extraterrestrial Life-Forms—Two-Header

Figure 7.7.

Mission 7

Intelligent Life on Planet Z

Extraterrestrial Life-Form Attributes—Two-Header

Two-Header. Physically, this life-form is very unusual looking—it has two heads. Its taller head is responsible for the senses of hearing, sight, and sensing the presence of a mate. Its lower head acts mainly as a mouth. The taller head sticks up out of the tall grasses to see prey at a distance. A Two-Header has scaly skin, and is cold-blooded like Earth reptiles. It has two small forearms with weak, small fingers on almost useless hands; two powerful jumping legs, and a long, spiked tail. It hops like an Earth kangaroo.

A Two-Header weighs between 450 and 475 kilograms, about the size of an Earth horse, and has some characteristics similar to the extinct Earth dinosaur Tyrannosaurus rex, namely its short forearms and large mouth with sharp teeth. Unlike Tyrannosaurus rex, a Two-Header has a larger brain, about 9 percent of its body size, because both heads have rather large brains that connect together. The feeding head and the sensing head act cooperatively to find and catch prey. Swipes of the Two-Header's weapon-like tail, kicks from the strong back legs, and bites from the biting head immobilize its prey. This carnivorous life-form mainly eats other life-forms. Two-Headers do not cooperate, nor do they hunt in packs. This Two-Header is very aggressive and is feared by most other life-forms on Planet Z.

A Two-Header reproduces sexually, requiring a male and a female to mate. The male impregnates the female. Gestation lasts 24 months. At birth, the two heads are side by side on short necks; the necks grow longer as they mature. The young are able to care for themselves, but they may watch adult Two-Headers, learning how to hunt by observation.

Mission 7

Intelligent Life on Planet Z

Extraterrestrial Life-Forms—Monoid

Figure 7.8.

Mission 7

Intelligent Life on Planet Z

Extraterrestrial Life-Form Attributes—Monoid

Monoid. The Monoid looks a little like an Earth salamander but it weighs about 22 to 25 kilograms, about the size of an Earth dog. It is covered with white hair and has numerous flat, leathery, green-colored plates on its back. These plates can be raised or lowered like a sail on a sailboat. The Monoid is a burrower that digs quickly with its sharp claws and webbed feet. It usually keeps its body below the surface, with its single large eye sticking up above the surface on a flexible stalk. When the eye senses light, the green-colored plates are raised; when the eye does not sense light, the green-colored plates remain flat against its body. The Monoid has unique "antifreeze" chemicals in its blood, like some Earth fish that live in cold Arctic waters. These chemicals prevent the Monoid from freezing. The Monoid has a very small mouth, and does not seem to eat very often. It does not hunt for prey, but keeps its mouth open, waiting to eat small creatures that literally "walk into its mouth."

The Monoid is hermaphroditic, which means each individual has both sex organs, but needs another individual to mate. Monoids know it is time to find a mate when there are 16 hours of sunlight in a day. Each Monoid mates once in its life. This is the only time that a Monoid meets another Monoid. After two Monoids mate, they both store sperm within their bodies. They use this sperm to fertilize two or three eggs each year. They lay these eggs underground and abandon them. The babies are completely able to care for themselves.

Mission 7

Intelligent Life on Planet Z

Attribute Matrix

Name:

Date:

Name of life-form:_____

Habitat(s) of life-form:

Mission 7

Intelligent Life on Planet Z
Mission Briefing

Name:

Date:

Dr. Dave Milne, Exobiologist on the SETI Academy Team

In this mission, you will be introduced to some fictitious extraterrestrial life-forms that might exist somewhere in the Milky Way Galaxy. We will assume that they do exist—on Planet Z. Your job will be to figure out: 1) what their habitats are likely to be, 2) which of their physical traits and behaviors may indicate intelligence, and 3) which life-form is most likely to have the greatest intelligence. You will help this one life-form to develop the additional abilities needed to form a culture, and to later form a civilization.

What Do You Think?

1. Based on intelligent Earth life-forms, what traits and behaviors should intelligent extraterrestrial life-forms have?

2. How would an intelligent extraterrestrial life-form need to evolve to be able to form a civilization?

From *The Rise of Intelligence and Culture.* © 1995. Teacher Ideas Press. (800) 237-6124.

Mission 7

Intelligent Life on Planet Z

Tiny Extraterrestrials

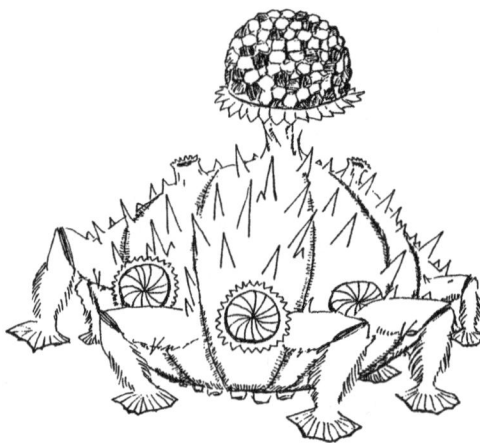

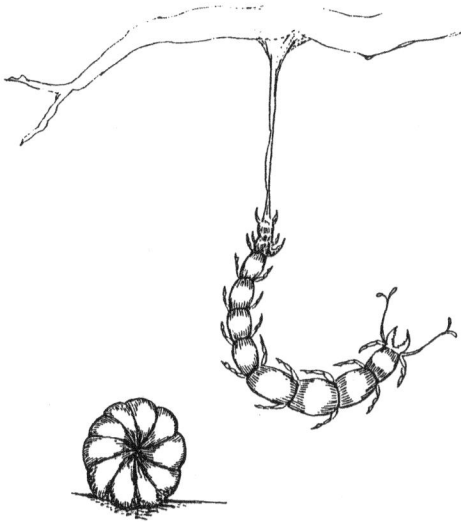

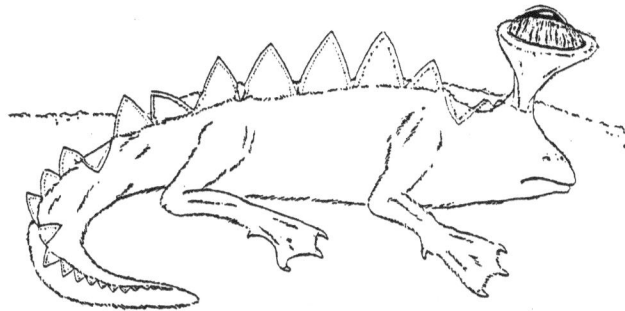

Mission 7

Intelligent Life on Planet Z

Helping Your Life-Form Survive (Part 1)

Name:

Date:

1. Put a check mark in the box on the table (see page 137) for the physical traits and behaviors that you think each Planet Z life-form has. Refer to the blank attribute matrix form you filled out earlier.

2. Add up the number of check marks for each life-form, and record this number in the "Total" column.

3. Rank the seven life-forms according to their levels of intelligence, from 1 to 7 ("7" = the most intelligent life-form, the one with the most check marks; "1" = the least intelligent).

Table 7.10—Physical Traits and Behaviors Matrix.

Life-Forms	1	2	3	4	5	6	7	8	9	10	11	12	13	14	15	16	17	18	19	20	21	22	Total ✓s	Rank
Aquatica																								
Bat-Rat																								
Hawkroach																								
Spheroid																								
Segmenter																								
Monoid																								
Two-Header																								

Mission 7

Intelligent Life on Planet Z

Helping Your Life-Form Survive (Part 2)

Name:

Date:

1. Work with your group to complete the following:

Continent:

Habitat:

Names of group members:

_____

_____

_____

_____

_____

2. In the table below, enter the five physical traits and behaviors your class has chosen to change.

Table 7.11—Data Table.

Physical Trait or Behavior	Description of Change
Size and Weight	
Position of Eyes	
Skull Size	
Use and Length of Appendages	
Sensory Ability (Change Ability to Get Input)	

3. For each trait or behavior, work with your group to decide how you would change that trait or behavior to make the life-form more intelligent. Record your decisions in the second column of the table above.

4. Have your teacher review your choices before you go on to Part 3.

From *The Rise of Intelligence and Culture.* © 1995. Teacher Ideas Press. (800) 237-6124.

Mission 7

Intelligent Life on Planet Z

Helping Your Life-Form Survive (Part 3)

Name:

Date:

1. Work with your group to sketch your "evolved" life-form in pencil. Make sure your group is in agreement about the changes to the life-form before you begin drawing.

2. Agree on a name for your life-form.

Name of your life-form: _____

Draw your Planet Z life-form here:

Mission 7

Intelligent Life on Planet Z

What Do You Think, Now?

Name:

Date:

After you have completed this mission, please answer the following questions:

1. Based on intelligent Earth life-forms, what traits and behaviors should intelligent extraterrestrial life-forms have?

2. How would an intelligent extraterrestrial life-form need to evolve to be able to form a civilization?

Mission 8

Cultures Evolve on Planet Z
How Might an Extraterrestrial Culture Develop?

Overview

In mission 8, students create cultural evolution on Planet Z, and observe how cultures may or may not change over time, with some developing a civilization. How might an extraterrestrial culture change?

In mission 8.1, students create intelligent cultures on Planet Z and observe how these cultures change or do not change over time. Students work in teams to create eight fictional cultures for Planet Z using specified guidelines. In mission 8.2, Planet Z's cultures evolve on separate landmasses in different climates, along lines similar to cultural evolution on Earth, as students play a game to simulate the evolution of each fictional culture and make posters to indicate their culture in action. In mission 8.3, students continue the simulation, while playing the game and observing how ocean trade affects the development of culture. In mission 8.4, students finish their simulation and analyze the development of culture.

Concepts

- In the history of Western culture, our "modern technology" developed as one invention or idea led to others.

- Cultural changes may be classified in "phases," according to the amount of technology the culture has developed.

- On Earth, some cultures survived successfully for thousands of years without developing "modern" technology, and still survive that way today.

- Cultures do not all develop in the same way, or at the same rate. An extraterrestrial culture might develop in many ways.

Notes

In mission 7, students met fictional extraterrestrial life-forms that were adapted to alien habitats on Planet Z. From among these, they selected one intelligent life-form and evolved its physical traits and behaviors to give it the abilities needed to form a culture.

- Environment affects the exact form of the culture that develops. (For example, cultures without clay will not create pottery.)

Skills

- Analyzing characteristics of culture.

- Making decisions.

Mission 8.1

Materials

For the Class

- Overhead projector

- Transparency of the logbook sheet "Stage One (Whole Class—A, B, C)" (see pages 157-159)

- Transparency of the logbook sheet "Planet Z Grassland Habitat" (see page 95)

- Dice

- Colored marker

- Meter stick

- 4 meters of adding machine tape

For Each Student

- SETI Academy Cadet Logbook

- Pencil

Getting Ready

One or More Days Before Class

1. Review the "Teacher Background Information" for this mission in the appendix.

2. Make a transparency of "Stage One (Whole Class—A, B, C)" and write the word *Grasslands* into the blank at the top of the page. Make a transparency of "Planet Z Grassland Habitat" (see page 95).

Just Before the Lesson

1. Set up the overhead projector.

2. Tape the 4 meters of adding machine tape to the chalkboard.

Classroom Action

1. **Mission Briefing.** Have the class refer to the "Mission Briefing" (see page 156) for mission 8 in their student logbooks as one student reads it aloud.

2. **What Do You Think?** Read aloud and discuss the pre-activity questions on the "Mission Briefing." Have students answer the questions in their logbooks. Invite them to share their answers in a class discussion. Remind students that all humans evolved from the same hominid line, yet we have many different cultures and many different physical appearances because we evolved in different habitats. Stress that culture evolves according to two variables:

   • the physical structure and bodily needs of the life-form itself, and

   • the resources available in the physical environment or habitat in which the life-form lives.

   Write these on the board for students to refer to throughout all parts of this mission.

3. **Lecture.** Tell students that they will be playing a game, first as a class and then in student teams. It is a game to design a culture for the life-form that they evolved in mission 7.

4. **Demonstration.** Put the transparency of "Stage One (Whole Class—A, B, C)" on the overhead projector. Explain that the class will do the first part of cultural evolution together. Have a student read this page aloud from their logbook.

   Put the "Planet Z Grassland Habitat" transparency on the overhead projector. Ask students to imagine and explain what their life-form's shelters and tools would be. Note that the tools are not yet intentionally shaped from found objects.

5. **Activity.** Explain that the class will use dice to show the chance factor in cultural evolution. For each roll, the class will use one die and record the culture's inventions and discoveries on the class timeline starting at the left end. Point out the adding machine tape attached to the chalkboard at the front of the classroom.

For this part of the game, each roll of the die equals 100,000 years, or 1 meter.

Have a student roll the die, call out the number that comes up, and read the directions for step 1 on the logbook sheet "Stage One (Whole Class—A, B, C)."

Demonstrate how to record a roll on the timeline. Consider the left-hand end of the tape as the beginning of the culture. For the first roll, measure 100 cm (1 meter) from the end of the tape and mark it with a vertical line. Label that line with the discovery or invention as shown in figure 8.1.

Teacher's Note: *Students will be tempted to go step by step, ignoring the directions to "Go to" other steps than the next successive step. Be sure to make students aware of this possible mistake.*

Figure 8.1—Sample Timeline.

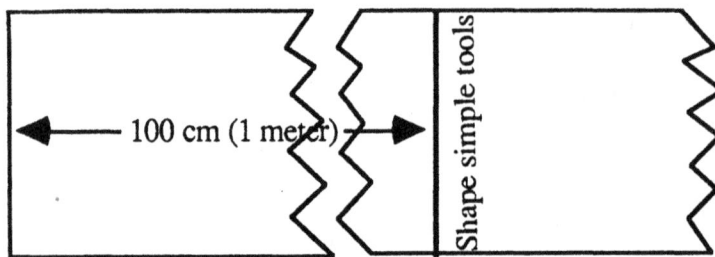

Have another student roll the die and call out the number that comes up. Record on the class timeline as before. Repeat this process until you arrive at step 5.

6. **Lecture.** Explain that by evolving their extra-terrestrial life-form through the first stage of culture this way, the class is modeling what scientific evidence suggests happened on Earth. Hominids, or early humans, emerged in the grasslands of Africa and migrated, perhaps about 100,000 years ago, to East Asia and from there eventually into Australia, Europe, Siberia, North America, and South America. The subsequent cultural adaptations to new habitats for the life-form will be modeled in mission 8.2. Student teams will be assigned a Planet Z habitat and appropriate directions.

7. **Wrap Up.** Have students open up their log-books to the "Describing Your Planet Z Culture" sheet (see page 159) for stage one and answer the questions.

Mission 8.2

Materials

For the Class

- A roll of adding machine tape

For Each Team

- 1 meter of adding machine tape

- One die

- Art materials; poster supplies

For Each Student

- SETI Academy Cadet Logbook

- Pencil

Getting Ready

A Day or Two Before Class

1. Organize students into eight teams.

2. Make a set of directions for each of eight student groups. On pages 160-162 are three *different* sets of directions. They are coded by letter: These letters are included in the title of each set of directions. The sets can be used for the various habitats as shown in table 8.1 (page 146).

   Make three copies of set C (two for rain forest and one for ice). Make two copies of set B (two for desert). Make three copies of set A (one for mixed forest, one for mountains, and one for grasslands). Make none for aquatic. Label and code each set appropriately using table 8.1.

3. Copy "Planet Z Habitat" logbook sheets from mission 6: two each for rain forest and desert; one each for mixed forest, ice, mountain, and grassland. Make none for aquatic.

Table 8.1—Codes for Cultural Evolution Packets.

Code	Habitat	Final Level of Technology
Set C	Rain Forest	Low
Set B	Desert	Medium
Set A	Mixed Forest	High
None	Aquatic	NA
Set C	Ice	Low
Set A	Mountain	High
Set A	Grassland	High

4. Copy the matching game (step) directions for each "Stage Two" coded "Your Planet Z Culture Evolves" (see pages 163-168).

5. Copy the appropriate "Stage Two" coded "Describing Your Planet Z Culture" sheets (see pages 169, 172, and 175).

6. Copy the appropriate "Stage Two" coded "Illustrating Your Planet Z Culture" sheets (see pages 170, 173, and 176).

Classroom Action

1. **Review.** Explain that Planet Z's cultural evolution will continue in this part of mission 8. Review what happened in mission 8.1, including a review of the two limitations on cultural evolution (the physical structure and bodily needs of the life-form itself, and the resources available in the physical environment or habitat in which the life-form lives). Summarize where the life-form ended up culturally after stage one's evolution.

   Have students share some of the answers they came up with in mission 8.1 for their "Describing Your Planet Z Culture" logbook sheet for stage one. Do they fit the limitations? If not, give some examples of how they could be made to fit.

2. **Activity.** Explain to students that they are to assume that parts of the original population of their life-form have relocated to other habitats, maybe even other continents! (They could have walked over land bridges in the past, when some of the continents were connected, or they might have built rafts or other floating vessels to cross over the sea.) Many life-forms will get a new habitat.

To each team, hand out a set of directions, the appropriate habitat picture, 1 meter of adding machine tape, and 1 die. See table 8.1 above for the packet codes.

Review the "Instructions" sheets for sets A, B, and C, emphasizing the differences from the activity in mission 8.1. From the "Planet Z Map" (which now has "landmasses" pasted on) logbook sheets from mission 6, each team will choose a continent that has their assigned habitat to colonize. During this part of the mission there will be four rolls of the die, with each roll equal to 20,000 years and 20 cm (the scale is still 1 meter = 100,000 years). At the end of the forth roll, the teams will stop and answer the questions on the "Describing Your Planet Z Culture" logbook sheet for stage two and prepare for possible "culture contact"! Most important, students should keep the effects of this second stage of cultural evolution a secret (from other teams) including the poster they created!

When teams understand their assignment, have them begin.

Mission 8.3

Materials

For the Class

- 8 slips of paper

- Box to hold slips of paper

For Each Team

- Art materials; poster supplies or posters begun in mission 8.2

For Each Student

- SETI Academy Cadet Logbook

- Pencil

Teacher's Note: *As teams finish the dice-rolling part of this activity, they should approach you for confirmation of their work and the supplies necessary to go on to the next step, as described in mission 8.3, completing the "Illustrating Your Planet Z Culture" logbook sheet. Be ready with art supplies as listed in the materials section of mission 8.3 (scratch paper, poster paper, pencils, markers, paint, and crayons).*

Getting Ready

One or More Days Before Class

1. On one of the eight slips of paper write "Ocean Travel." Fold each slip of paper in half and put it into the box.

Just Before the Lesson

1. Supply a set of colored markers for each group.

Classroom Action

1. **Activity.** Tell the class that teams will be sharing their posters of their Planet Z cultures today. Have the teams polish up their posters.

2. **Review.** Have students summarize what has happened so far in the cultural evolution simulation. The life-form first evolved in grasslands on one continent. About 100,000 years ago, groups of the species began to split off and relocate to different habitats and continents, where they continued to evolve. Ask them, given the history of Earth life-forms, what could happen next? At some point, extraterrestrial life-forms might travel to different habitats and continents and meet other, differently evolved life-forms of the same species. They might even share ideas with one another.

   Tell students that ocean travel and cultural contact will happen next! Explain that, as a preview to official cultural contact, they are going to have a chance to view all the cultures via the posters the teams have designed.

3. **Activity.** When the posters are complete, have students "tour the planet," that is, walk around the room and look at the posters depicting the accomplishments of other cultures. Any of the ideas they see represented on other posters is fair game for their culture's future cultural evolution. When the cultures evolve for the last time, they may adopt discoveries and inventions from other cultures. You may also want to have teams present their posters, emphasizing the highlights of each culture.

4. **Preview.** Tell students that it is now time to figure out which culture was the first to achieve ocean travel! Show them the box with the eight folded slips of paper in it. Tell students that one

of the slips has "Ocean Travel" written on it while the rest are blank. Ask for a representative from each team to come up and take a folded slip of paper from the box. Have them unfold their papers all together. Announce the traveling culture! Tell students that mission 8.4 will be a simulation of cultural contact.

Mission 8.4

Materials

For the Class

- One copy of the "Culture Contact—Intention and Reaction Cards" (3 sheets) (pages 173-175), cut apart

- Whole-class culture timeline from mission 8.1

- Student-team culture timelines

For Each Team

- 3-by-5-inch index cards (6)

For Each Student

- SETI Academy Cadet Logbook

- Pencil

Getting Ready

A Day or Two Before Class

1. Locate index cards.

2. Cut the "Cultural Contact" sheets into cards.

3. Clear a bulletin board and set up the 4-meter timeline the class made together in mission 8.1. Leave room for team timelines as shown in figure 8.2 (see page 150).

Just Before the Lesson

1. Distribute the index cards and the "Culture Contact Cards" to each team as described in Classroom Action 3 Activity below.

Figure 8.2—Timeline Display.

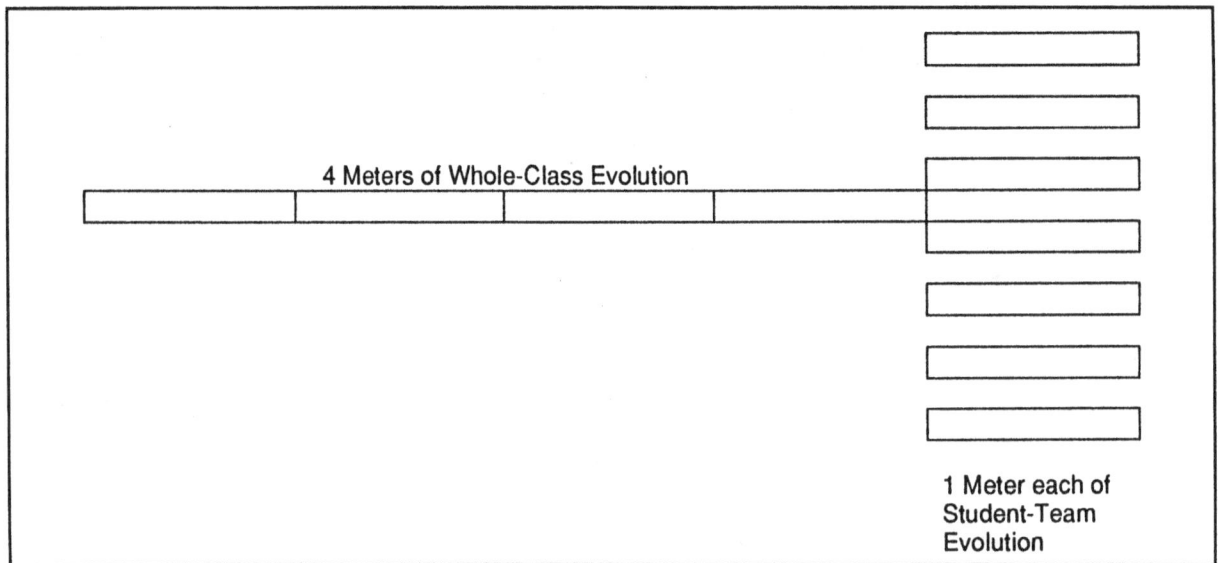

Classroom Action

1. **Activity.** Instruct each culture group to make a set of cultural accomplishment cards using 3-by-5-inch index cards. The cards should state the culture's accomplishments up to the time ocean travel was invented. The cards should list the following cultural achievements, one achievement per card: tools, clothing and decoration, shelter, religion, transportation, and food.

   Teacher's Note: *The culture that first achieved ocean travel will need six sets of their cards. If a photocopier is handy, immediately copy six sets of this culture's accomplishment cards so they may bring them along on their travels to use for trade with other cultures. Alternatively, have volunteers copy extra sets by hand.*

2. **Lecture.** Ask students to imagine what would happen if the first culture to achieve ocean travel explored the rest of the continents and cultures on Planet Z. Point out that each visited culture would be at a different level in its development. Explain that the next activity will focus on what the visiting and visited cultures see and experience when this *does* happen. Read the following brief summaries about how different Earth cultures reacted to first contacts with other cultures.

   The Polynesians began ocean travel approximately 1500 BCE. They encountered and colonized unpopulated islands in the Pacific Ocean. They traveled to find new places to live.

   Phoenicians sailed around Africa about 600 BCE, seeking information and riches. They had to stop for months at a time to grow their own food, so it is unlikely that they met many native cultures.

   Teacher's Note: *To reflect modern, nondenominational usage, CE (for Common Era) is used instead of AD, and BCE (for Before Common Era) is used instead of BC.*

The ancient Greeks began ocean travel approximately 600 BCE. They traveled originally with the intent of exploration and trade. The Greek sailor, Pytheas, sailed to England and traded cloth for tin. He continued north to the Arctic Circle before going back to Greece.

The Vikings sailed from Norway, west around Britain and Ireland and discovered Greenland. More recent Vikings also discovered the east coast of North America, about 986 CE.

In 1492 CE, Columbus sailed from Spain to San Salvador. His intent was to find gold and to trade with the local peoples. He also wanted to colonize other lands and convert the native cultures to Christianity.

An Englishman, John Cabot, sailed from England to Canada in 1497 CE. He was a merchant who wanted to find a way to transport spices from England to China and back again.

Overall, sailing cultures brought an assortment of things to the societies they visited. Both diseases and religions were spread around the globe by travelers. Plant and animal resources were shared by sailors who carried seeds and livestock with them. When the Spaniards landed on the California coast and rode their horses inland, the Native Americans thought they were amazing creatures and possibly gods. Later the Native Americans adopted horses as a means of transportation. Elaborate trade routes were established by merchant sailors who were trading goods all over the globe by the 1500s. Sometimes slaves were captured from one country and traded for goods in another country.

Summarize the possibilities for intent and response by reading the cards on the three "Culture Contact—Intention and Reaction Cards" logbook sheets. Ask students to come up with suggestions for other possible reactions and record them on the blank cards in their logbooks. The teacher should record some of these suggested reactions on the two blank reaction cards for each intention card.

3. **Activity.** Give the visiting culture team a random choice of one of the three intention cards before they begin their travels. Pass out to the cultures that will be visited the seven reaction cards that correspond to the visiting team's intention card. Instruct the visiting team to go and visit each of the other landmasses' cultures.

As members of the visiting group meet briefly with each of the other cultures, they take turns reading the intention and reaction cards, and then giving or taking each other's accomplishment cards as instructed on the reaction card. When this cultural contact portion of the activity is complete, instruct each team to return to their work areas and once again describe their culture using the "Stage Two" coded "Describing Your Planet Z Culture" logbook sheets. Their answers this time must take into account how their cultures were affected by making contact with a new culture.

You may wish to do the final cultural evolution the next day.

4. **Activity.** Have the teams turn to the final set of directions—the logbook sheet "Your Modern Planet Z Culture," (see pages 176-178). Review the directions. Allow teams to work on their final stage of evolution.

When the timelines are complete, collect and add them to the bulletin board as shown in figure 8.2 on page 150.

Closure

1. **Discussion.** Point out that the cultural evolution game for Planet Z is based upon Earth's cultural evolution, as it occurred in the Western world. It was set up so that the average time to reach each level would be similar to human cultural evolution. The levels 1) hunter/gatherer with fire, 2) metal, 3) writing, and 4) ocean travel and technology also correspond to human cultural evolution. (See the appendix for more information.)

Discuss some or all of the following questions about Earth culture:

- How did your culture change after getting information from other cultures?

- What have cultures done when exploring other cultures?

- Have all cultures developed at the same speed?

- Is development always progress?

Teacher's Note: *Now is a good time to discuss value judgments. As members of Western culture, we tend to worship progress and tend to believe that cultures who haven't developed modern technology are backwards. We call other counties "undeveloped" or "developing." You may wish to point out that other cultures value stability, or that some of the "less advanced" cultures are not polluting the environment and using up resources as fast as the "developed countries."*

- What parts of your culture do you like?

- What parts of your culture would you like to change?

- Does each landmass have only one culture?

- Does each landmass have only one habitat?

- Why do you think a culture develops faster and faster as time goes on?

2. **What Do You Think, Now?** Have students answer the post-activity questions on the logbook sheet "What Do You Think, Now?" (see page 179). Invite students to share their responses and their drawings. Ask them how their opinions have been changed by this mission.

Going Further

Creative Arts Activity: Summing Up Your Civilization

Have students demonstrate how their cultures changed by creating a play, a diorama, a comic strip, a puppet show, or an entry in a particular life-form's diary.

Research: Earth History

Have students take any two Earth cultures that have discovered each other and research the ways in which they interacted upon contact. Have students write a play depicting this "first contact" and perform it for the class.

Mission 8

Cultures Evolve on Planet Z

Stage One (Whole Class—A, B, C)

Instructions

Assumptions for the _____ habitat:

You can assume that the life-forms in your extraterrestrial culture live by eating plants or animals. They do not build shelters, but they do take advantage of naturally occurring shelters such as caves or plants. They have a nomadic lifestyle. Tools and weapons are objects that can be found in the habitat (stones, bones, grass, branches, leaves, etc.). The life-forms in your culture have not yet domesticated any animals, so work needs to be done by your life-form. Your culture has not invented the wheel or discovered how to start a fire.

Step 1. (500,000 to 400,000 years ago)
If you roll a . . .
1, 2, or 3 = your culture has learned to keep and make fire.
Go to—**Step 2a.**
4, 5, or 6 = your culture has learned how to shape simple bone and wood tools.
Go to—**Step 2b.**

Step 2a. (400,000 to 300,000 years ago)
If you roll a . . .
1, 2, or 3 = your culture has learned how to make simple bone tools.
Go to—**Step 3a.**
4, 5, or 6 = your culture has learned how to make simple stone tools.
Go to—**Step 3a.**

Step 2b. (400,000 to 300,000 years ago)
If you roll a . . .
1, 2, or 3 = your culture has learned to make fire.
Go to—**Step 3b.**
4, 5, or 6 = your culture has learned to keep fire.
Go to—**Step 3b.**

Step 3a. (300,000 to 200,000 years ago)
If you roll a . . .
1, 2, or 3 = your culture has learned to make dye from plants and paint from rocks.
Go to—**Step 4a.**
4, 5, or 6 = your culture has learned how to preserve and store food.
Go to—**Step 4b.**

Step 3b. (300,000 to 200,000 years ago)
If you roll a . . .
1, 2, or 3 = your culture has learned how to preserve and store food.
Go to—**Step 4b.**
4, 5, or 6 = your culture has learned how make dye from plants and paint from rocks.
Go to—**Step 4a.**

Step 4a. (200,000 to 100,000 years ago)
If you roll a . . .
1, 2, or 3 = your culture has learned how to salt or smoke meat.
Go to—**Step 5.**
4, 5, or 6 = your culture has learned how to dry fruit and store seeds.
Go to—**Step 5.**

Step 4b. (200,000 to 100,000 years ago)
If you roll a . . .
1, 2, or 3 = your culture has learned how make dye from plants.
Go to—**Step 5.**
4, 5, or 6 = your culture has learned how to make paint from rocks.
Go to—**Step 5.**

Step 5. When all of these inventions and discoveries have been made, cooperate to answer the questions on the logbook sheet "Describing Your Planet Z Culture" for stage one.

Mission 8

Cultures Evolve on Planet Z

Mission Briefing

Name:

Date:

Dr. Anthony Garcia, Cultural Anthropologist on the SETI Academy Team

Intelligent life on other worlds will not only be different from us in physical form, but also in culture. To imagine how intelligent cultures might differ from habitat to habitat, we would like you to remember the summary of the development of some early cultures on Earth. Then, each team will imagine how intelligent cultures might have developed on your Planet Z continent. Please keep your culture's accomplishments a "secret" so that you can make some real discoveries later as you search Planet Z for other cultures!

What Do You Think?

1. Is it reasonable to suppose that cultural evolution might occur differently on other planets? Why or why not?

2. What might some of the cultural differences be?

Mission 8

Cultures Evolve on Planet Z

Stage One (Whole Class—A, B, C)
Describing Your Planet Z Culture

Name:

Date:

1. **Work**—Is work divided up? Who does what tasks?

2. **Clothing**—Do your life-forms need protection for their bodies? What do they wear for decoration and protection?

3. **Group Control**—What guidelines for group control does your culture have? What do you do when life-forms refuse to live by the guidelines? Do you have leaders? How are they chosen?

4. **Ownership**—What do individuals own? What do groups own? What does the whole community own?

5. **Learning**—What do your life-forms need to learn? How do they learn it?

6. **Mobility**—How do your life-forms get around?

7. **Water**—From what source does your culture get fresh water for drinking and keeping clean?

Mission 8

Cultures Evolve on Planet Z

Stage Two (A)

Date:

Instructions

Your team's culture lives in the Planet Z _____ habitat. You will use information from your "Planet Z Habitat" logbook sheets and these directions to discover what your cultural evolution will be like in stage two.

For this part of the cultural evolution, your team will need

1 meter of adding machine tape
1 die
colored pens
a metric ruler

1. Use the maps of Planet Z from mission 6 in your logbook to choose a continent that has the habitat where your life-form will experience further cultural evolution. Circle this location.

2. Based on the cultural evolution from stage one and your answers to stage one's culture questions, decide what capabilities your culture starts with. Record them in the area below.

3. You will roll a die four times. Each roll will equal 20,000 years; 20,000 years = 20 cm (scale is still 100,000 years = 1 meter, or 100 cm). The number you roll will indicate what your life-form's cultural inventions and discoveries are. For each time-period roll, measure 20 cm on your timeline and record by drawing a line and writing in your life-form's cultural discoveries and inventions, as shown below. For this part of mission 8, *keep your work a secret!*

Figure 8.3—Timeline.

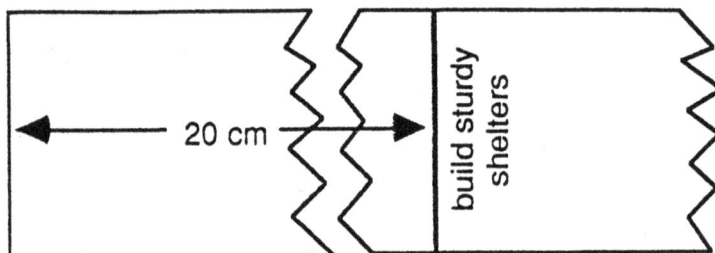

From *The Rise of Intelligence and Culture.* © 1995. Teacher Ideas Press. (800) 237-6124.

Mission 8

Cultures Evolve on Planet Z

Stage Two (B)

Date:

Instructions

Your team's culture lives in the Planet Z _____ habitat. You will use information from your "Planet Z Habitat" logbook sheets and these directions to discover what your cultural evolution will be like in stage two.

For this part of the cultural evolution, your team will need

1 meter of adding machine tape
1 die
colored pens
a metric ruler

1. Use the maps of Planet Z from mission 6 in your logbook to choose a continent that has the habitat where your life-form will experience further cultural evolution. Circle this location.

2. Based on the cultural evolution from stage one and your answers to stage one's culture questions, decide what capabilities your culture starts with. Record them in the area below.

3. You will roll a die four times. Each roll will equal 20,000 years; 20,000 years = 20 cm (scale is still 100,000 years = 1 meter or 100 cm). The number you roll will indicate what your culture's inventions and discoveries are. For each time period roll, measure 20 cm on your timeline and record by drawing a line and writing in your life-form's cultural discoveries and inventions, as shown below. For this part of mission 8, *keep your work a secret!*

Figure 8.4—Timeline.

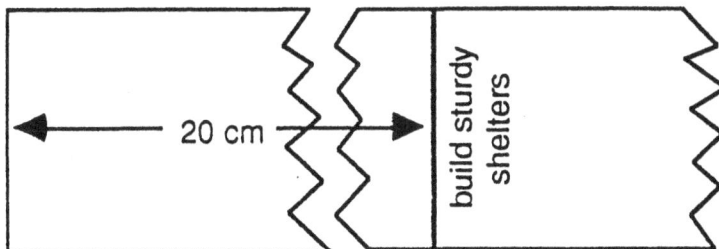

From *The Rise of Intelligence and Culture.* © 1995. Teacher Ideas Press. (800) 237-6124.

Mission 8

Cultures Evolve on Planet Z

Stage Two (C)

Date:

Instructions

    Your team's culture lives in the Planet Z _____ habitat. You will use information from your "Planet Z Habitat" logbook sheets and these directions to discover what your cultural evolution will be like in stage two.

    For this part of the cultural evolution, your team will need

    1 meter of adding machine tape
    1 die
    colored pens
    a metric ruler

1. Use the maps of Planet Z from mission 6 in your logbook to choose a continent that has the habitat where your life-form will experience further cultural evolution. Circle this location.

2. Based on the cultural evolution from stage one and your answers to stage one's culture questions, decide what capabilities your culture starts with. Record them in the area below.

3. You will roll the die four times. Each roll will equal 20,000 years; 20,000 years = 20 cm (scale is still 100,000 years = 1 meter or 100 cm). The number you roll will indicate what your culture's inventions and discoveries are. For each time period roll, measure 20 cm on your timeline and record by drawing a line and writing in your life-form's cultural discoveries and inventions, as shown below. For this part of mission 8, *keep your work a secret!*

Figure 8.5—Timeline.

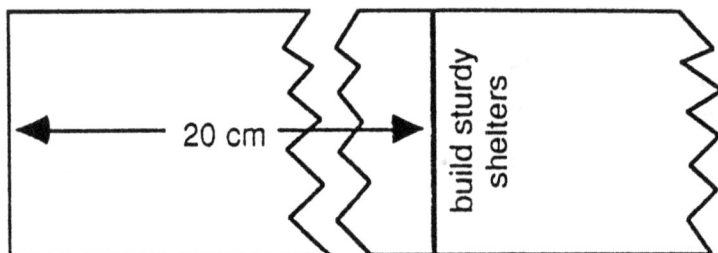

Mission 8

Cultures Evolve on Planet Z

Stage Two (A)
Your Planet Z Culture Evolves

Step 6. (100,000 to 80,000 years ago)
If you roll a . . .
1, 2, or 3 = your culture has learned how to build simple shelters; they have
also invented a ceremony.
Record and Go to—**Step 7a.**
4, 5, or 6 = your culture has learned how to make better tools by shaping them;
they begin to bury their dead.
Record and Go to—**Step 7b.**

Step 7a. (80,000 to 60,000 years ago)
If you roll a . . .
1, 2, or 3 = your culture has learned how to combine materials (like bone and wood)
to make better tools; they have also invented a story to explain birth.
Record and Go to—**Step 8a.**
4, 5, or 6 = your culture has learned how to cooperate to find and collect food; they
have also invented some new tools.
Record and Go to—**Step 8b.**

Step 7b. (80,000 to 60,000 years ago)
If you roll a . . .
1, 2, or 3 = your culture has learned to build sturdy shelters by important
natural resources; they also take care of their older members.
Record and Go to—**Step 8a.**
4, 5, or 6 = your culture has learned how to make bricks from clay; they have
also invented a story to explain the seasons.
Record and Go to—**Step 8b.**

Step 8a. (60,000 to 40,000 years ago)
If you roll a . . .
1, 2, or 3 = your culture has learned how to prepare a new food; they also
make ceremonial clothing.
Record and Go to—**Step 9a.**
4, 5, or 6 = your culture has learned how to cooperate to find and collect food; they
have also invented body decorations.
Record and Go to—**Step 9b.**

Step 8b. (60,000 to 40,000 years ago)
If you roll a . . .
1, 2, or 3 = your culture has discovered a new food plant or animal; they also carve wood, stone, and bone.
Record and Go to—**Step 9a.**
4, 5, or 6 = your culture has learned how to make planks from wood; they have also invented a story to explain the weather.
Record and Go to—**Step 9b.**

Step 9a. (40,000 to 20,000 years ago)
If you roll a . . .
1, 2, or 3 = your culture has learned how to record numbers by notching a stick or a bone; they have also invented a story to explain why the Sun rises and sets.
Record and Go to—**Step 10.**
4, 5, or 6 = your culture has learned how to tell a story by painting figures on a wall; they have also invented a story to explain why the moon changes shape.
Record and Go to—**Step 10.**

Step 9b. (40,000 to 20,000 years ago)
If you roll a . . .
1, 2, or 3 = your culture has learned how to keep track of the days between full moons; they have also invented a story to explain why the stars move.
Record and Go to—**Step 10.**
4, 5, or 6 = your culture has learned how to tell a story by carving figures into rocks and bones; they have also invented a story to explain eclipses.
Record and Go to—**Step 10.**

Step 10. When you are finished rolling and recording, cooperate to answer the questions on the logbook sheet "Describing Your Planet Z Culture" for stage two. On a separate piece of paper, include pictures of your inventions and discoveries.

Mission 8

Cultures Evolve on Planet Z

Stage Two (B)
Your Planet Z Culture Evolves

Step 6. (100,000 to 80,000 years ago)
If you roll a . . .
1, 2, or 3 = your culture has learned how to build simple shade shelters; they have also invented a ceremony.
Record and Go to—**Step 7a.**
4, 5, or 6 = your culture has learned how to make better tools by shaping them; they have a ceremony for their dead members.
Record and Go to—**Step 7b.**

Step 7a. (80,000 to 60,000 years ago)
If you roll a . . .
1, 2, or 3 = your culture has learned how to combine materials (like bone and wood) to make better tools; they have also invented a story to explain birth.
Record and Go to—**Step 8a.**
4, 5, or 6 = your culture has learned how to cooperate to find and collect food; they have also invented some new tools.
Record and Go to—**Step 8b.**

Step 7b. (80,000 to 60,000 years ago)
If you roll a . . .
1, 2, or 3 = your culture has learned to build light-weight, mobile (transportable) shelters; they also take care of their older members.
Record and Go to—**Step 8a.**
4, 5, or 6 = your culture has learned how to make pottery from clay; they have also invented a story to explain the seasons.
Record and Go to—**Step 8b.**

Step 8a. (60,000 to 40,000 years ago)
If you roll a . . .
1, 2, or 3 = your culture has learned how to prepare a new food; they also make ceremonial clothing.
Record and Go to—**Step 9a.**
4, 5, or 6 = your culture has learned how to cooperate to find and collect food; they have also invented body decorations.
Record and Go to—**Step 9b.**

Step 8a. (60,000 to 40,000 years ago)
If you roll a . . .
1, 2, or 3 = your culture has learned how to prepare a new food; they also make ceremonial clothing.
Record and Go to—**Step 9a.**
4, 5, or 6 = your culture has learned how to cooperate to find and collect food; they have also invented body decorations.
Record and Go to—**Step 9b.**

Step 8b. (60,000 to 40,000 years ago)
If you roll a . . .
1, 2, or 3 = your culture has discovered a new food plant or animal; they also carve wood, stone, and bone.
Record and Go to—**Step 9a.**
4, 5, or 6 = your culture has learned how to find water in difficult situations; they have also invented a story to explain the weather.
Record and Go to—**Step 9b.**

Step 9a. (40,000 to 20,000 years ago)
If you roll a . . .
1, 2, or 3 = your culture has learned how to record numbers by notching a stick or a bone; they have also invented a story to explain why the Sun rises and sets.
Record and Go to—**Step 10.**
4, 5, or 6 = your culture has learned how to tell a story by painting figures on a rock; they have also invented a story to explain why the moon changes shape.
Record and Go to—**Step 10.**

Step 9b. (40,000 to 20,000 years ago)
If you roll a . . .
1, 2, or 3 = your culture has learned how to keep track of the days between full moons; they have also invented a story to explain why the stars move.
Record and Go to—**Step 10.**
4, 5, or 6 = your culture has learned how to tell a story by carving figures into rocks and bones; they have also invented a story to explain eclipses.
Record and Go to—**Step 10.**

Step 10. When you are finished rolling and recording, cooperate to answer the questions on the logbook sheet "Describing Your Planet Z Culture" for stage two. On a separate piece of paper, include pictures of your inventions and discoveries.

Mission 8

Cultures Evolve on Planet Z

Stage Two (C)
Your Planet Z Culture Evolves

Step 6. (100,000 to 80,000 years ago)
If you roll a . . .
1, 2, or 3 = your culture has learned how to build simple shelters; they have also invented a ceremony.
Record and Go to—**Step 7a.**
4, 5, or 6 = your culture has learned how to make better tools by shaping them; they have a ceremony to celebrate their dead.
Record and Go to—**Step 7b.**

Step 7a. (80,000 to 60,000 years ago)
If you roll a . . .
1, 2, or 3 = your culture has learned how to combine materials (like bone and wood) to make better tools; they have also invented a story to explain birth.
Record and Go to—**Step 8a.**
4, 5, or 6 = your culture has learned how to cooperate to find and collect food; they have also invented some new tools.
Record and Go to—**Step 8b.**

Step 7b. (80,000 to 60,000 years ago)
If you roll a . . .
1, 2, or 3 = your culture has learned to build sturdy shelters by important natural resources; they also take care of their older members.
Record and Go to—**Step 8a.**
4, 5, or 6 = your culture has learned how to make bricks from natural resources; they have also invented some toys and games.
Record and Go to—**Step 8b.**

Step 8a. (60,000 to 40,000 years ago)
If you roll a . . .
1, 2, or 3 = your culture has learned how to prepare a new food; they also make play an important part of their day.
Record and Go to—**9a.**
4, 5, or 6 = your culture has learned how to cooperate to find and collect food; they have also invented body decorations.
Record and Go to—**9b.**

Step 8b. (60,000 to 40,000 years ago)
If you roll a . . .
1, 2, or 3 = your culture has discovered a new food plant or animal; they also
carve wood, stone, and bone.
Record and Go to—**Step 9a.**
4, 5, or 6 = your culture has learned how to make planks from wood; they have
also invented a story to explain how the world was made.
Record and Go to—**Step 9b.**

Step 9a. (40,000 to 20,000 years ago)
If you roll a . . .
1, 2, or 3 = your culture has learned how to record numbers by notching a bone;
they have also invented a new toy.
Record and Go to—**Step 10.**
4, 5, or 6 = your culture has learned how to tell a story by painting figures on a
wall; they have also invented a story to explain why the moon changes shape.
Record and Go to—**Step 10.**

Step 9b. (40,000 to 20,000 years ago)
If you roll a . . .
1, 2, or 3 = your culture has learned how to drill small objects so they can be hung on
a thread; they have also invented a story to explain why it rains or snows.
Record and Go to—**Step 10.**
4, 5, or 6 = your culture has learned how to tell a story by carving figures into
bones; they have also invented a new game.
Record and Go to—**Step 10.**

Step 10. When you are finished rolling and recording, cooperate to answer
the questions on the logbook sheet "Describing Your Planet Z Culture" for stage two.
On a separate piece of paper, include pictures of your inventions and discoveries.

Mission 8

Cultures Evolve on Planet Z

Stage Two (A)
Describing Your Planet Z Culture

Name:

Date:

1. **Work**—Is work divided up? Who does what tasks?

2. **Clothing**—Do your life-forms need protection for their bodies? What do they wear for decoration and protection?

3. **Group Control**—What guidelines for group control does your culture have? What do you do when life-forms refuse to live by the guidelines? Do you have leaders? How are they chosen?

4. **Ownership**—What do individuals own? What do groups own? What does the whole community own?

5. **Learning**—What do your life-forms need to learn? How do they learn it?

6. **Beliefs**—What are your life-forms' beliefs, rituals, and ceremonies? What do they believe happens to them when they die?

7. **Trade**—What does your culture trade?

8. **Mobility**—How do your life-forms get around?

9. **Water**—From what source does your culture get fresh water for drinking and keeping clean?

From *The Rise of Intelligence and Culture*. © 1995. Teacher Ideas Press. (800) 237-6124.

Mission 8

Cultures Evolve on Planet Z

Stage Two (B)
Describing Your Planet Z Culture

Name:

Date:

1. **Work**—Is work divided up? Who does what tasks?

2. **Clothing**—Do your life-forms need protection for their bodies? What do they wear for decoration and protection?

3. **Group Control**—What guidelines for group control does your culture have? What do you do when life-forms refuse to live by the guidelines? Do you have leaders? How are they chosen?

4. **Ownership**—What do individuals own? What do groups own? What does the whole community own?

5. **Learning**—What do your life-forms need to learn? How do they learn it?

6. **Beliefs**—What are your life-forms' beliefs, rituals, and ceremonies? What do they believe happens to them when they die?

7. **Trade**—What does your culture trade?

8. **Mobility**—How do your life-forms get around?

9. **Water**—From what source does your culture get fresh water for drinking and keeping clean?

Mission 8

Cultures Evolve on Planet Z

Stage Two (C)
Describing Your Planet Z Culture

Name:

Date:

1. **Work**—Is work divided up? Who does what tasks?

2. **Clothing**—Do your life-forms need protection for their bodies? What do they wear for decoration and protection?

3. **Group Control**—What guidelines for group control does your culture have? What do you do when life-forms refuse to live by the guidelines? Do you have leaders? How are they chosen?

4. **Ownership**—What do individuals own? What do groups own? What does the whole community own?

5. **Learning**—What do your life-forms need to learn? How do they learn it?

6. **Beliefs**—What are your life-forms' beliefs, rituals, and ceremonies? What do they believe happens to them when they die?

7. **Trade**—What does your culture trade?

8. **Mobility**—How do your life-forms get around?

9. **Water**—From what source does your culture get fresh water for drinking and keeping clean?

Mission 8

Cultures Evolve on Planet Z

Stage Two (A)
Illustrating Your Planet Z Culture

For this part of the cultural evolution, your team will need

scratch paper and poster paper
pencils
colored markers or crayons or paint

1. Make sure that all of your life-forms' inventions and discoveries are based on the physical structure and bodily needs of the life-form itself and the resources available in the physical environment or habitat.

2. Have your teacher check over your work so far. If it is okay, your teacher will give you the materials you need to illustrate your Planet Z culture!

3. Use your answers to the cultural questions so far to draw a rough draft of a picture showing a typical community in action. Show or describe each important characteristic of your culture. Feature your intelligent life-form and be sure to include plants, other animals, and the landscape.

4. Make sure everyone in your team agrees on the picture. Have your teacher check your rough draft before going on.

5. On the poster paper, create your final, full-color version of the typical community in action.

Rough Draft:

Mission 8

Cultures Evolve on Planet Z

Stage Two (B)
Illustrating Your Planet Z Culture

For this part of the cultural evolution, your team will need

scratch paper and poster paper
pencils
colored markers or crayons or paint

1. Make sure that all of your life-forms' inventions and discoveries are based on the physical structure and bodily needs of the life-form itself and the resources available in the physical environment or habitat.

2. Have your teacher check over your work so far. If it is okay, your teacher will give you the materials you need to illustrate your Planet Z culture!

3. Use your answers to the cultural questions so far to draw a rough draft of a picture showing a typical community in action. Show or describe each important characteristic of your culture. Feature your intelligent life-form and be sure to include plants, other animals, and the landscape.

4. Make sure everyone in your team agrees on the picture. Have your teacher check your rough draft before going on.

5. On the poster paper, create your final, full-color version of the typical community in action.

Rough Draft:

Mission 8

Cultures Evolve on Planet Z

Stage Two (C)
Illustrating Your Planet Z Culture

For this part of the cultural evolution, your team will need

scratch paper and poster paper
pencils
colored markers or crayons or paint

1. Make sure that all of your life-forms' inventions and discoveries are based on the physical structure and bodily needs of the life-form itself and the resources available in the physical environment or habitat.

2. Have your teacher check over your work so far. If it is okay, your teacher will give you the materials you need to illustrate your Planet Z culture!

3. Use your answers to the cultural questions so far to draw a rough draft of a picture showing a typical community in action. Show or describe each important characteristic of your culture. Feature your intelligent life-form and be sure to include plants, other animals, and the landscape.

4. Make sure everyone in your team agrees on the picture. Have your teacher check your rough draft before going on.

5. On the poster paper, create your final, full-color version of the typical community in action.

Rough Draft:

Mission 8

Cultures Evolve on Planet Z

Culture Contact—Intention and Reaction Cards

Intention 1

Table 8.2—Culture Contact Cards.

Intention Card 1	Reaction Card (1A)
1. Intentions are peaceful; the sailing culture is interested in trade of goods and resources, as well as exchange of knowledge.	Your response is to be aggressive and fight the sailing culture to save your culture's way of life. You win. You get all the sailing culture's cards and give up none of your own.
Reaction Card (1B) Your response is to be friendly and assist the sailing culture in any way possible. Trade any of your cards for any of their cards.	**Reaction Card (1C)** Your response is to be frightened and timid. You are interested in self-preservation without warfare. Let the sailing culture choose two of your cards. Take one of theirs.
Reaction Card (1D) Your response is to be very curious and intellectually interested in the sailing culture. You trade all of your cards for all of their cards.	**Reaction Card (1E)** Your response is to be in awe of the sailing culture. Your culture worships and idolizes the mysterious visitors. You take all their cards and give up all but one of your own.
Reaction Card (1F)	**Reaction Card (1G)**

From *The Rise of Intelligence and Culture.* © 1995. Teacher Ideas Press. (800) 237-6124.

Mission 8

Cultures Evolve on Planet Z

Culture Contact—Intention and Reaction Cards

Intention 2

Table 8.3—Culture Contact Cards.

Intention Card 2	Reaction Card (2A)
2. Intentions are righteous; the sailing culture is looking for other beings to convert to their culture's religion.	Your response is to be friendly and interested in trade of goods and resources, and in the exchange of knowledge. Trade any of your cards for any of their cards.
Reaction Card (2B) Your response is to be aggressive and fight the sailing culture to save your culture's way of life. You get all the sailing culture's cards and give up two of your own.	**Reaction Card (2C)** Your response is to be friendly and interested in learning the sailing culture's religion. You trade all your cards for their religion card.
Reaction Card (2D) Your response is to be frightened and interested in self-preservation; all but the weakest hide. You get all the sailing culture's cards and give up none of your own.	**Reaction Card (2E)** Your response is to be aggressive and fight the sailing culture to practice your religion on them by cannibalizing the ship's crew. You get all the sailing culture's cards and give up none of your own.
Reaction Card (2F)	**Reaction Card (2G)**

Mission 8

Cultures Evolve on Planet Z

Culture Contact—Intention and Reaction Cards

Intention 3

Table 8.4—Culture Contact Cards.

Intention Card 3	Reaction Card (3A)
3. Intentions are warlike; the sailing culture is interested in conquering more land, and in taking slaves to be laborers and warriors in their homeland.	Your response is to fight the sailing culture to save your own way of life. Give up half your cards and accept three of theirs.
Reaction Card (3B) Your response is to be friendly and interested in assisting the sailing culture in any way possible. You trade three of your cards for all of their cards.	Reaction Card (3C) Your response is to be warlike. You are interested in cannibalizing the sailors. Give up two of your cards and accept one of theirs.
Reaction Card (3D) Your response is to be frightened and run away in the interest of self-preservation. Give up one of your cards and take all of theirs.	Reaction Card (3E) Your response is to be frightened and timid. You are interested in self-preservation without warfare. Let the sailing culture choose any of your cards. Take one of theirs.
Reaction Card (3F)	Reaction Card (3G)

Mission 8

Cultures Evolve on Planet Z

Stage Three (A)
Your Modern Planet Z Culture

For this part of the cultural evolution, your team will need

your timeline
metric ruler
markers

1. Stage three will evolve your life-form's culture up to the present day. You have been visited by (or visited) other cultures on Planet Z and are aware of what their inventions and discoveries are. You may incorporate any of these into this last stage only if they fit naturally into the guidelines set forth by following these directions.

2. Because of the resources available to the life-forms in your culture, they have

   invented metal and the wheel,

   discovered the use of wind and water to generate power,

   learned how to raise plants and animals,

   mastered the ability to tame and ride larger animals,

   invented an alphabet,

   invented a code of law,

   discovered how to build roadways,

   discovered how to build huge structures,

   discovered how to get energy from a non-renewable resource (like gasoline),

   discovered how to make synthetic "creature-made" materials (like plastics),

   discovered electromagnetic waves (like radio and television), and

   discovered how to make "thinking" machines (like computers).

3. Record these events on your timeline.

4. Below and on the back of this page, describe what your culture is like now. Draw your new inventions. Describe any environmental problems that have arisen because of your culture's use of technology. Describe what your culture is like now.

Mission 8

Cultures Evolve on Planet Z

Stage Three (B)
Your Modern Planet Z Culture

For this part of the cultural evolution, your team will need

your timeline
metric ruler
markers

1. Stage three will evolve your life-form's culture up to the present day. You have been visited by (or visited) other cultures on Planet Z and are aware of what their inventions and discoveries are. You may incorporate any of these into this last stage only if they fit naturally into the guidelines set forth by following these directions.

2. Because of the resources available to the life-forms in your culture, they have

   invented metal and the wheel,

   discovered the use of wind to generate power,

   learned how to raise plants and animals,

   mastered the ability to tame and ride larger animals,

   invented an alphabet,

   invented a code of law,

   discovered how to build roadways, and

   discovered how to build huge structures.

3. Record these events on your timeline.

4. Below and on the back of this page, describe what your culture is like now. Draw your new inventions. Describe any environmental problems that have arisen because of your culture's use of technology. Describe what your culture is like now.

Mission 8

Cultures Evolve on Planet Z

Stage Three (C)
Your Modern Planet Z Culture

For this part of the cultural evolution, your team will need

your timeline
metric ruler
markers

1. Stage three will evolve your life-form's culture up to the present day. You have been visited by (or visited) other cultures on Planet Z and are aware of what their inventions and discoveries are. You may incorporate any of these into this last stage only if they fit naturally into the guidelines set forth by following these directions.

2. Because of the resources available to the life-forms in your culture, they have

   invented the wheel,

   discovered the use of water to generate power,

   learned how to raise plants and animals,

   mastered the ability to tame and ride larger animals,

   invented an alphabet, and

   invented a code of law.

3. Record these events on your timeline.

4. Below and on the back of this page, describe what your culture is like now. Draw your new inventions. Describe any environmental problems that have arisen because of your culture's use of technology. Describe what your culture is like now.

Mission 8

Cultures Evolve on Planet Z

What Do You Think, Now?

Name:

Date:

After you have completed this mission, please answer the following questions:

1. Is it reasonable to suppose that cultural evolution might occur differently on other planets? Why or why not?

2. What might some of the cultural differences be?

Mission 9

Extraterrestrial Communication Can We Talk to Anybody Out There?

Overview

Cultures, such as those evolved in mission 8, might eventually develop technology that can communicate over interstellar distances. If there are civilizations on other planets in our galaxy, how can we best communicate with them? In mission 9, students consider what technology a civilization needs to communicate with other planets.

In mission 9.1, students consider different methods of communication on Earth and in space. They discuss and analyze different methods of communicating in space. In mission 9.2, students model two methods of interstellar communication to determine the more practical method of communicating with a distant extraterrestrial civilization.

Concepts

- Some methods of communication used on Earth do not work in outer space.

- Some methods of communication will take too long to cover the vast reaches of space that exist between us and an extraterrestrial civilization.

- Traveling to another solar system in a space-craft, using currently available technology, would not be practical, because it would take many human lifetimes.

Skills

- Building models.

- Applying mathematics to real life.

- Understanding large numbers: million, billion.

Notes

In mission 8, students observed the cultural evolution of intelligent cultures on Planet Z.

181

Mission 9.1

Materials

For the Class

- A piece of butcher paper or a chalkboard

- Two dusty chalkboard erasers

- A flashlight

- (optional) Flour

- (optional) VCR and monitor

- (optional) videotape of *Reading Rainbow*, "Space Case" episode (see "Resources" in the appendixes)

For Each Student

- SETI Academy Cadet Logbook

- Pencil

- (optional) Calculator

Getting Ready

One or More Days Before Class

1. Review the "Teacher Background Information" for this mission in the appendixes.

2. You may wish to practice the demonstration of sending light through space with chalkboard erasers and a flashlight. If any students have allergies to chalk dust, try the demonstration with flour.

3. If you choose to show "Space Case," preview the tape and queue it to the section of the tape you choose to show.

Just Before the Lesson

1. Hang the butcher paper on a wall at the front of the classroom.

2. (optional) Set up VCR and monitor.

Classroom Action

1. **Mission Briefing.** Have the class refer to the "Mission Briefing" for mission 9 in their student logbooks as one student reads it aloud.

2. **What Do You Think?** Read aloud and discuss the pre-activity questions on the "Mission Briefing." Have students answer the questions in their logbooks. Invite them to share their answers in a class discussion.

3. **Discussion.** How can we communicate? Ask students for their ideas about how we communicate with one another on Earth. Record student suggestions on the butcher paper (or on the chalkboard). Items on the list might include: talking, writing, songs, television, telephone, smoke signals, radio, cellular phones, sign language, and newspapers.

   Remind students that in the mission briefing they were challenged to find the most *practical* method of communicating with a distant extraterrestrial civilization. What is practical? What are our limiting factors? Allow time for student discussion. Write their ideas on the chalkboard. Time, distance, and money are some of the limiting factors students should come up with.

   Ask students which methods of communication would work in space. Circle the methods on the list that could work in space. Discuss why those methods work. You may want to read the following information to your students or show them the episode of *Reading Rainbow* entitled "Space Case."

   Ask students why we think extraterrestrials would use radio to communicate, and not light, for example, or even more exotic methods such as gravity waves. One big advantage of radio waves is that they go easily through the dust that floats between the stars. Although this dust is very thin, space is very large, so when we look toward the center of the Milky Way, we can only see about one-tenth of the way to the center, about 3,000 light-years, before the dust blocks our view. So anyone signaling with ordinary light would be limited by this dusty fog to fairly nearby "listeners" (viewers).

   Another point is that stars put out a lot of light and this would tend to confuse the signal.

Finally, most light beams such as those from a high-powered laser are very narrow: You have to know exactly where the listener is in order to "hit" them with your beam of light. Radio beams are easily made very wide, and can cover a lot of sky. So, unless some extraterrestrials know exactly where we are (or vice versa), there's a greater chance that we'll be in someone's radio beam than in their optical (light) beam.

4. **Demonstration.** Use a flashlight to illustrate the concept of light getting absorbed in cosmic dust. To do this, darken the room and turn on a flashlight as you direct the beam of light at the chalkboard. Discuss the size of the circle of light projected on the board. Ask students if they can make any observations about the beam of light itself. They should be able to see particles of dust floating around within the beam. Next, turn off the flashlight and clap two chalkboard erasers together as you tell students that this dust you are making represents the cosmic dust in space. Once again, direct the beam of light at the chalkboard through the cosmic dust. Ask students if they can observe any differences about the circle of light projected by the flashlight or any difference in the beam of light itself. They should be able to see an increase in the amount of dust particles in the beam of light and a reduction in the brightness of the projected circle of light.

Narrow down the student list to three methods of communicating with a distant extraterrestrial civilization. To elicit the correct answers, ask students questions such as:

- Which method of interstellar communication (on the list) is the fastest way to send a message to another planet?

- Which method of interstellar communication (on the list) is probably the least expensive way to send a message to another planet?

The list should be narrowed down to spacecraft, radio waves, and light waves. Explain to students that, of these three methods, light waves and radio waves both travel at the speed of light. Spacecraft speed will be referred to as probe speed, because that is what actual spacecraft are called, like the *Pioneer* space probes, for example. (They are called probes because they are probing or investigating the unknown.)

Mission 9.2

Materials

For the Class

- 140 meters of string

- Meter stick

- Transparent tape

- 3-by-5-inch index cards (10)

For Each Student

- SETI Academy Cadet Logbook

- Pencil

- (optional) Calculator

Getting Ready

One or More Days Before Class

1. Locate a large outdoor area such as a playing field or blacktop area that measures at least 108 meters in length or 108 meters diagonally.

2. Cut the string, or have a student cut the string, into the following lengths: one 8-meter length of string, one 19.5-meter length of string, one 108-meter length of string.

3. Write, or have a student write, the names of the planets and the Sun on index cards, one name per card.

Just Before the Lesson

1. Take the materials for the class (for constructing a model solar system) outdoors to the large area selected earlier.

2. Remind students of conduct rules for an outdoor activity.

Classroom Action

1. **Lecture.** Explain that students will now do an activity to help them determine which of two ways is the most practical in terms of cost, distance, and time. They will build a model of the solar system, as shown in figure 9.1, to help them act out how practical probe speed and speed of light are as methods of communicating through space.

Figure 9.1—Probe Speed Versus Light Speed.

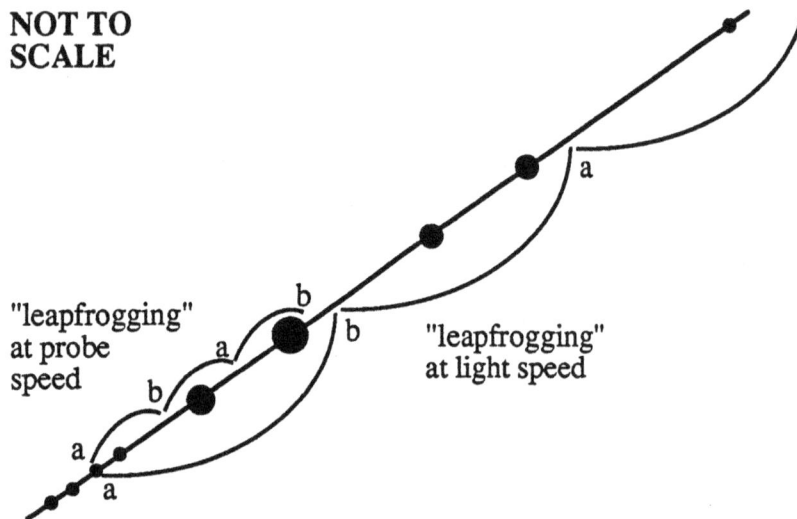

NOT TO SCALE

"leapfrogging" at probe speed

"leapfrogging" at light speed

2. **Activity.** Go outdoors to a large playing field or outdoor blacktop area. Pass out the index cards with planet names. Give the 108-meter string to the student with the Sun card. Instruct this student to stand at the corner of the field or blacktop, holding the string by one end. Have the student with the Pluto card hold the other end of the 108-meter string. Instruct these students to extend the string to its full length, diagonally across the field or blacktop area. Tell the students with the Sun and Pluto cards to tape their index cards to the ends of the string.

   With a meter stick and the Planet Distances chart (table 9.1), measure, or have a student measure, the distances between planets along the string. When a distance of 1 meter, 5 centimeters is measured from the Sun, call for the student with the Mercury card and have him/her tape the card to the string and stand by their card beside the string. Continue doing this until all the planets (students) and cards are in place.

Table 9.1—Planet Distances.

Planet	Distance from Sun	Distance from Previous Planet
Mercury	1 m, 5 cm	NA
Venus	1 m, 97 cm	92 cm
Earth	2 m, 73 cm	76 cm
Mars	4 m, 15 cm	1 m, 42 cm
Jupiter	14 m	10 m
Saturn	26 m	12 m
Uranus	52 m	26 m
Neptune	82 m	30 m
Pluto	108 m	26 m

Your model is complete. Students may now act out probe speed and the speed of light. Tell the class that they will act out the time and distance requirements to get to Pluto at probe speed and at the speed of light. First, they will act out probe speed. Have two students (student A and student B) who want to represent the probe hold the ends of the 8-meter string, which represents the distance a probe can travel in one year.

Ask the class at what point in the solar system they should begin measuring. Make sure students understand that Earth is the starting point. Have the 8-meter string holders begin next to the person with the Earth card. Tell student A to stand by the Earth person as student B extends the string out toward Pluto, staying alongside the string of planets. When the string is taut and student B can go no farther, have the students not currently involved in the action call out, "One year at probe speed!"

Next, student A should extend the end of the string in the direction of Pluto, "leapfrogging" around student B and then alongside the string of planets, until the string becomes taut again. Students should now call out, "Two years at probe speed!" Have students continue this process until either student A or student B reaches Pluto, which will be "13 years at probe speed!" Have one student be responsible for remembering the probe speed total.

Repeat this simulation for the speed of light, using two other students and the 19.5-meter length of string. Remind the class that this string represents the distance that light travels in one *hour*, and compare this to the distance traveled in an entire *year* at probe speed. Students should call out, "One hour at the speed of light!" and so on, continuing until Pluto is reached—"5.5 hours at the speed of light!" Have another student be responsible for remembering the light speed total.

Closure

1. **Lecture.** In the classroom, instruct students to turn to their logbook sheet "Sending Messages." This worksheet shows students the time and distance involved in sending a message to Pluto and to the star system nearest our solar system, the Proxima Centauri system. You may want to explain that the playing field outdoors where they built the model of the solar system was barely big enough to act out sending a message to Pluto at the speed of a probe and at the speed of light. It would take more than 740 km (4.44 miles) to build a scale model that could include Proxima Centauri, the star nearest our solar system.

2. **Activity.** Have the students responsible for remembering the totals for probe and light speeds write their numbers on the chalkboard for students to refer to during this activity. Allow time for students to complete "Sending Messages," including figure 9.2 (page 193). Circulate to help as needed. You may choose to guide students through this worksheet as a whole-class activity.

Answers to the "Sending Messages" Logbook Sheet

See logbook sheet, pages 191-193.

1. When you measured with the 8-meter string, you learned that it would take *13 years* to send a message to Pluto at the speed of a probe.

When you measured with the 19.5-meter string, you learned that it would take *5.5 hours* to send a message to Pluto at the speed of light.

2. *55 hours* ÷ 24 = *.23 days* to send a message to Pluto at the speed of light.

.23 days ÷ 365 = *.0006 years* to send a message to Pluto at the speed of light.

3. 40,000 ÷ 5.8 = *6,896.5* times farther.

Proxima Centauri is *7,000* times farther away from Earth than Pluto is!

4. *13 years* x ÷ 7,000 = *91,000 years*

.0006 years x ÷ 7,000 = *4.2 years*

---

3. **Discussion.** Ask students what method they would use to try to communicate with extraterrestrials. Encourage them to present their viewpoints with supporting information and to debate and question other students. Consider the practicality of each method—cost, time, and energy.

4. **What Do You Think, Now?** Have students answer the post-activity questions on the logbook sheet "What Do You Think, Now?" Invite students to share their responses and their drawings. Ask them how their opinions have been changed by this mission.

Going Further

Research: No, No, UFO!

Have students calculate how long it would take an extraterrestrial life-form to reach Earth in a spaceship from Alpha Centauri? Is this likely to happen?

Mission 9

Extraterrestrial Communication
Mission Briefing

Name:

Date:

Dr. Seth Shostak, Radio Astronomer on the SETI Academy Team

Now we would like you to consider how we might communicate with an extraterrestrial civilization. There are many possible methods, but we challenge you to find ones that are practical.

What Do You Think?

1. Given our current scientific knowledge, can we have a "quick" conversation with an extraterrestrial?

2. Can we go to an extraterrestrial world? Explain why or why not.

Mission 9

Extraterrestrial Communication

Sending Messages

Name:

Date:

The Challenge: Find out how long it will take to send a message to both Pluto and Proxima Centauri (the star nearest our solar system) by probe and by radio (the speed of light).

Table 9.2—Data.

Average distance from Earth to Pluto	5.8 billion kilometers
Distance from Earth to Proxima Centuri	40,000 billion kilometers
Speed of probe	61,000 kilometers per hour (about half a billion kilometers per year)
Speed of light	300,000 kilometers per second (about 1 billion kilometers per hour)

1. You worked with a team of students to take measurements of a scale model of the solar system. Using two different lengths of string, you measured the trip between Earth and Pluto.

   ☞ When you measured with the 8-meter string, you learned that it would take _____ *years* to send a message to Pluto at the probe speed.

   ☞ When you measured with the 19.5-meter string, you learned that it would take _____ *hours* to send a message to Pluto at the speed of light.

2. Notice that the times listed above are in different units of measurement. Probe speed is in *years*, and light speed is in *hours*. The next step is to figure out how long it would take to send a message to Proxima Centauri. Use the equations below to convert the hours it takes to send a message by light speed into years so that you will have the same unit of measurement for your answers.

   ☞ _____ *hours* ÷ 24 = _____ *days* to send a message to Pluto at the speed of light.

   ☞ _____ *days* ÷ 365 = _____ *years* to send a message to Pluto at the speed of light.

From *The Rise of Intelligence and Culture.* © 1995. Teacher Ideas Press. (800) 237-6124.

3. Now you know how long, in years, to send a message to Pluto by probe speed and by light speed. You can use this information to discover how long it would take to send a message to our nearest star, Proxima Centauri. Pluto is 5.8 billion kilometers from Earth and Proxima Centauri is 40,000 billion kilometers from Earth. To find out how many times farther from Earth Proxima Centauri is than Pluto, complete the following equation:

   ☞ 40,000 ÷ 5.8 = _____ times farther.

   ☞ Round this number off to the nearest thousand and enter it on the line in the next sentence. Proxima Centauri is _____ times farther away from Earth than Pluto is! This number is your multiplier. You will multiply this number by the number of years it takes to get from Earth to Pluto by probe speed and by light speed. You will discover how many years it would take to send a message to Proxima Centauri by each of these two methods.

4. You will need some of your calculations from numbers 1 and 2 of this sheet to complete the following equations:

   ☞ _____ *years* x _____ = _____ *years*
      years from Earth to Pluto at probe speed   multiplier

   ☞ _____ *years* x _____ = _____ *years*
      years from Earth to Pluto at light speed   multiplier

Figure 9.2—*Pioneer* Plaque.

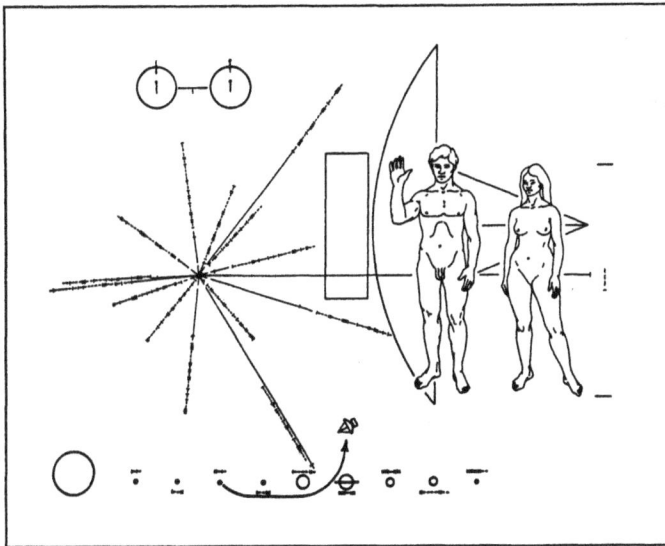

☞ If I were to send a message by a space probe, like the plaque on the *Pioneer* probe (left), it would be _____ *years* before it would arrive at the nearest star, Proxima Centauri.

☞ If I were to send a message at the speed of light, like the radio message from Arecibo (right), it would be _____ *years* before it would arrive at the nearest star, Proxima Centauri.

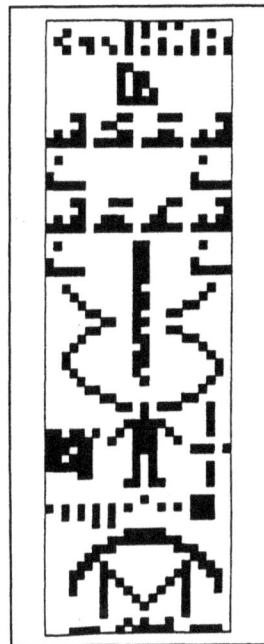

Mission 9

Extraterrestrial Communication

What Do You Think, Now?

Name:

Date:

After you have completed this mission, please answer the following questions:

1. Given our current scientific knowledge, can we have a "quick" conversation with an extraterrestrial?

2. Can we go to an extraterrestrial world? Explain why or why not.

Mission 10

Decoding an Extraterrestrial Message
Figuring Out a "Message from ET"

Overview

What would an extraterrestrial message look like? How would we decode it? In mission 10, students learn to translate a radio signal into information that Earthlings can interpret. In mission 10.1, students hear a sample message and discuss codes. In mission 10.2, students have a chance to decode a complex "practice" extraterrestrial message made by a SETI scientist.

Concepts

- Extraterrestrials might not speak an Earth language.

- A message from an extraterrestrial civilization might be difficult to interpret.

- The laws of mathematics and the laws of physics apply everywhere in the universe, so they will be the same for us as they are for any extraterrestrial cultures.

- An extraterrestrial culture might use mathematical concepts such as prime numbers to encode nonverbal ideas as a message.

- A message from an extraterrestrial civilization might appear in the form of a picture.

Skills

- Decoding messages.

- Recognizing prime numbers.

- Recognizing patterns.

Notes

In mission 9, students determined the most practical method of communicating with a distant extraterrestrial civilization.

195

Mission 10.1

Materials

For the Class

- Overhead projector

- Tape recorder

- Blank tape

- Two different noise makers

For Each Student

- SETI Academy Cadet Logbook

- Pencil

Getting Ready

One or More Days Before Class

1. Review the "Teacher Background Information" for this mission in the appendixes.

2. Using two different sounds (they don't have to be "beep" and "click"), tape record the following message:

   beep, click, click, click, click, click, beep, beep, click, beep, beep, beep, click, beep, beep, click, beep, click, beep, click, beep, beep, click, beep, beep, beep, click, beep, beep, click, click, click, click, click, beep.

   Make sure that the recording is slow enough to distinctly hear the two sounds.

Just Before the Lesson

1. Set up overhead projector.

2. Draw a 5-by-7 grid on the chalkboard or the overhead projector.

Classroom Action

1. **Mission Briefing.** Have the class refer to the "Mission Briefing" for mission 10 in their student logbooks as one student reads it aloud.

Teacher's Note: *Before beginning this activity, make sure that students know about the concept of prime numbers. If necessary, review or present this crucial concept.*

2. **What Do You Think?** Read aloud and discuss the pre-activity questions on the "Mission Briefing." Have students answer the questions in their logbooks. Invite them to share their answers in a class discussion.

3. **Lecture.** Explain to students that SETI scientists currently are exploring radio frequencies for signs of intelligent life in the universe. They expect a signal of intelligent origin to have a pattern that could not be made by a naturally occurring object. They also hope that a signal would contain interesting and helpful information. But how does one translate a radio signal into information that Earthlings can interpret?

4. **Demonstration.** Announce that you have an example of a radio message. Request that they listen carefully for information. Play the beep-click tape. Ask if anyone got useful information from the message. Explain that radio astronomers do not expect to be able to understand an extraterrestrial message right away. They assume that they will need to decode it first.

   Allow students a few minutes to try and detect a pattern in the sequence they just listened to. Let them try to find a sequence of English words, sequences of numbers, and so forth.

   Have students open up their logbooks to the sheet "Decoding a Radio Message." Ask a student to read number one. Explain that they just listened to the beep-click message written below the first statement. Ask students if it is any easier to get information out of the message when it is written down. Emphasize that extraterrestrial life-forms probably don't speak any Earth language.

   Have another student read number two. Any two forms of signal can communicate two-symbol messages (dots and dashes, two different tones, pulses and blanks). Extraterrestrials may not know any Earth language, but we assume that they will know math.

   Ask students why a picture from an extraterrestrial culture would be more useful than their printed language. It is more useful because we probably won't be able to read their language.

Have another student read number three. Ask a student to demonstrate how to properly fill in the 5-by-7 grid you drew on the chalkboard or overhead projector, as in figure 10.1: beep (leave blank), click (fill in), click (fill in), beep (leave blank), and so forth.

Figure 10.1—Grid Showing Messages.

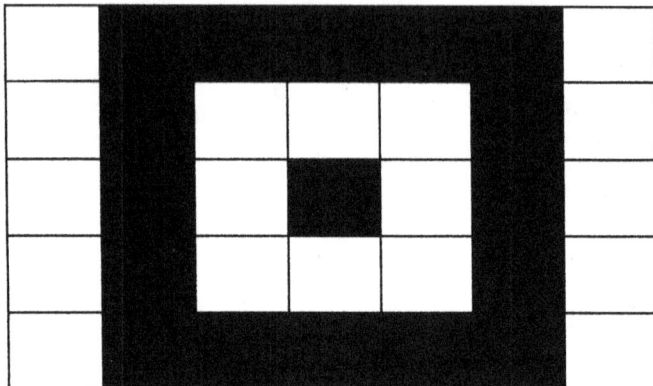

5. **Activity.** Have students complete the grids on the logbook sheet "Decoding a Radio Message." Make sure students understand the assignment.

6. **Discussion.** Ask students which arrangement of beeps and clicks made the most sense. They should have found that the second one made more sense because it formed a shape instead of scattered squares. Tell students that they will be seeing several real messages intentionally sent by scientists from Earth into space, hopefully to some unknown civilization. Ask students to consider what methods for sending the messages the scientists might have chosen and what information the messages might contain.

Mission 10.2

Materials

For Each Team

- Five-page "Practice Message" (pages 203-207)

For Each Student

- SETI Academy Cadet Logbook

- Pencil

Getting Ready

One or More Days Before Class

1. Try to decode the five-page logbook message yourself.

2. Group students into teams of two to four each.

Classroom Action

1. **Activity.** Announce that you have a message that might be like something an extraterrestrial civilization would send. (This message was created by a SETI scientist.) Explain that the message has been *decoded* from a radio signal into a series of five images or pictures. Tell students that the challenge is to *interpret* it to the best of their abilities. In other words, "If such a message were really received from an alien civilization, what do you think it might mean?"

2. Hand out the five-page "Practice Message" logbook sheets that contain the communication. Divide the class into teams and give them 20 to 30 minutes to work.

3. Ask the students to look at the first image and invite student teams to say what they think it might mean. When all ideas have been exhausted, go on to the next image. Accept all ideas equally, and resist any requests to say what it really means, by telling them that if a message is actually received from an alien civilization, no one on Earth would know for certain what was intended. A sample discussion of the kinds of ideas that students frequently come up with is included in the appendix.

Closure

1. **What Do You Think, Now?** Have students answer the post-activity questions on the logbook sheet "What Do You Think, Now?" Invite students to share their responses and their drawings. Ask them how their opinions have been changed by this mission.

Going Further

Class Activity: Designer Messages

Have students design a message for another class to decode. Or divide the class into teams and have them make, trade, and decode messages.

Mission 10

Decoding an Extraterrestrial Message
Mission Briefing

Name:

Date:

Dr. Kent Cullers, Signal Processing Expert on the SETI Academy Team

You will receive a "practice" extraterrestrial message that was actually invented by one of our SETI scientists. If we receive a message from an intelligent civilization, we will need to interpret it, so use this one to refine your skills.

What Do You Think?

1. What do you need to know about an extraterrestrial civilization to decode one of its messages?

2. What do you think such a message might say?

Mission 10

Decoding an Extraterrestrial Message

Decoding a Radio Message

Name:

Date:

1. SETI radio astronomers expect to receive an extraterrestrial message in the form of a radio signal. It might sound like two different noises if you were to listen to it on a radio. Here is an example:

    beep, click, click, click, click, click, beep,
    beep, click, beep, beep, beep, click, beep,
    beep, click, beep, click, beep, click, beep,
    beep, click, beep, beep, beep, click, beep,
    beep, click, click, click, click, click, beep.

2. In the hope that this message contains information, the receiving radio astronomer would count up the total number of sounds and attempt to organize them in some way. Notice that there are 35 clicks and beeps. The number 35 is only divisible by 35 and 1 or 5 and 7. This suggests that the beeps and clicks can be organized on a grid that is either 5 by 7 or 7 by 5.

Figure 10.2—Grids for Translating Signals.

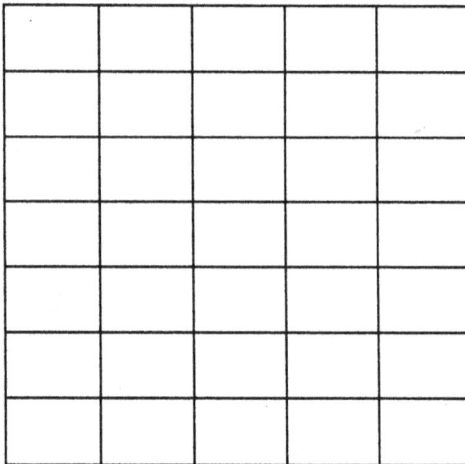

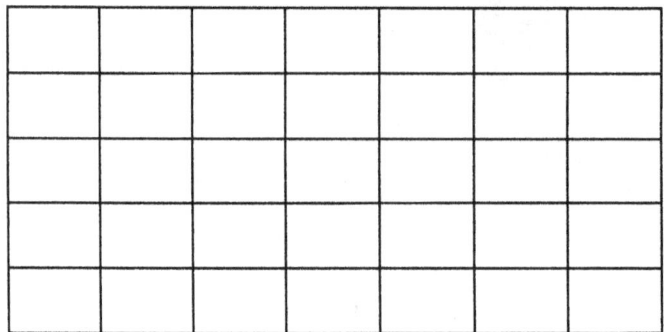

3. Work carefully to translate the beeps and clicks into a grid picture. For each beep, leave one square blank; for each click, fill in one square. Work horizontally, from left to right. Be accurate! One mistake and all the information will be incorrect (using a pencil is a good idea).

Mission 10

Decoding an Extraterrestrial Message

Message (Page 1)

Figure 10.3.

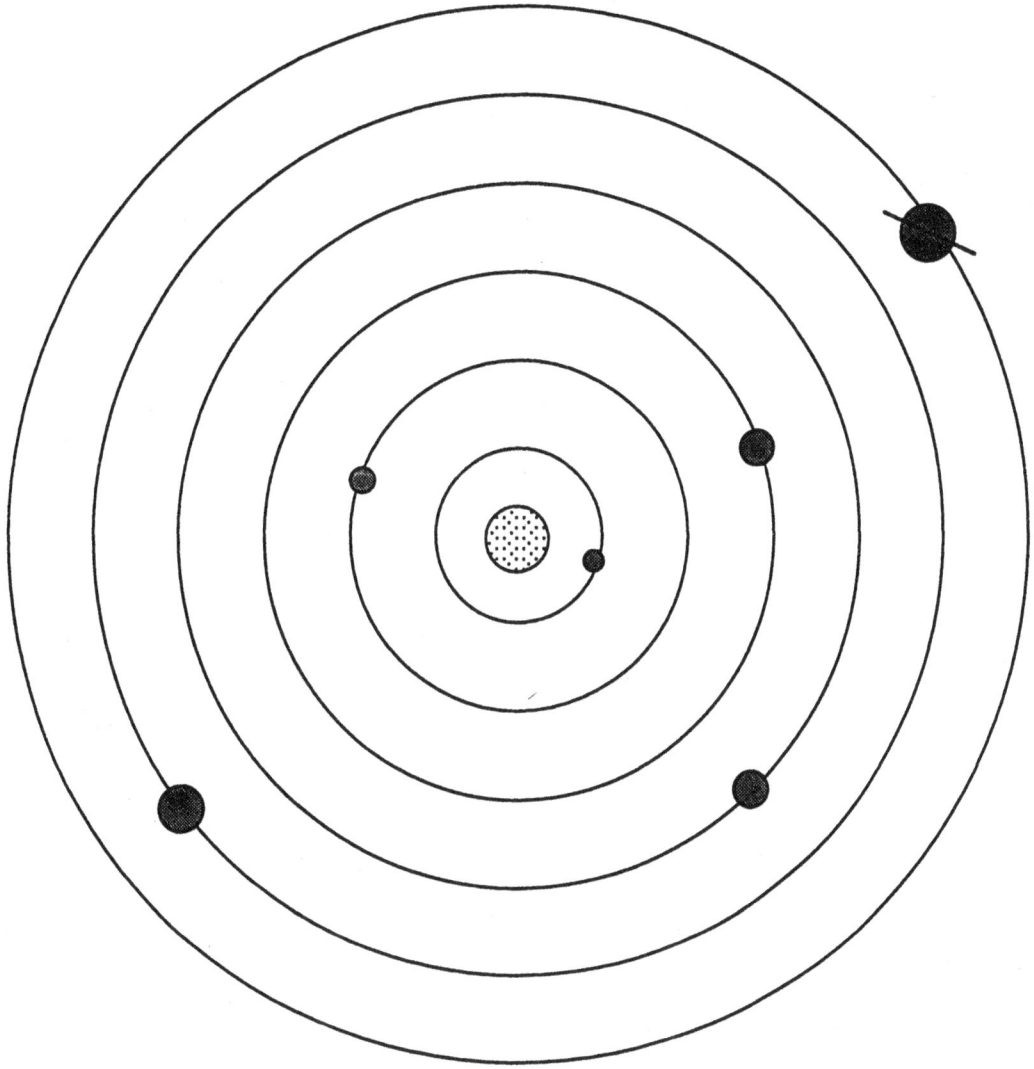

Mission 10

Decoding an Extraterrestrial Message

Message (Page 2)

Figure 10.4.

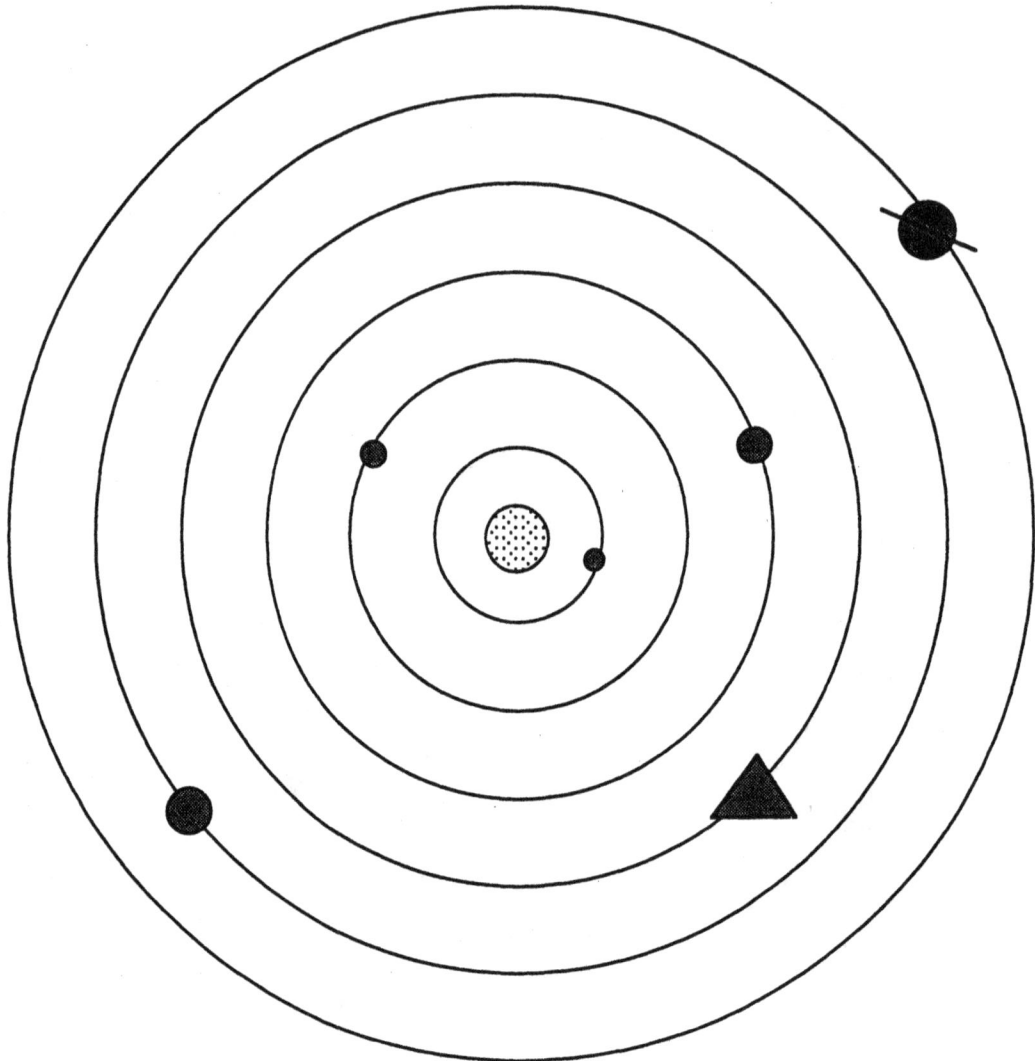

Mission 10

Decoding an Extraterrestrial Message

Message (Page 3)

Figure 10.5.

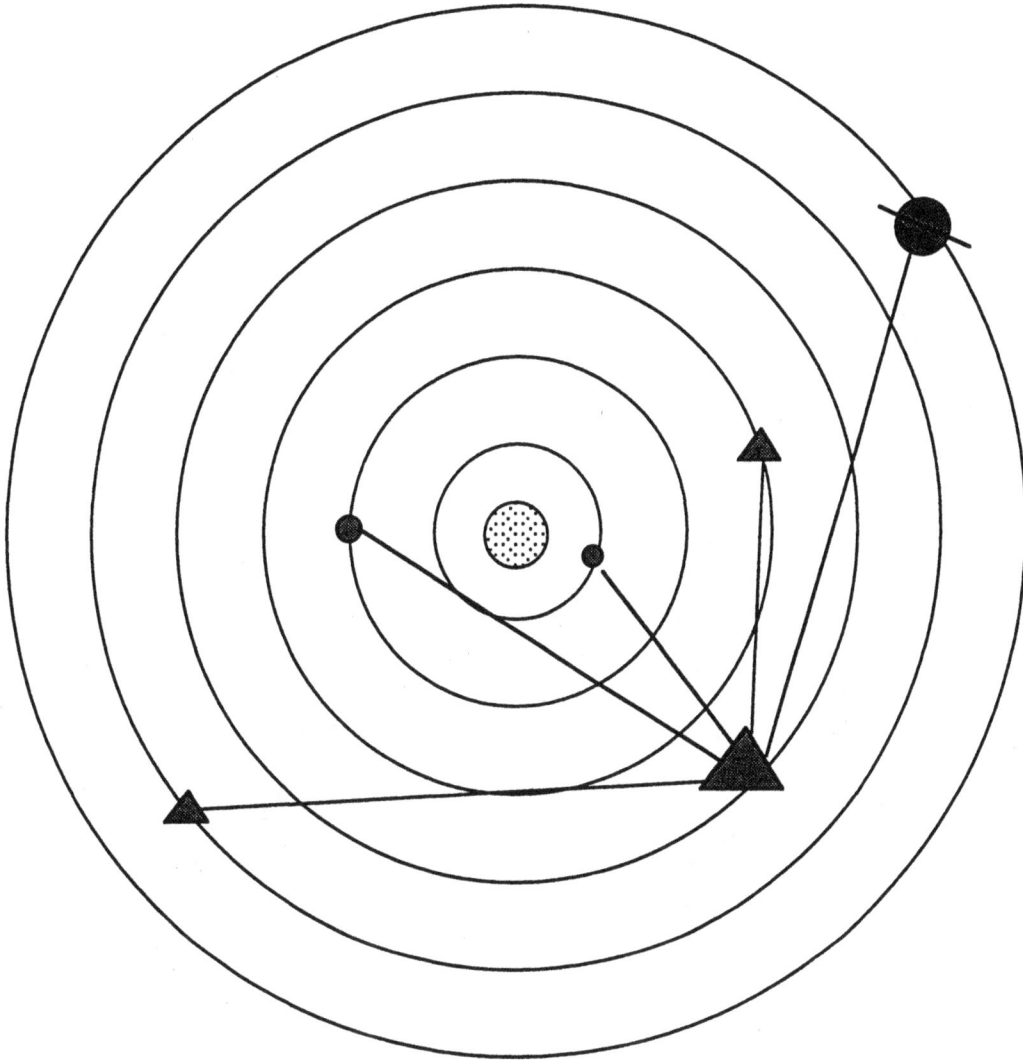

Mission 10

Decoding an Extraterrestrial Message

Message (Page 4)

Figure 10.6.

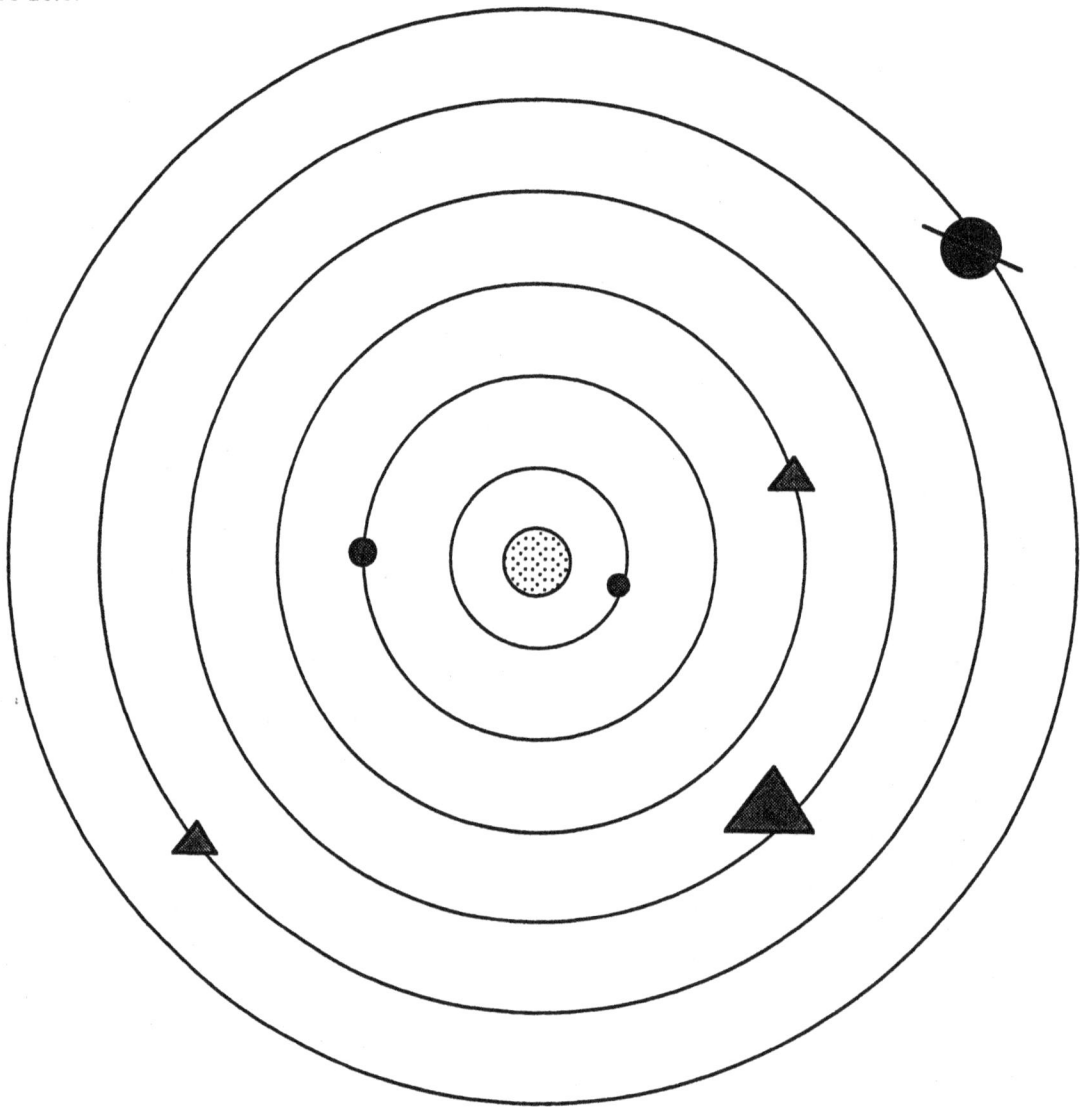

Mission 10

Decoding an Extraterrestrial Message

Message (Page 5)

Figure 10.7.

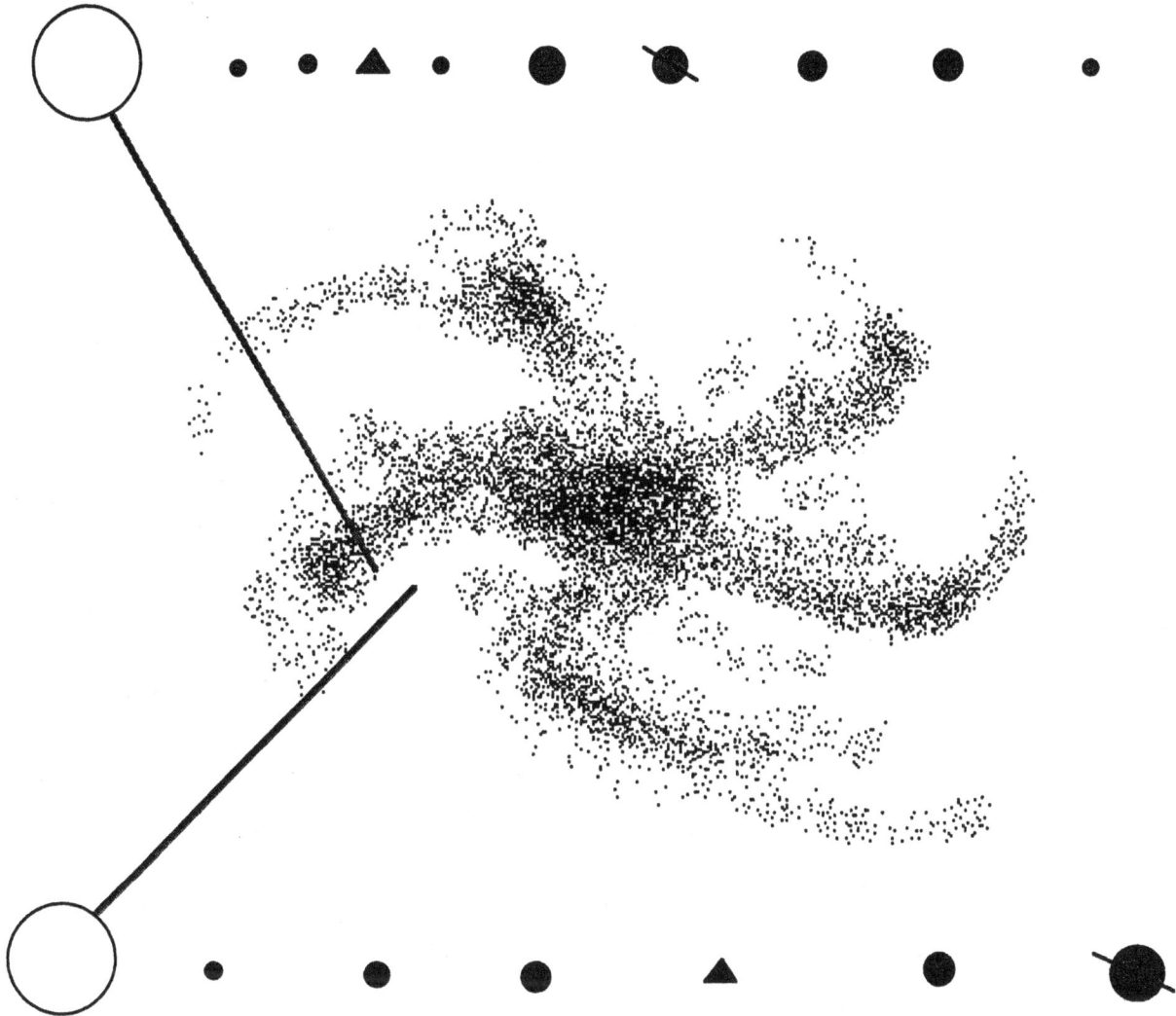

Mission 10

Decoding an Extraterrestrial Message

What Do You Think, Now?

Name:

Date:

After you have completed this mission, please answer the following questions:

1. What do you need to know an about extraterrestrial civilization to decode one of its messages?

2. What do you think such a message might say?

Mission 11

What Do We Say, and How Do We Say It?
What Information Do We Want to Send?

Overview

What should we say, and how should we say it? In mission 11, students figure out the components of a "good space message" (one that another civilization can decode), and they write and decode messages from cultures on Planet Z.

In mission 11.1, students compare and contrast the "practice" extraterrestrial message with three actual messages sent into space by scientists from Earth. In mission 11.2, students decide what information about their Planet Z cultures would be appropriate to send into space, and prepare messages from Planet Z. Students form Planet Z culture groups and send their messages to other teams in the classroom. The messages are interpreted and responses are sent.

Concepts

- A message from one planet to another needs to rely on universal concepts, such as mathematics.

- The interpretation of a message may be different than the meaning that was intended.

Skills

- Critical thinking.

- Decoding a message.

- Interpreting and sending messages.

- Comparing and contrasting messages.

Notes

In mission 10, students learned to translate a radio signal into information that Earthlings can interpret.

Mission 11.1

Materials

For the Class

- Overhead projector

- Transparencies of the "Practice Message" from mission 10

- Transparencies of the three "Earth Message" logbook sheets (pages 216-218)

- 2 sheets of butcher paper

- Markers

For Each Pair

- Paper

For Each Student

- SETI Academy Cadet Logbook

- Pencil

Getting Ready

One or More Days Before Class

1. Review the "Teacher Background Information" for this mission in the appendixes.

2. Make transparencies of the five-page "Practice Message" from mission 10 and the three "Earth Message" logbook sheets.

Just Before the Lesson

1. Hang the blank butcher paper on the chalkboard and have markers handy.

2. Set up the overhead projector.

Classroom Action

1. **Mission Briefing.** Have the class refer to the "Mission Briefing" for mission 11 in their student logbooks as one student reads it aloud.

2. **What Do You Think?** Read aloud and discuss the pre-activity questions on the "Mission

Briefing." Have students answer the questions in their logbooks. Invite them to share their answers in a class discussion.

3. **Discussion.** Put the transparencies of the five-page "Practice Message" on the overhead projector. Have student pairs share their ideas about what the message says, and why. Discuss why it was or was not easy to decide what it said.

   Have students begin a list of characteristics of a "good space message," such as "it is a picture," "it shows recognizable objects like a galaxy," and so on. Record their ideas on the butcher paper (save this paper for mission 11.2).

4. **Lecture.** Tell students that you have three messages that were sent into space by scientists from Earth. Ask students to analyze the messages for more characteristics of a "good space message."

   Put the transparency of the Arecibo message on the overhead projector. Challenge students to attempt to decode it as if they were intelligent Planet Z life-forms. What does this message communicate to another civilization? Add good communication characteristics to the list, such as "shows important concepts like DNA," "shows what a human looks like," "shows the solar system," and "teaches about how to decode it by showing numbers."
   Repeat this procedure for the *Pioneer* and *Voyager* messages.

5. **Discussion.** Have students decide what assumptions should be used when deciding to send an interstellar message from Planet Z. Record them on the second sheet of butcher paper (save this paper for mission 11.2).

   For example, assume that

   - your audience does not speak your language,

   - your audience has never heard of Planet Z nor of Planet Z's solar system,

   - the life-forms who might receive the message live on a faraway planet orbiting another star, and

- the receivers of your message are *not* Earthlings.

6. **Activity.** Have students work in their Planet Z culture teams to brainstorm what ideas, concepts, and images they would like to include in an interstellar message from Planet Z.

7. **Discussion.** Have a short class discussion to consider students' topics for messages. Ask students which was harder, deciding what to say or deciding how to say it. Ask students to describe what ways their messages could be misinterpreted.

Mission 11.2

Materials

For the Class

- Butcher paper lists from mission 11.1

For Each Student

- SETI Academy Cadet Logbook

- Pencil

Getting Ready

1. Make sure the two lists from mission 11.1 are displayed where all students can see them.

Classroom Action

1. **Discussion.** Remind students that they recently worked with their Planet Z culture teams to brainstorm what ideas, concepts, and images they would like to include in an interstellar message. From the lists, review the characteristics of a "good space message" and the assumptions that should be considered when deciding what information to send into space.

2. **Activity.** Instruct students to design messages from Planet Z to an unknown civilization. Ask them to do a rough draft on scratch paper and have it approved by the teacher before making the final version. Hand out scratch paper to the

student pairs and allow time for them to work. As you approve the rough drafts, have students record their final drafts on the logbook page, "Message from Planet Z." Collect all final drafts.

3. **Lecture.** How do we interpret messages? Explain to students that they will do the next activity from the point of view of Earth-based scientists. They will have to put aside what they know about Planet Z and act purely as Earthlings. Tell them you will be handing out mysterious, extraterrestrial messages for their analysis. You will also be handing out scratch paper for students to record their ideas about the message they have received before they make final interpretive decisions. Once they feel like they really understand the extraterrestrial message, they should record their translations on the logbook sheet "Interpreting an Extraterrestrial Message."

4. **Activity.** Mix up the "Message from Planet Z" logbook sheets and distribute them. Hand out scratch paper and allow time for students to decode the messages. Have students make their final interpretations. Collect the messages and interpretations and return them to their originators. Have students look them over to see how successful they were at getting their message across.

5. **Discussion.** Have students share ideas about which part of their messages worked and which didn't. Discuss how they could make their messages more clear.

Closure

1. **Lecture.** Tell students that SETI scientists and radio astronomers all over the globe recently began a massive search of the radio spectrum in the hopes of finding a message like the ones students have been creating.

2. **What Do You Think, Now?** Have students answer the post-activity questions on the logbook sheet "What Do You Think, Now?" Invite students to share their responses and their drawings. Ask them how their opinions have been changed by this mission.

Going Further

Activity: More Messages

Now that students have had practice, give them a chance to refine their technique and revise their messages.

Mission 11

What Do We Say, and How Do We Say It?
Mission Briefing

Name:

Date:

Dr. Frank Drake, Radio Astronomer on the SETI Academy Team

Your mission is to figure out the components of a "good space message" (one that another civilization can decode). We'd like you to start with some messages that SETI scientists have already sent into space, in the hope that they will someday be detected by an extraterrestrial civilization. Then we'd like you to imagine what message *you* would send into space if you were in charge of informing an extraterrestrial civilization about Earth.

In this mission, your Planet Z culture team will design and send a message from your culture. Acting as SETI scientists, your team will also receive one of these "extraterrestrial messages." The challenge is to interpret it to the best of your ability. When your group is done, give it back to the team that sent it so they can see how successful they were. Good luck!

What Do You Think?

1. What is the most important information you want to get across to an extraterrestrial civilization? How will you send that message?

2. How could the interpretation of the message be different than the meaning you intended?

Mission 11

What Do We Say, and How Do We Say It?

Earth Message—Arecibo

This message was transmitted for 10 minutes from the giant radio telescope at the Arecibo Observatory, Puerto Rico, on November 16, 1974. The message was sent by switching between two nearby radio frequencies to achieve a binary pattern. When decoded it shows binary representations of numbers and a series of images.

Figure 11.1.

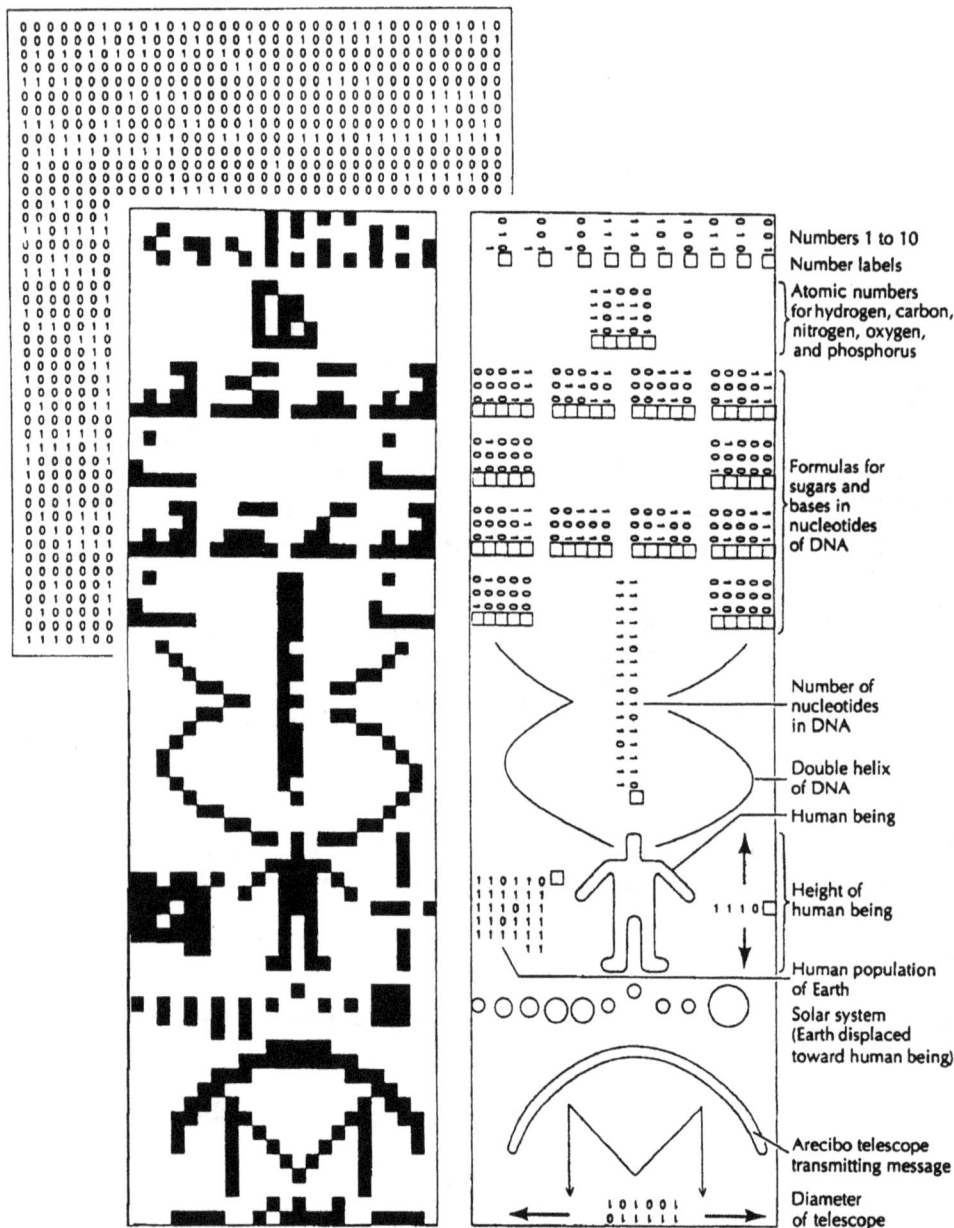

From *The Rise of Intelligence and Culture.* © 1995. Teacher Ideas Press. (800) 237-6124.

Mission 11

What Do We Say, and How Do We Say It?

Earth Message—Pioneer 10

This engraved aluminum plate was attached to protected locations on the outside of the two *Pioneer 10* spacecrafts. *Pioneer 10* left our solar system in 1983.

Figure 11.2.

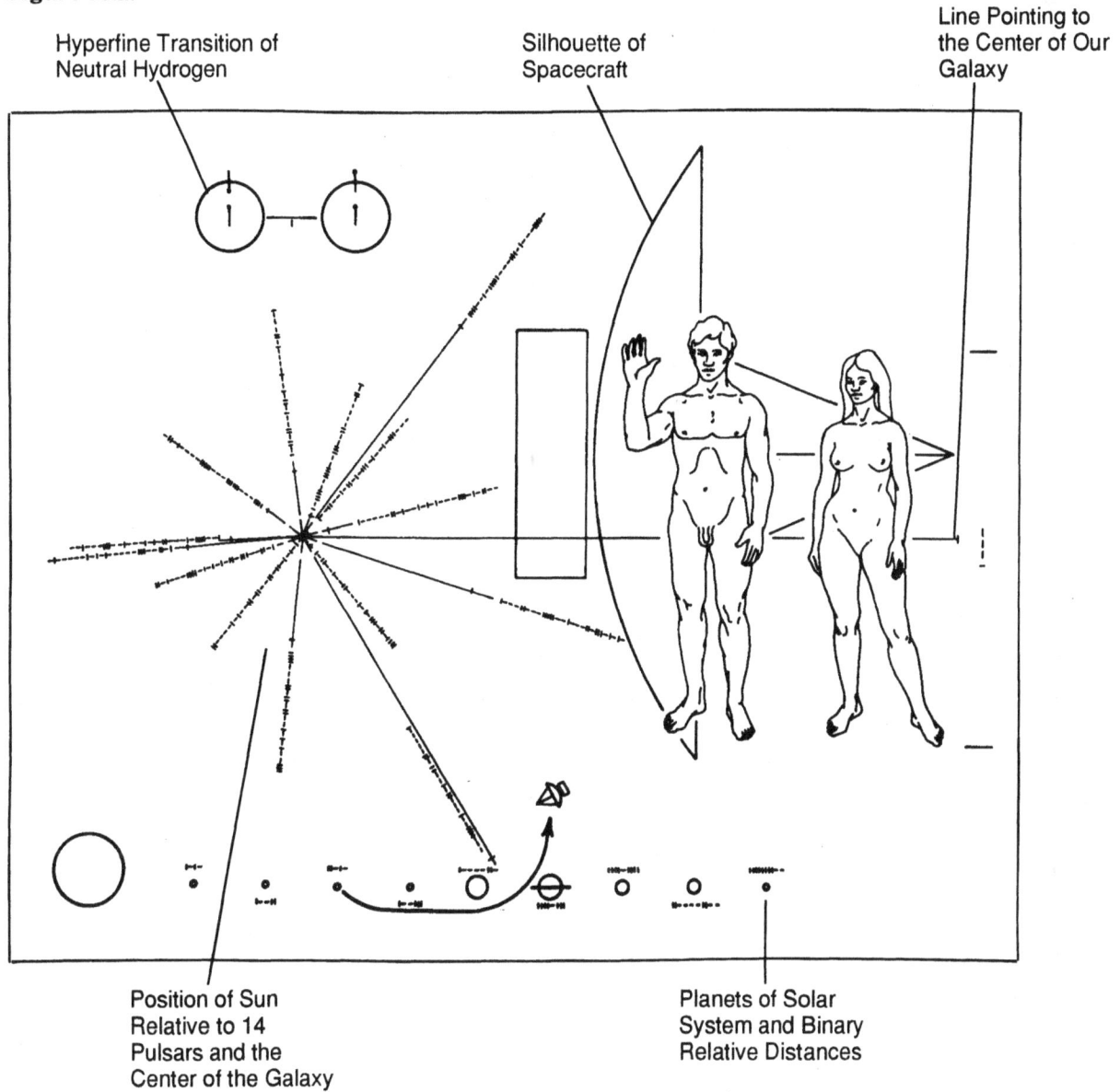

Hyperfine Transition of Neutral Hydrogen

Silhouette of Spacecraft

Line Pointing to the Center of Our Galaxy

Position of Sun Relative to 14 Pulsars and the Center of the Galaxy

Planets of Solar System and Binary Relative Distances

Mission 11

What Do We Say, and How Do We Say It?

Earth Message—Voyager

This information is contained on a 12-inch copper disk (record) along with a ceramic cartridge, stylus, and directions for making a record player. The pictures are binary like the Arecibo message. The record will also play sounds, starting with a greeting in Sumerian, animal sounds and music, and ending with an English-speaking child saying, "Hello from the children of Planet Earth."

Figure 11.3.

PICTURES (in sequence)

calibration circle	fetus diagram	vertebrate evolution diagram	children with globe	artisan with drill
solar location map	fetus	seashell (Xancidae)	cotton harvest	factory interior
mathematical definitions	diagram of male and female	dolphins	grape picker	museum
physical unit definitions	birth	school of fish	supermarket	X-ray of hand
solar system parameters (2)	nursing mother	tree toad	diver with first	woman with microscope
the sun	father & daughter (Malaysia)	crocodile	fishing boat, nets	Pakistan street scene
solar spectrum	group of children	eagle	cooking fish	India rush-hour traffic
Mercury	diagram of family ages	South African waterhole	Chinese dinner	modern highway (Ithaca)
Mars	family portrait	Jane Goodal, chimps	licking, eating, drinking	Golden Gate Bridge
Jupiter	continental drift diagram	sketch of bushman	Great Wall of China	train
Earth	structure of earth	bushmen hunters	African house construction	airplane in flight
Egypt, Red Sea, Sinai, Pen., Nile (from orbit)	Heron Island (Australia)	Guatemalan man	Amish construction scene	airport (Toronto)
chemical definitions	seashore	Balinese dancer	African house	Antarctic expedition
DNA structure	sand dunes	Andean girls	modern house (Cloudcroft)	radio telescope (Westbrook)
DNA structure magnified	Monument Valley	elephant	house interior with artist & lire	radio telescope (Arecibo)
cells and cell division	leaf	Turkish man with beard and glasses	Taj Mahal	book page (Newton's System of the World)
anatomy (8)	fallen leaves	old man with dog and flowers	English city (Oxford)	astronaut in space
human sex organs (drawing)	sequoia	mountain climber	Boston	Titan Centaur launch
conception diagram	snowflake	Cathy Rigby	UN building (day)	sunset with birds
conception photo	tree with daffodils	Olympic sprinters	UN building (night)	string quartet
fertilized ovum	flying insect, flowers	schoolroom	Sydney Opera House	violin with score

GREETINGS IN MANY TONGUES (alphabetically)

Akkadian	Czech	Hindi	Kechua (Peru)	Nyanja (Malawi)	Russian		Thai
Amoy (Min. dialect)	Dutch	Hittite	Korean	Oriya (India)	Serbian		Turkish
Arabic	English	Hungarian	Latin	Perians	Sinhalese (Sri Lanka)		Ukrainian
Aramaic	French	Ila (Zambia)	Luganda (Uganda)	Polish	Sotho (Lesotho)		Urdu
Armenian	German	Indonesian	Mandarin	Portuguese	Spanish		Vietnamese
Bengali	Greek	Italian	Marathi (India)	Punjabi	Sumerian		Welsh
Burmese	Gujarati (India)	Japanese	Nepali	Rajasthani	Swedish		Wu (Shanghai dialect)
Cantonese	Hebrew	Kannada (India)	Nguni (SE Africa)	Romanian	Telugu (India)		

SOUNDS OF EARTH (in sequence)

whales	volcanoes	cricket frogs	chimpanzee	blacksmith shop	sawing	horse and carriage	kiss
planets (audio analog of orbital velocity)	mud pots	birds	footsteps and heartbeats	herding sheep	riveter	train whistle	baby
	rain	hyena	laughter	dogs (domestic)	Morse code	truck	life signs: EEG, EKG
	surf	elephant	fire	tools	horse and cart	Saturn 5 rocket liftoff	pulsar

MUSIC (in sequence)

Bach: Brandenberg Concerto #2, 1st m.	Bach: Partita #3 for violin	Bulgaria: shepherdess song—"Izlel Delyo hajdulin"
Java: court gamelan—"Kinds of Flowers"	Mozart: "Queen of the Night" (from "The Magic Flute")	Navajo: night chant
Senegal: percussion	Georgia (USSR): folk chorus—"Chakrulo"	English 15th cent.: "The Fairie Round"
Zaire: "Pygmy girls" Initiation song	Peru: pan pipes	Melanesia: pan pipes
Australia: horn and totem song	Louis Armstrong: "Melancholy Blues"	Peru: women's wedding song
Mexico: mariachi—"El Cascabel"	Azerbaijan: two flutes	China: ch'in (zither)—"Flowing Streams"
Chuck Berry: "Johnny B. Goode"	Stravinsky: "Rite of Spring" conclusion	India: raga—"Jaat Kahan Ho"
New Guinea: men's house	Bach: Prelude and Fuge #1 in C Major	Blind Willie Johnson: "Dark Was the Night"
Japan: shekuhachi (flute) — "Depicting the Cranes in Their Nest"	Beethoven: Symphony #5, 1st m.	Beethoven: String Quartet #13. "Cavatina"

Mission 11

What Do We Say, and How Do We Say It?

Message From Planet Z

Name:

Date:

Please sketch out your message below. Remember that language or symbols may not be understood by an extraterrestrial civilization.

Mission 11

What Do We Say, and How Do We Say It?

Interpreting an Extraterrestrial Message

Name:

Date:

Carefully examine the "extraterrestrial" message designed by another team. Write your interpretation of the message below:

Mission 11

What Do We Say, and How Do We Say It?

What Do You Think, Now?

Name:

Date:

After you have completed this mission, please answer the following questions:

1. What is the most important information you want to get across to an extraterrestrial civilization? How will you send that message?

2. How was the interpretation of the message different than the meaning you intended?

3. How would you change your message to get the meaning across better?

Mission 12

Detection: What Could Happen?
What Will We Do When We Detect a Signal?

Overview

How might our civilization deal with the detection of an extraterrestrial civilization? In mission 12.1, students consider what should be done in the event that we do detect an extraterrestrial message. Students write about what it would mean to Earthlings.

Concepts

- An announcement by SETI scientists of the reception of an intelligent extraterrestrial radio signal would undoubtedly affect every culture on Earth.

Skills

- Critical thinking.

Mission 12.1

Materials

For Each Student

- SETI Academy Cadet Logbook

- Pencil

Getting Ready

Just Before the Lesson

1. Review the "Teacher Background Information" for this mission in the appendixes.

2. Make sure scratch paper is available.

In Mission 11, students decoded messages.

223

Classroom Action

1. **Mission Briefing.** Have the class refer to the "Mission Briefing" for mission 12 in their student logbooks as one student reads it aloud.

2. **What Do You Think?** Read aloud and discuss the pre-activity questions on the "Mission Briefing." Have students answer the questions in their logbooks. Invite them to share their answers in a class discussion.

3. **Activity.** Give students time to write short opinion essays (they should do rough drafts on lined notebook paper) about what humans should do in the event of successful detection of extraterrestrial intelligence. Invite several students to read their essays to the class. Give the class a chance to discuss their personal opinions in a supportive atmosphere. Have students rewrite their essays into their logbooks on the sheet "Reflecting on Radio Detection."

Closure

1. **What Do You Think, Now?** Have students answer the post-activity questions on the logbook sheet "What Do You Think, Now?" Invite students to share their responses and their drawings. Ask them how their opinions have been changed by this mission.

Going Further

Drama Activity: Press Conference

Have students hold a press conference to announce the detection of an extraterrestrial radio signal.

Creative Writing: People React Around the World!

Have students write a series of vignettes showing how different cultures or groups of people might respond to the news of the discovery of an extraterrestrial civilization.

Mission 12

Detection: What Could Happen?

Mission Briefing

Name:

Date:

Dr. Margaret Race, Environmental Impact Analyst, on the SETI Academy Team

As scientists, we always need to think about the implications of our work. What if an extraterrestrial message is actually received? What might that mean, to realize that we are not alone in the universe? In this mission, you will work on your own to write a page or so about what it would mean to Earthlings if we really do make contact with an extraterrestrial civilization.

What Do You Think?

1. What would be the one biggest change on Earth caused by making contact with extraterrestrials?

Mission 12

Detection: What Could Happen?

Reflecting on Radio Detection

Name:

Date:

What might it mean to Earthlings to realize that we are not alone in the universe?

Mission 12

Detection: What Could Happen?

What Do You Think, Now?

Name:

Date:

After you have completed this mission, please answer the following question:

1. What would be the one biggest change on Earth caused by making contact with extraterrestrials?

From *The Rise of Intelligence and Culture.* © 1995. Teacher Ideas Press. (800) 237-6124.

Mission 13

Mission Completed!
What Have You Learned?

Overview

In mission 13.1, students write and draw what they have learned about the rise of intelligence and culture, as well as interstellar communication. To assess how much students have learned and which of their ideas have changed as a result of their study of intelligence and culture, compare their writings and drawings in this mission to those from mission 1.

Mission 13.1

Materials

For Each Student

- SETI Academy Cadet Logbook

- Pencil

- Crayons, markers, and other drawing materials

Getting Ready

No preparation is necessary.

Classroom Action

1. **Discussion.** Encourage a wrap-up class discussion and invite students to share what they learned as they completed the missions in *The Rise of Intelligence and Culture*. Refer to the information on mission 13 in the appendix and review as needed for students.

2. **Mission Briefing.** Have the class refer to the "Mission Briefing" for mission 13 in their student logbooks as one student reads it aloud.

3. **What Do You Think?** Read aloud and discuss the pre-activity questions on the "Mission Briefing." Have students answer the questions

Notes

In mission 12, students worked on their own to write about what it would mean to humanity if we really do achieve a detection of an extraterrestrial civilization.

in full and complete sentences, in as much detail as possible (have them use extra paper if necessary). Have students make their drawings as elaborate and detailed as possible.

Closure

1. **Discussion.** Have students share and discuss the drawings, ideas, and question answers from their logbooks. Focus the discussion on what was learned.

Going Further

Research: Astronomy and Much More

The missions may be over, but there are dozens of spin-offs that students or the class as a whole could pursue. They might have developed an interest in astronomy or in evolution. This curriculum ties in with many others.

Mission 13

Mission Completed!
Mission Briefing

Name:

Date:

Dr. Jill Tarter, Chief Project Scientist of the SETI Academy Team

Congratulations, you have now finished *The Rise of Intelligence and Culture*, the third phase of missions at the SETI Academy. Please answer the questions below and then draw an intelligent Earth life-form and an intelligent extraterrestrial life-form on the next two pages.

What Do You Think, Now?

1. What do you think are the most important events in human history? Number these events in order of their occurrence, from first to last.

2. What is *culture*? Is modern technology necessary to culture?

3. What enabled humans to create culture?

4. What is the best way of detecting an extraterrestrial civilization? Explain why you think so.

From *The Rise of Intelligence and Culture.* © 1995. Teacher Ideas Press. (800) 237-6124.

Mission 13

Mission Completed!

Draw planet Earth's most intelligent life-form. Label the things that make it exceptional.

Mission 13

Mission Completed!

Draw an intelligent life-form from a fictional planet. Label the things that make it exceptional.

Achievement Award

This Certifies That

_____

Has Successfully Completed the Course

SETI Academy

The Rise Of Intelligence and Culture.

On _____ , 19___ .

Thomas Pierson
Mr. Thomas Pierson, Executive Director

Jill Tarter
Dr. Jill Tarter, Chief Scientist

Glossary

Adaptation. The ability of a plant or animal to adjust to its environment. Adaptations can be passed on to the offspring of the organism.

Behavior. The ways in which a living organism responds to the environment or the way something reacts to a change of any kind.

Biologic. Having to do with the science that deals with the origin, history, and life processes of plants and animals.

Biome. A large, general geographic area that shares a type of climate, with average temperatures and rainfall, such as a rain forest or a desert.

Characteristic. A distinguishing trait or quality.

Civilization. The culture of a people, at a time when that people is considered to have reached a high level of social or technological development.

Cranial. Having to do with the skull, which surrounds and protects the brain.

Culture. The customs, techniques, ideas, beliefs, language, equipment, skills, and arts of a given people in a given period.

Environment. All the surroundings of an organism, including all matter and forms of life with which the organism is interdependent.

Evolution. The theory that groups of organisms change over time into very different creatures.

Extraterrestrial. Anything not of or from our Earth.

Galaxy. A group of stars and gas and dust that are gathered together by gravitation, such as our Milky Way Galaxy, a collection of about 400 billion stars.

Habitat. The specific place an organism lives, which is the specific environment to which an organism is adapted.

Hominid. A primate of the family Hominidae, of which modern man is the only living species. The group known as *Australopithecus*, which lived about 5.5 million years ago, are the first known fossil hominids.

Instinct. Inflexible behavior caused by genetics. Instinct does not adapt to new situations.

Intelligence. The ability to learn, to solve problems, and to adapt to changing situations, as opposed to instinct. This definition shall be refined by students through discussion to include attributes such as the ability to cooperate with others.

Intelligent being. A creature that exhibits intelligence.

Natural selection. The way that evolution works. Organisms with better variations live and pass on the good traits to their young.

Opposable thumb. A finger or digit capable of being placed opposite other fingers or digits to make a grasping hand.

Organism. A living thing that carries on life functions.

Primate. An order (group) of animals that includes monkeys, apes, fossil hominids, and man.

Resource. A source of supply, support, or aid.

SETI. Search for Extraterrestrial Intelligence.

Stereoscopic vision. The ability to see or perceive three dimensions; the ability to mentally superimpose two different viewpoints and see them as one.

Trait. A distinguishing feature or quality; a characteristic.

Appendixes

Suggestions for Cutting Costs

1. **Options.** Omit some or all of the optional materials. These materials are indicated in the tables that follow.

2. **Teams.** We recommend working with students in teams of two for more hands-on interaction. However, to save money and materials, have students work in teams of four (or even more). This will cut the cost of many of the needed materials in half (or even more). The materials are indicated in the tables that follow.

3. **Substitutions.** Some substitutions can be made. These substitutions are indicated in the tables that follow.

Required Materials List

Table A.1—Office, Art, and General Supplies.

Material	Substitutions or Alternatives. Optional Items Are Indicated.	Quantity per Pair, Team, or Center	Quantity for Each Class of 32	Reusable in Each Class	Used in Activity
Pencil or pen			32	Yes	All
Drawing materials	Use pencil or pen				1, 8
Marking pens or crayons		1 set		Yes	2, 3, 7, 11
Thumb tacks		4		Yes	2
Bag of peanuts		4 peanuts		No	2
Stopwatches	Clocks or watches with a second hand	1		Yes	2
Trash/waste cans	Anything to put trash in	1		Yes	2
Cups	Small containers	4 cups		Yes	2
Small, flat objects	Coins, paper clips, washer, etc.	40		Yes	2
Masking tape		1 roll		No	2
Scissors		1 pair		Yes	2, 7
Calculator	Optional	1		Yes	2, 4, 9
Butcher paper	Other large paper	Variable		No	3, 8, 9, 11
Earth globe	Flat Earth map		1	Yes	5, 6
Map pins	Straight pins		≈ 28	Yes	5
Tiny labels	Optional		≈ 28	Yes	5
Physical map of the world	Social studies textbook or an atlas		1	Yes	6
Transparent tape	Paste		1 roll	No	7, 9
Meter stick	Straight edge	1 (8)	1 (9)	Yes	8, 9
Adding machine tape		6 meters	2 or 3 rolls	Yes	8
Dice		2 dice		Yes	8
Index cards	Cut tagboard	6 (8)	20 (9)	No	8
String	Kite string, heavy thread		≈ 250 meters	Yes	9
Dusty chalkboard erasers	Flour		2	Yes	9
Flashlight			1	Yes	9
Blank cassette			1	Yes	10
Cassette recorder			1	Yes	10
Two noise makers			2	Yes	10

Table A.2—Audiovisual Equipment.

Material	Substitutions or Alternatives. Optional Items Are Indicated.	Quantity per Pair, Team, or Center	Quantity for Each Class of 32	Reusable in Each Class	Used in Activity
Overhead projector	Handouts		1	Yes	4, 7, 8, 10, 11
VCR and monitor	Optional				9
Reading Rainbow episode "Space Case"	Optional				9

Teacher Background Information

You do not need to have all the answers to begin teaching your students about SETI! However, many teachers have asked for more information about the various topics presented in this unit. Therefore, the following notes about missions are included (not all missions are addressed). Please keep in mind that this section is written at an adult level, and it is not intended to be read to students. Enjoy!

Note: To reflect modern, nondenominational usage, CE (for Common Era) is used instead of AD, and BCE (for Before Common Era) is used instead of BC.

Missions 1 and 2: The Rise of Human Intelligence and Human Physical Traits and Behaviors

The terms *culture* and *civilization* are often used as synonyms, but in this guide we have tried to maintain a distinction. By definition, *culture* is "the customs, techniques, ideas, beliefs, language, equipment, skills, arts, and so forth of a given people in a given period." *Civilization* is defined as "the culture of a people at a time when that people is considered to have reached a high level of social or technological development." The use of these two terms can embody prejudice, as any culture might call itself "civilized" and all other cultures "uncivilized."

Logically, it is often assumed that once a species has evolved physical traits and behaviors that enable it to develop culture, the rise of some sort of civilization occurs as a naturally ensuing step. The rise of Western civilization, as we know it, transpired within the last 6,000 years. The rise of intelligence, the primary building block of culture and civilization, began to develop much earlier in the evolutionary process. It is usually assumed that many animals have some intelligence, but that only humans have true culture.

Focusing attention on the intelligence of humans and their ape-like ancestors (hominids), one can identify some characteristics of intelligence that have contributed to the rise of humans as the dominant species on Earth. Characteristics of intelligence fall into two categories: physical traits (such as physiological makeup and abilities, and methods of mobility) and behaviors. The first category includes opposable thumbs, large brain size compared to other animals, walking upright, and stereoscopic vision (eyes on the front of the head). The second group consists of social behavior, use of language, and living in groups. Anthropologists believe that these physical traits and behaviors arose over millions of years of evolutionary change. See the background information for mission 4 (below) for further discussion about hominids evolving the physical traits and behaviors that led to increased intelligence and to the rise of culture.

Mission 3: Physical Traits and Behaviors of Earth Animals

It is a basic intellectual challenge among humans, young and old, to comprehend the nature of the cognitive experiences of other species. Those of us who live with animals are generally convinced of their intelligence, and we wonder if thoughts and feelings occur only in human beings. The issue of animal of intelligence has, historically, had many sides. Philosophers throughout history have debated the issue.

Scientists have, for the most part, remained uninquisitive about the mental experiences of the animals whose behavior they study.

Pig (Domestic)

Physical Traits of Intelligence

1. Does it have stereoscopic vision? *Yes, but very little, as its eyes are on the sides of its head.*

2. Does it easily adapt its diet to a variety of foods? *Yes. A pig will eat nearly anything.*

3. Does it walk upright on two feet? *No.*

4. Does it have an appendage that it uses to grasp? *No.*

5. Brain size: *A pig has a moderate ratio of brain weight to body weight, indicating a moderate level of intelligence.*

Physical Behaviors of Intelligence

1. Does it communicate with others of its species? *Yes. Pigs communicate by scent and by sound.*

2. Does it learn from others? *Yes. Pigs are considered intelligent by animal trainers because they learn tricks easily.*

3. Does it make shelters or nests? *No. Pigs wallow in mud but do not make any shelters. Domesticated pigs live in stalls or barns.*

4. Does it adapt easily to new or changing situations? *Indeterminate.*

5. Does it live in organized groups? *No. Pigs are domesticated, so the groups are determined by people.*

6. Does it make or use tools? *No.*

7. Does it protect its group and coordinate group efforts? *Indeterminate.*

Gorilla

Physical Traits of Intelligence

1. Does it have stereoscopic vision? *Yes.*

2. Does it easily adapt its diet to a variety of foods? *Yes. Gorillas are vegetarian and herbivorous. Their diet includes bark, stems, roots, fruits, and leaves.*

3. Does it walk upright on two feet? *No. A gorilla walks partially upright on two feet while placing its knuckles on the ground.*

4. Does it have an appendage that it uses to grasp? *Yes, opposable thumbs like humans.*

5. Brain size: *A gorilla has a ratio of brain weight to body weight that is nearly equal to that of a chimpanzee, so they are very intelligent.*

Physical Behaviors of Intelligence

1. Does it communicate with others of its species? *Yes. Gorillas communicate through grunts, screams, and postures and gestures such as beating their chests.*

2. Does it learn from others? *Yes. Gorilla young are totally defenseless and dependent on the mother for protection and nourishment. It takes about three years for a gorilla to mature and therefore it has a long time in which to learn from its mother about foods that are safe to eat and animals that are to be avoided. "Toddler age" gorillas play together, mimicking the behavior of their elders.*

3. Does it make shelters or nests? *Yes. At night, sleeping platforms are built for the mother and young; the male sleeps and guards at the base of the tree.*

4. Does it adapt easily to new or changing situations? *Yes, but not to captivity.*

5. Does it live in organized groups? *Yes. Gorillas live in family groups of females and their offspring are led by a dominant male. Males may stay in the group until they develop a silver back, a sign of maturity, at which time they leave the group to live alone or with other males. They can come back to the group to mate without challenging the lead male.*

6. Does it make or use tools? *No.*

7. Does it protect its group and coordinate group efforts? *Yes. The lead male is very protective of his group.*

Elephant

Physical Traits of Intelligence

1. Does it have stereoscopic vision? *No.*

2. Does it easily adapt its diet to a variety of foods? *Yes. Elephants are herbivorous. Their diet includes fresh and dry grasses, leaves, twigs, bark, and occasionally fruit.*

3. Does it walk upright on two feet? *No.*

4. Does it have an appendage that it uses to grasp? *Yes, a trunk with which it can pick up and grasp objects.*

5. Brain size: *An elephant's brain is large, but much of it is dedicated to controlling its enormous body. Elephants have moderate intelligence.*

Physical Behaviors of Intelligence

1. Does it communicate with others of its species? *Yes. Elephants communicate by touching with their trunks. They also communicate by trumpeting to alert others of danger or when one male challenges another. Elephants also emit sounds so low that humans cannot hear them. The low sounds are intended to attract mates. Elephants also "purr" from their stomachs. They do this when they are not in sight of the rest of the herd and stop when danger comes near. This sudden stop of purring alerts the other elephants in the herd. Elephants also communicate with secretions from glands in their bodies.*

2. Does it learn from others? *Yes. Elephants take a long time to grow up and spend a lot of time being educated by their mothers. The matriarch teaches her family where to find food and water and how to avoid dangers.*

3. Does it make shelters or nests? *No. Elephants are nomadic grazing animals and spend most of their time on the plains.*

4. Does it adapt easily to new or changing situations? *Yes. An elephant can be captured as an adult and adapt well to living in captivity.*

5. Does it live in organized groups? *Yes. Elephants are social animals that live in tightly knit groups or herds. The herd consists of family units led for 60 to 70 years by a matriarch. When the matriarch dies, her oldest daughter becomes the new matriarch. Adult males leave the herd just before maturity to live independently until the need to mate draws them back to the herd.*

6. Does it make or use tools? *No.*

7. Does it protect its group and coordinate group efforts? *Yes. Females will protect their young. Males will challenge one another for mating purposes. A social ritual has been observed where a mating couple is encircled by cows and young elephants. Female elephants who go into the thick underbrush to give birth are accompanied by another female. No one knows if this is for protection or for assistance.*

Ant (Leaf-Cutter)

Physical Traits of Intelligence

1. Does it have stereoscopic vision? *No. Most ants have simple eyes, called ocelli, on top of their heads as well as a compound eye with many lenses on each side of the head. However, their vision is very poor.*

2. Does it easily adapt its diet to a variety of foods? *No. Leaf-cutter ants are not easily adaptable to many foods, having a very restricted diet. Their diet consists of one type of fungus, which the ants cultivate for themselves.*

3. Does it walk upright on two feet? *No. Ants are insects and have six legs.*

4. Does it have an appendage that it uses to grasp? *Yes. Leaf-cutter ants can carry bits of fungus food and nesting material with one set of their jaws.*

5. Brain size: *A leaf-cutter ant's brain consists of a few cells at the end of a nerve cord. They are not intelligent; they operate on instinct.*

Physical Behaviors of Intelligence

1. Does it communicate with others of its species? *Yes. Leaf-cutter ants communicate by tapping their antennae. Also, using their antennae, they are able to recognize their nest and other members of the colony.*

2. Does it learn from others? *No. There is no evidence that leaf-cutter ants' behaviors are learned; they are, rather, instinctive.*

3. Does it make shelters or nests? *Yes. This social invertebrate cuts away pieces of leaves and flowers to feed the fungus. They carry the food into underground chambers, linked by tunnels, that house the fungus gardens. When it is time for a new colony to develop, a piece of the fungus garden is taken away by a female ant who uses it to start a new one in a new location constructed by herself and her mate.*

4. Does it adapt easily to new or changing situations? *Indeterminate.*

5. Does it live in organized groups? *Yes. Ants live in colonies. Each ant has its role or position within the colonial structure.*

6. Does it make or use tools? *No, though it uses one set of its jaws to cut away pieces of leaf and flower to gather food for the fungus garden.*

7. Does it protect its group and coordinate group efforts? *Yes. Ants can instantly detect an intruder from another colony by its smell. Some scientists infer from the varied, effective, and highly integrated behavior of leaf-cutter ants that they might think consciously about digging underground chambers, leaf gathering, tending of the fungus by feeding it and removing inedible fungus, as well as caring for eggs and larvae. It is difficult to assume that instinct is entirely accountable for this complex way of life.*

Horse

Physical Traits of Intelligence

1. Does it have stereoscopic vision? *Yes, but only partially, as its eyes are more toward the sides of its head than they are toward the front of its head.*

2. Does it easily adapt its diet to a variety of foods? *Yes. Horses are probably the most adaptable with respect to diet of all the animals that humans have domesticated. Their digestive tract processes quickly. A horse can eat grass that is fresh, just cut, or dry and coarse; and fruits and vegetables. It won't starve from poor quality—it just eats more.*

3. Does it walk upright on two feet? *No.*

4. Does it have an appendage that it uses to grasp? *No.*

5. Brain size: *Horses have moderate intelligence.*

Physical Behaviors of Intelligence

1. Does it communicate with others of its species? *Yes. Horses communicate by sound. They have a "pecking order" like pack animals such as wolves. Hierarchy is indicated by their actions.*

2. Does it learn from others? *Yes. Females teach their young what food to eat.*

3. Does it make shelters or nests? *No.*

4. Does it adapt easily to new or changing situations? *Yes, though a horse is easily spooked.*

5. Does it live in organized groups? *Yes. Feral horses live in stable family units consisting of a male and his harem. Young foals and fillies tend to leave the family unit to find mates in other groups. This prevents inbreeding.*

6. Does it make or use tools? *No.*

7. Does it protect its group and coordinate group efforts? *Yes. The roving herd structure is protection—safety in numbers. Males don't defend territories, and fights between males are rare.*

Dolphin

Physical Traits of Intelligence

1. Does it have stereoscopic vision? *No. Dolphins' vision (as well as sense of smell) is actually very poor. They have an excellent sense of echo-location, which is quite useful to an animal that lives under water.*

2. Does it easily adapt its diet to a variety of foods? *No. Their food comes from the ocean and includes fish, shrimp, and squid.*

3. Does it walk upright on two feet? *No. Though the dolphin swims and lives in water, it evolved from land mammals. Forearms are modified in whales and dolphins into flippers, and all that remains of the hind legs are two small internal bones. The tail is split and spread horizontally unlike the vertically oriented tale of a fish.*

4. Does it have an appendage that it uses to grasp? *Yes. Dolphins carry things in their mouths and have been witnessed supporting injured pod members to help them to the surface.*

5. Brain size: *A dolphin has a high ratio of brain weight to body weight, indicating a high level of intelligence.*

Physical Behaviors of Intelligence

1. Does it communicate with others of its species? *Yes. Dolphins communicate through a variety of sounds and whistles. Each dolphin has its own identity whistle, which is also used by other dolphins to attract its attention.*

2. Does it learn from others? *Yes. Young dolphins are cared for by their mothers for a period of time that does not exceed four months while they learn which sea animals are enemies. Dolphins are easily trained by humans. They are even used in certain military maneuvers that involve collecting "dud" torpedoes.*

3. Does it make shelters or nests? *No. Dolphins do not need to make shelter—they like being wet! It is necessary for the dolphin to remain in the water for the buoyancy it provides. If a dolphin should become stranded on the land, the weight of its body could crush the animal's internal organs, causing it to suffocate.*

4. Does it adapt easily to new or changing situations? *Yes. It cannot change its aquatic habitat, but the species seems well adapted to living in captivity.*

5. Does it live in organized groups? *Yes. Their groups are called pods. Dolphins swim and hunt for schools of fish in groups; there is no dominant leader in these groups. They support each other in protecting and raising their young.*

6. Does it make or use tools? *No. However, they have been trained by humans to play with balls and rings.*

7. Does it protect its group and coordinate group efforts? *Yes. Dolphins have been witnessed supporting an injured pod member to help it to the surface. Dolphins herd schools of fish into tighter, smaller areas in order to feed more efficiently. Dolphins have exhibited problem-solving behavior by changing their swimming patterns to stay near a tuna fishing boat.*

Snake (Boa Constrictor)

Physical Traits of Intelligence

1. Does it have stereoscopic vision? *No. But they do have color vision, and most reptiles have the ability to adapt to and accommodate their environment visually.*

2. Does it easily adapt its diet to a variety of foods? *No. Snakes are carnivorous. They eat small animals; some eat eggs.*

3. Does it walk upright on two feet? *No. Snakes are legless and slither on their abdomens. Their abdominal scales lift slightly, allowing snakes to push as they move their bodies forward sinuously.*

4. Does it have an appendage that it uses to grasp? *No. But a boa constrictor can wrap its entire body around its prey and hold on to it until the prey has suffocated.*

5. Brain size: *A boa constrictor has a very small brain, indicating a low level of intelligence.*

Physical Behaviors of Intelligence

1. Does it communicate with others of its species? *Yes. But snakes have no need to communicate with others of their species, except for courtship and reproductive purposes. Males locate females through chemical senses of olfactory chemical detection using a sensory structure called Jacobson's organ. In some species of snake, males perform a courtship dance or a graceful sparing match to gain a mate.*

2. Does it learn from others? *Yes. In laboratory experiments, newly hatched snakes that had never eaten were given a choice of extracts of foods that their mother would eat and those that their mother would not eat. They chose to eat the extracts of the food that their mother would naturally eat but were then trained to eat the extracts of foods that were not ordinarily part of their species' diet.*

3. Does it make shelters or nests? *No. But snakes will seek shelter in crevices between rocks and holes in the ground.*

4. Does it adapt easily to new or changing situations? *Indeterminate.*

5. Does it live in organized groups? *No. Snakes live solitary lifestyles, only coming together to mate.*

6. Does it make or use tools? *No.*

7. Does it protect its group and coordinate group efforts? *Indeterminate.*

Kangaroo

Physical Traits of Intelligence

1. Does it have stereoscopic vision? *Yes.*

2. Does it easily adapt its diet to a variety of foods? *Yes. Kangaroos are grazing animals that feed on grasses, twigs, insects, and worms.*

3. Does it walk upright on two feet? *No. Kangaroos hop with their strong hind legs. The red kangaroo can run at speeds of up to 90 kilometers per hour and can leap horizontal distances of nearly 3 meters.*

4. Does it have an appendage that it uses to grasp? *Yes. Kangaroos use their forearms to hold onto things, though no opposable thumbs are present.*

5. Brain size: *A kangaroo has a brain significantly smaller than that of a placental mammal of comparable size, such as a deer.*

Physical Behaviors of Intelligence

1. Does it communicate with others of its species? *Indeterminate.*

2. Does it learn from others? *Yes. Mothers show their young what types of grasses are safe to eat.*

3. Does it make shelters or nests? *No. Kangaroos are grazing animals and do not usually need shelter.*

4. Does it adapt easily to new or changing situations? *Yes. They adapt well to living in zoo settings.*

5. Does it live in organized groups? *Yes. Kangaroos live in groups called "mobs," which are led by a male.*

6. Does it make or use tools? *No.*

7. Does it protect its group and coordinate group efforts? *Yes. Males will fight enemies (such as dingoes), and they will fight one another for a mate. Females can hop faster than males, which could well be an adaptation for protecting offspring held in their pouches.*

Monkey (New-World)

Physical Traits of Intelligence

1. Does it have stereoscopic vision? *Yes. Monkeys evolved stereoscopic vision for depth perception and distance perception. They also see in color.*

2. Does it easily adapt its diet to a variety of foods? *Yes. A monkey's diet consists mainly of fruit, nuts, seeds, leaves, flowers, bird's eggs, and spiders.*

3. Does it walk upright on two feet? *No. Monkeys swing from branch to branch with their arms, occasionally holding on with their tail. However, they can and do walk on their back feet a few steps at a time if they use their front limbs for balance and support.*

4. Does it have an appendage that it uses to grasp? *Yes. New-World monkeys have a prehensile tail that can be used to help them hang onto and navigate their way around trees. A few species have an opposable thumb to use much as a human does.*

5. Brain size: *New-World monkeys have a very high level of intelligence.*

Physical Behaviors of Intelligence

1. Does it communicate with others of its species? *Yes. Monkeys communicate by sound, and they scream to alarm others that a predator is near. Elders in a social group are very patient with young members of the group, and contribute to their protection and education.*

2. Does it learn from others? *Yes. Baby monkeys are totally dependent on their mothers for nourishment, warmth, and transportation. They learn what is safe to eat and about dangers that exist. In some cultures, humans have trained monkeys to perform (monkeys that accompany accordion players, for example) and to climb trees and harvest coconuts.*

3. Does it make shelters or nests? *Yes. Monkeys live in treetops about 100 meters above the ground. There they raise their young, sleep, and eat, away from the dangers of most predators.*

4. Does it adapt easily to new or changing situations? *Yes.*

5. Does it live in organized groups? *Yes. Monkeys are very social animals and live in groups lead by a dominant male. They groom each other. Some mate for life. As in other primate groups, the young males tend to leave the group, seeking out others when it is time to mate.*

6. Does it make or use tools? *No.*

7. Does it protect its group and coordinate group efforts? *Yes. Monkeys protect their young and their social group.*

Parrot

Physical Traits of Intelligence

1. Does it have stereoscopic vision? *Yes. Parrots also have monocular vision and can see in color. They have difficulty seeing what is directly in front of them; this is why they cock their heads.*

2. Does it easily adapt its diet to a variety of foods? *Yes. A parrot's diet consists of fruit, nuts, and seeds.*

3. Does it walk upright on two feet? *No. For the most part, parrots fly, but they can walk (stiffly) on their legs, which are used mostly for perching.*

4. Does it have an appendage that it uses to grasp? *Yes. Parrots use their bills to give them support when clambering from perch to perch (a trait that can be fatal when climbing on power lines).*

5. Brain size: *A parrot has a small brain with large eyeballs and optic nerves, indicating a low level of intelligence. Also, the cerebrum is very smooth.*

Physical Behaviors of Intelligence

1. Does it communicate with others of its species? *Yes. Parrots call to advertise territories, to attract mates, to keep in contact with the flock, and to give warnings about danger.*

2. Does it learn from others? *Yes. Parrots are skilled at mimicry of other sounds. Scientists have trained a gray parrot named "Alex" to use a vocabulary of 40 words, which it can relate to objects.*

3. Does it make shelters or nests? *Yes. Parrots build nests in trees.*

4. Does it adapt easily to new or changing situations? *Yes. Parrots adapt well to living in captivity.*

5. Does it live in organized groups? *Yes. Parrots tend to migrate and roost in flocks.*

6. Does it make or use tools? *No.*

7. Does it protect its group and coordinate group efforts? *Yes. Parrots use their skills of mimicry and voice throwing to fool predators about their location and species.*

Mole

Physical Traits of Intelligence

1. Does it have stereoscopic vision? *No. Moles are nearly blind. They have tiny eyes that can only tell light from dark.*

2. Does it easily adapt its diet to a variety of foods? *No. Moles eat worms, slugs, and snails. A mole needs to consume almost its body weight in food each day. Moles do not adapt their diet easily.*

3. Does it walk upright on two feet? *No. Moles burrow through tunnels with very large paddle-like appendages. They move fairly quickly underground, but not very fast on land.*

4. Does it have an appendage that it uses to grasp? *No.*

5. Brain size: *Moles have a moderate level of intelligence.*

Physical Behaviors of Intelligence

1. Does it communicate with others of its species? *Yes. Moles mark their tunnels with secretions from glands on their abdomen. They have not been observed to make any vocal noises.*

2. Does it learn from others? *Yes. Young are dependent on the mother for food until their fur comes, at about three to four weeks of age, at which time they leave.*

3. Does it make shelters or nests? *Yes. The female builds a nest of soft grasses and "tidies up" the tunnels before she gives birth.*

4. Does it adapt easily to new or changing situations? *Indeterminate.*

5. Does it live in organized groups? *No. Moles are very solitary animals. They search out other moles only when it is time to mate.*

6. Does it make or use tools? *No.*

7. Does it protect its group and coordinate group efforts? *Yes. Females protect their young by isolating them from predators.*

Cat (Domestic)

Physical Traits of Intelligence

1. Does it have stereoscopic vision? *Yes. Cats eyes are positioned on the front of their heads, allowing stereoscopic vision, which is necessary for pouncing and jumping.*

2. Does it easily adapt its diet to a variety of foods? *No. Cats are carnivores. Sometimes they will nibble at grass or plants. In the wild, cats are strictly meat-eaters; domestic cats, however, have slightly longer intestines than wild cats and can digest a greater variety of foods.*

3. Does it walk upright on two feet? *No. Cats can jump and run quickly, and they use their tails as a rudder for balance.*

4. Does it have an appendage that it uses to grasp? *No. But cats use their claws to climb trees.*

5. Brain size: *Cats have a moderate level of intelligence.*

Physical Behaviors of Intelligence

1. Does it communicate with others of its species? *Yes. Cats communicate with scent markings, visual signals, body language, and with vocal signals. Cats leave scent markings with urine or from rubbing glands on their bodies against objects or living things. They do this to mark their territory and to make their reproductive status known to other cats. Cats also claw trees and furniture to leave a visual signal to other cats about territory. Cats communicate aggression through flattened, rotated ear positions; a thrashing of the tail; and a low growling sound for a warning. Cats will meow to gain their owner's attention in order to have a need met, such as food. Loud meowing, such as in a cat fight, is another "statement" of aggressive intentions. Purring and soft meows are a statement of contentment.*

2. Does it learn from others? *Yes. Cats learn to meow from hearing their mother. Cats learn from their mother to hunt and kill prey.*

3. Does it make shelters or nests? *Yes. When preparing to give birth, female cats will seek out a dry, comfortable, secluded area.*

4. Does it adapt easily to new or changing situations? *No. Cats will tolerate changes, such as a new human baby in the family, but they don't seem to adjust well to new residences.*

5. Does it live in organized groups? *No. Cats tend to be solitary animals. Female cats care for their young during the first several months.*

6. Does it make or use tools? *No.*

7. Does it protect its group and coordinate group efforts? *Yes. Female cats will protect their young. Occasionally, group hunting and "torture" of prey, such as a mouse or a rat, has been observed among domestic cats. It is believed that such behavior occurs because cats were not able to learn from their mothers about hunting, catching, and killing prey.*

Dog (Domestic)

Physical Traits of Intelligence

1. Does it have stereoscopic vision? *Yes. Dogs have mostly stereoscopic vision. This allows for a certain amount of depth perception, which they need to jump and to catch objects with their mouths.*

2. Does it easily adapt its diet to a variety of foods? *Yes. Dogs will eat just about anything, though they are classified as carnivores. Domestication has changed the diet of the dog to include many different types of foods.*

3. Does it walk upright on two feet? *No.*

4. Does it have an appendage that it uses to grasp? *Yes. Dogs use a firm bite to carry objects.*

5. Brain size: *Dogs have a moderate level of intelligence.*

Physical Behaviors of Intelligence

1. Does it communicate with others of its species? *Yes. Dogs communicate by scent, vocal signals, and body language signals. Vocal signals include barking, growling, and whining. Dogs have a very strong sense of smell and communicate and receive information from other dogs by marking objects or territory with urine. Body signals such as tail wagging, relaxed ear position, and open mouth indicate happiness. The opposite—stiff, still tail; erect, forward-facing ears; and snarling, bared teeth—indicate aggression.*

2. Does it learn from others? *Yes. Dogs are eager to please their masters, and can be trained to perform many tasks. They can learn from experience, but are rarely able to apply previously learned skills to new situations.*

3. Does it make shelters or nests? *Yes. Dogs prefer a comfortable, dry space for sleeping, usually a pillow or rug in a basket. Dogs turn around two or three times and scratch at their bedding before lying down. In the wild, this behavior is used for sleeping outside where leaves have fallen beneath a tree—the scratching of the leaves stirs up the scent of the tree, masking the odor of the dog—and sleeping among the roots of a tree offers protection from wind.*

4. Does it adapt easily to new or changing situations? *Yes. Dogs adapt very well to new situations, such as a new home or a human baby in the family, although the latter situation has been known to cause undesirable behaviors from dogs, out of jealousy or envy over attention that the new family member is receiving, until the new member is accepted into the "pack."*

5. Does it live in organized groups? *Yes. Instinctively, dogs are social, pack animals, like wolves, and thrive in a situation such as a family offers. Domestic dogs have an instinctive sense of rank, and defer to a human being.*

6. Does it make or use tools? *No.*

7. Does it protect its group and coordinate group efforts? *Yes. Dogs are protective of their young and of their human families. Wild dogs hunt in packs.*

There are two different perspectives regarding animal behavior and consciousness. The first is from a cognitive view: An animal thinks about what it is doing. The second is from a behaviorist view: An animal adapts its behavior to changing circumstances and conditions. The following table (see page 252) is a an example of behaviors that imply cognitive thinking, according to some animal behaviorists, and the animals that display each trait or behavior.

Mission 4: Cranial Changes

The volume of the braincase is an important attribute examined by paleontologists and anthropologists when comparing and assessing the fossil remains of hominid skulls. According to *The Encyclopedia of Evolution* by Richard Milner, the basic method to measure the braincase of hominids involves filling the skull through the hole at its base with buckshot or seeds until it is full. The seeds are then removed and measured for volume in cubic centimeters (cc).

To track cranial changes through 3 million years of human ancestry, consider the size of the braincase of each human ancestor in the fossil record. *Australopithecus* had a cranial capacity that averaged 450 cc, which is similar to the brain size of the average living chimpanzee. *Homo habilis* had a cranial capacity of about 750 cc. *Homo erectus* came next, with a brain size of 1,000 cc. Last is *Homo sapiens*, which includes modern man, with an average brain size of 1,000-1,800 cc. This increase in the cranial capacity of human ancestors occurred over a span of 3 million years. In general, a bigger brain (as compared to the body weight) does indicate greater intellectual abilities.

As brain size increased, tool use and other skills developed.

However, when looking at individuals within a species, brain size does *not* directly correspond to intelligence. This is proved by the fact that one of the largest human brains ever studied belonged to an "idiot," while the brain of a very intelligent writer was far below average in size. There are special characteristics of brains, other than size, that may indicate the intelligence of an individual, such as the shape of the lobes, grooves, and veins of the brain. Scientists study these differences from interior molds of skulls.

The cumulative accomplishments of hominids (members of the genus *Homo*) have been made possible by a combination of changes in physical traits, mastery of physical abilities, and behavioral characteristics. An opposable thumb is a trait unique to the order Primate, which includes monkeys, apes, and humans. It has enabled these groups to pick up, hold, and grasp objects. The opposable thumb and the abilities associated with it contributed greatly to the rise of intelligence.

Table A.3—Cognitive thinking in animals.

Behavior	Animals
Cooperation	**Wild dogs** cooperate when hunting large prey as do some of the large cats such as **lions. Humans** cooperate on many levels. **Humpback whales** have been observed cooperating; see Capturing prey below. **Beavers** cooperate in the building of dams that benefit both food gathering and protection. Social insects, such as **ants, termites,** and **bees,** cooperate to build shelters that benefit all individuals involved.
Use tools	Many different animals use natural objects as tools. For example, **chimpanzees** find a long, thin stick from a tree or bush, trim it down, and take it to a termite mound into which the stick is inserted and pulled out; then it's inspected for termites that the chimp eagerly eats. **Gulls** drop shellfish onto hard surfaces until the shell breaks. **Sea otters** use rocks to bang shellfish open. **Egyptian vultures** throw rocks at ostrich eggs to break them.
Adaptability to changing circumstances	This behavior is difficult to observe outside of a laboratory setting. **Humans** are able to adapt to chaining circumstances. **Dogs** and **cats** can adapt to changing circumstances such as a change in the location of their food. **Chimps** and laboratory **rats** have displayed adaptability in controlled settings.
Building shelters	**Leaf-cutter ants**—Some scientists infer from the varied, effective, and highly integrated behavior of leaf-cutter ants that they might think consciously about digging underground chambers, leaf (fungus food) gathering, tending of the fungus by feeding it and removing inedible fungus as well as caring for eggs and larvae. **Beavers** construct complex dams to create deeper areas of water using tree limbs they cut off and drag with their teeth.
Capturing prey and gathering food	**Leaf-Cutter Ants**—This social invertebrate cuts away pieces of leaves to carry into underground chambers linked by tunnels. The leaf pieces are used as food for the fungus garden that is tended inside the ant burrows (invertebrate agriculture?). The fungus serves as the primary food source for these ants. It is difficult to assume that this complex way of life is entirely accountable by instinct. When it is time for a new colony to develop, a piece of the fungus garden is taken away by a female ant who uses it to start a new one in a new location constructed by herself and her mate. **Humpback whales** have been observed cooperating to capture food by releasing tiny bubbles in a circular pattern that cause small fish and invertebrates to shy away from the bubbles resulting in a mouthful of water that has a higher concentration of food.
Storing food	**Rats, squirrels,** some other rodents, and some species of **birds** store food when it is abundant for times when it is scarce.
Communication	**Vertebrates** generally rely on visual signals in communication because of the perfect structure of the vertebrate eye. When parent **birds,** for example, see their offspring begging for food, they fly off to get some. **Dogs** and **cats** also communicate with their sense of smell. **Honey bees** communicate through a dance language. Some types of **monkeys** have screams of alarm for different types of danger.
Learning and problem solving	When food or water is withheld from a **cat** or **dog,** it will figure out a way to obtain the attention of the food/H^2O provider in such a way to receive the nutrient it wants. **Dolphins** have exhibited problem-solving behavior by changing their swimming patterns when a tuna fishing boat is within sight, and when trapped in a net by rising close to the surface to get the attention of the fishermen in the boat. **Song sparrows** must learn their songs from their parents. **Chimpanzees** stack boxes to get to hanging bananas.

Early hominids walked on all fours. It is uncertain when the structure of the hip bone changed, resulting in a primate that could stand and walk on two feet, another trait associated with intelligence. This uncertainty represents a "missing link" between other hominids present in the fossil record and *Australopithecus afarensis*, who lived 3 million years ago. "Lucy" (a member of *Australopithecus afarensis*) is the oldest known hominoid that walked upright on two feet. Many anthropologists believe that Lucy's skeletal structure suggests that she was on the line that inevitably led to the human genus (*Homo*).

The ability to walk upright may have evolved as an adaptation to catastrophic environmental and climatic changes 5 million years ago. As the borders of the densely forested habitat of the early hominids retreated because of climatic changes (i.e., less rain so the area became drier), many primates were forced from the safety of the trees into the grasslands and low shrub environments that were becoming more common as the climate became drier. This change of habitat contributed to the need to walk erect on two feet in order to see approaching predators, and, ultimately, the need to survive.

Also visible in the fossil record where the skeletal remains of Lucy were discovered was evidence of the presence of many other individuals. This suggests that these primates lived together in groups. Some anthropologists surmise that severe drops in temperature and the expansion of ice sheets 2.5 million years ago caused the end of some hominid species in the genus *Australopithecus* that are believed to have used crude tools of bone, but these species had not developed the brain center responsible for articulate speech. It is not known why the *Homo* genus split away from *Australopithecus*, but some anthropologists think that it is related to climatic changes.

About the time that *Australopithecus* became extinct, 1.8 million years ago, *Homo habilis* (handy man) appeared, an event that is recorded in the fossil record. This hominid has been credited with the invention of stone tools. There is evidence that *Homo habilis* used tools in order to make other tools, a noteworthy indicator of intelligence. A primary difference between *Homo habilis* and the hominids whose existence overlapped theirs was brain size. The brain of *Homo habilis* was one-third larger than the brain of *Australopithecus afarensis*. Most importantly, the portion of the brain known as *Broca's area*, the region necessary for speech, was present in the skull of *Homo habilis* as well as in the skulls of all successive hominids. Experts agree that because of this, *Homo habilis* was necessarily neurologically capable of rudimentary speech. Greatly increased brain power and its associated abilities were crucial elements in the rise of intelligence and culture.

There are many aspects of intelligence and behavior that were not preserved in the fossil record. For example, there is no evidence that hominids had language, ideas, or beliefs until much later. Fossils of *Homo erectus* (who lived from 1.6 million years ago to .5 million years ago), the only known successor of *Homo habilis*, have been found in areas of Africa and Southeast Asia. This suggests that *Homo erectus* moved beyond Africa. There are many fossilized tools that date back to the time of *Homo erectus*. Fossilized ash layers and burnt bones discovered near remains of *Homo erectus* suggest that *Homo erectus* used fire similar to the way tools were used to make life easier. This discovery influenced ideas about the lifestyle of *Homo erectus*. It implies that they had the behavioral characteristic of living in groups, which suggests the tasks of hunting, gathering, and cooking food were shared.

The next human in the fossil record is *Homo sapiens* (who lived from 300,000 to 40,000 years ago). This hominid may represent a population of proto-Neanderthals that inhabited the northernmost fringes of the inhabited world. Tools had become more sophisticated, and included chipped-stone axe and spear heads. Fossils of Neanderthal *Homo sapiens* (who lived from 125,000 to 40,000 years ago), who are the contemporaries and eventual successors of the proto-Neanderthals, have been found in sites around Europe and the

Middle East. The similarities between modern humans and Neanderthals are ceremonial burial of the dead, use of fire and tools, and a larger brain, all of which indicate developing intelligence and culture. By about 30,000 years ago, modern *Homo sapiens* had spread to nearly all parts of the world. In addition to the physical and behavioral characteristics discussed above that connote intelligence and culture, modern *Homo sapiens* must have used language. Most anthropologists assume this ancestor must have had social organization from evidence that suggests group living as well as findings that show the use of symbolic representation. Cave paintings, simple musical instruments, and carvings are closely linked to language, as they utilize symbols to represent ideas and objects. Though there is no physical evidence, modern *Homo sapiens* must have had a spoken language. Physically, these people were just like people that live today.

Mission 5: Early Earth Cultures

The following descriptions illustrate further the early Earth cultures that are seen in the transparencies for this mission.

Mountain Habitat: South American Inca Culture

The Inca Empire extended 2,000 miles from Ecuador, through central Chile, from the desert coast of western South America to the high, rugged Andes Mountains. The civilizations that led up to the Inca Empire began about 3000 BCE. The Empire itself had a brief life (less than 100 years) ending in 1532 when the spaniard Pizarro killed the Inca leader Atahuallpa and imposed Spanish culture on the Incas. Inca civilization developed from a scattering of farming villages into regional states based on intensive agriculture and ruled by an emperor and strong armies. Agricultural practices consisted of hillside terraces on the sides of the steep mountains combined with the use of irrigation (bringing water to crops through ditches, canals, and aqueducts). Intensive agriculture increased food supplies, which provided food for a dense population (about 10 million people).

The Inca Empire was a complex society of different social classes and religious and political institutions with widespread trading and large armies. This stratified society was run very smoothly by priests, who were at the top of the social-class strata. Successively below the priests in the social order were the emperor (believed to be a descendant of the gods), the emperor's family, the army, and political officials. At the bottom of society were the peasants. Each social class was provided food from a different section of farmland; the higher the social class, the "closer" the section was to the gods. No family ever went without food. Milestones in Inca society included an extensive system of paved and maintained roads; stone fortresses and temples designed by skilled engineers; an abundance of metalwork with gold, platinum, copper, and bronze; as well as accomplished craftsmanship using weaving and cloth making. Physical requirements for human survival were found in or created from the local habitat.

Desert Habitat: African Egyptian Culture

The Nile River provided the ancient Egyptians with the riches of life on a yearly basis. The annual cycle of flooding, planting, and harvesting seasons was the inspiration for the Egyptian three-season calendar as well as the essence of Egyptian culture from 3000 BCE to 31 BCE. The yearly flooding of the Nile was used by farmers to irrigate food crops and to store water by damming it for later use. Egyptians were the first culture to make and use paper—papyrus reeds that grew along the banks of the Nile supplied the necessary fiber.

Egyptian society was divided into social classes. The highest class was the king, or Pharaoh. Egyptians believed that the Pharaoh *was* a god. Also in the upper level of society were government officials—tax collectors, and scribes, who were Egypt's writers. They learned and used hieroglyphics to keep records for the Pharaoh and to write official letters. Next in the social hierarchy were artisans and skilled workers. They included brick makers, who provided the materials for carpenters and builders to make homes for the upper classes. At the bottom of the social hierarchy were the workers under the Pharaoh, who built temples and pyramids out of stone. During the flood season, farmers also served the Pharaoh, by working on the pyramids. The pyramids were built with stone blocks. Each Pharaoh had his tomb built well in advance of his death.

Upper-class members of society spent a large part of their lives preparing for the afterlife. This aspect of Egyptian religion was very important. Egyptians believed life was truly wonderful and that the afterlife would be even better.

Egyptian culture lasted for nearly 3,000 years. In 31 CE, Mark Antony and Queen Cleopatra were defeated by Octavian and his Roman armies—Egypt became a Roman province.

Grassland Habitat: North American Plains Indian Culture

The Plains Indian tribes inhabited the grassland region of North America from about 2500 BCE to 1876 CE. For more than 1,000 years before the coming of Europeans the Plains tribes lived in semipermanent villages in the tall grass and short grass (steppe) regions. Plains Indian culture was distinguished by pottery making, burial mounds, semipermanent villages, and limited use of agriculture. Evidence of hunter/gatherer culture has also been associated with these tribes as well as an agriculture and trade-based economy as found in relics of later Plains culture (from about 600 CE to 1000 CE). Plains Indians of this later period lived in mud-covered lodges that were rectangular in shape. They used tools for gardening, such as digging sticks and hoes made from bison shoulder blades. Other tools included stone arrowheads. They stored extra food in underground pits and protected their villages with encircling ditches and stockades. Among all the Plains tribes throughout the centuries of their development, agricultural tasks were accomplished by the women and hunting responsibilities were performed by the men.

Spiritual visions and ceremonies were an important aspect of Plains Indian religion. Supernatural visions were sought by both men and women. Young adults would be sent off to isolated places in order to fast and await a vision, often in a dream of a spiritual guardian that would remain with a person, in spirit, throughout their life.

With the arrival of the white man in North America, horses were introduced into the Plains Indian culture. Plains tribes fought against the white man in efforts to save their lands and their way of life. Finally, in 1876, after hundreds of years of escalating warfare and decimation of the bison herds, the Battle of the Little Big Horn, between Col. George Custer and his armies and the Plains Indians, brought the dominance of the Plains Indian culture in North America to a sad end, leaving the remaining Indians to live on government-provided reservations and their primary food source (buffalo) destroyed.

Desert Habitat: Australian Aboriginal Culture

The Australian Aborigine culture inhabited the continent of Australia tens of thousands of years prior to the arrival of the white man. Aborigines were a nomadic, food-gathering people who lived in tribes consisting of several families that spoke a common language and participated in one another's ceremonies. Each tribe had a hunting territory the boundaries of which were outlined by naturally occurring features such as hills, rivers, creeks, or belts of vegetation. Between each tribal territory was a zone in which nobody was allowed to hunt, but families from the hunting grounds on either side could pass through. Boundaries were respected by all tribes, and no territorial expansion was attempted through efforts of peace or war. Aborigine tribes were friendly to one another, spoke similar languages, had similar tribal organization, and intermarried, but otherwise existed separately from one another. There were 91 different Aborigine tribes. Each tribe had a leader, usually the oldest father in the group. The leaders settled arguments, decided when to go to war, and passed laws that affected the people. Tribes traded with one another at gatherings called *corroborees*.

Work among the Aborigines was divided between the sexes. Men were hunters and protectors, and women were food gatherers and child bearers. Little is known about the religious life of the early Aborigines. They believed that the world as they knew it was created during their "dreamtime" by their ancestral spirits. These spirits were their guides and were said to be animals in form—kangaroos, emus, reptiles, and birds. Each spirit was the source of a different Aboriginal *totem*, a carved or painted emblem and reminder of the spirit guide. Each tribe had its own totem and believed that its members descended directly from that animal (a belief called *totemism*). Individuals never ate, hurt, or married someone of the same totem.

Death rites varied from tribe to tribe. Some tribes buried or cremated their dead; others disposed of bodies by putting them on a platform or in a tree, exposing them to the elements. There were instances of cannibalism in Aboriginal death rites—usually, they ate the dead as an act of mourning for a friend or loved one, or, in some instances, as a final act of contempt toward an enemy.

Rain Forest Habitat: African Pygmy Culture

The Ituri rain forest in the heart of Africa is the home of nomadic hunters called Pygmies. This lush habitat is where these wandering nomads find protection, food, water, clothing, and healing—everything they need to survive. Pygmies belong to a variety of different tribes, one of which is the Bambuti. The Bambuti Pygmy population is estimated to be 80,000 at present. Pygmies are a small people. An adult female reaches a height of about four feet. An adult male reaches a height between 4.5 and 5 feet.

Pygmy tribes consist of many clans. Each clan is made up of several groups. Groups have 20 to 30 people, which is enough to provide for themselves by hunting and gathering food. Each group sets up camp where they live for a few months before moving on. A group moves its camp because food resources become scarce or because of a dispute with another group or tribe. Pygmies are very independent in their actions. Families come and go from their group as they please. Pygmies live in harmony with their environment and other tribes in the area. They trade and participate in the ceremonies of other peoples. Work is divided between men and women. The women construct huts, tend the children, gather food, and cook. The men hunt. Pygmy religious beliefs center on the forest, thought of as their host and protector. A Pygmy's spiritual life is closely tied to real life. Each clan has a totem, a spirit guide embodied in the form of an animal or object. Folklore plays a significant part in Pygmy religion. Religion to the Pygmy is the spirits of the dead, the totems of each clan, as well as the spirit of the forest.

Mixed Forest Habitat: Early Asian Culture

The Khmer Empire existed from 500 CE to 1431 CE. It occupied the mixed forest region of present-day Cambodia and parts of Thailand, Laos, and Vietnam. The Funan was the earliest Khmer culture known to live beside the lower and middle Mekong River. The second known Khmer culture in this region was called the Chenla. Together they are called the Khmer. The best-known relic of early Khmer culture is Angkor Wat, a compound of buildings built in the seventh century. Angkor Wat was a large Buddhist sanctuary of sandstone temples and structures of extraordinarily beautiful and ornate architecture.

Khmer culture was influenced by Indian civilization in the areas of language and religion. Their primary religion was Sivaism; however, evidence of other religions, such as Buddhism, is notable throughout Khmer history. When someone died, there were several ways in which the Khmer disposed of the body. There was burial in water, earth, or by exposure to the elements and birds such as vultures. To mourn the loss of a loved one, the Khmer fasted for several days and shaved their heads.

The Khmer were a farming, hunting, and gathering society. Abundant resources attracted the Khmer to the locale where Angkor Wat was built. They lived in permanent villages consisting of raised huts made from bamboo with thatched-palm roofs. They used bamboo, palm trees, rushes, reeds, cotton, and silk (from silkworms) to make their tools and clothing. They raised rice in the monsoon-watered plains of Angkor Wat. They captured fish trapped in small lakes by flood waters during the monsoon season. Also available were a wide variety of tropical fruits. The roles of women and men are not completely recorded, but it is known that women held important roles in government.

The Khmer Empire fell in 1431 CE when the Siamese raided Angkor Wat and took over rule of the region.

Island Habitat: Ancient European Greek Culture

The Aegean Sea and the rugged mountains rising from its coastline helped define the ancient civilization of the Greeks. Greece was both a mainland (in Europe) and an island habitat, separated into regions by islands, bays, and inlets. Greek civilization consisted of many independent city-states that shared a common language and a common religion. By our standards, Greek culture was very advanced compared to other cultures existing at the same time (from 3000 BCE to 30 BCE). Unlike the nomadic tribes of the Pygmies and the Aborigines, the Greeks had a stable, farming lifestyle that enabled them to develop an alphabet, a democratic government, a religion not based on totemism, currency, and many cultural arts. Sports events were very important to the Greeks. They had a yearly competition called the Olympics (held in the city of Olympia), an event held to honor the god Zeus, who ruled over a pantheon of many gods.

Greeks, regardless of where they lived, worshipped Zeus and his family of gods. The Greeks believed that these gods controlled both the human world and the world of nature. Myths and legends of the Greeks explained the roles played by the gods in the creation of the world. Greeks made animal sacrifices to their gods in temples—each god had such a sanctuary—to thank them for answering prayers.

The Greeks of Athens, a city-state, developed a democratic government. The citizens of Athens enjoyed a pleasant life during their Golden Age. Greek society had much leisure time because the Greeks captured slaves from other places during war to do all the hard work for them. The use of slaves allowed the Greeks time to develop cultural arts, have debates about how to run Athens, and design and build exquisite buildings and temples in which to worship their gods. Boys attended school to learn how to read, write, and play musical instruments.

Wars occurred frequently throughout ancient Greek history. There was difficult span of time called the Dark Ages, which lasted from 1050 BCE to 750 BCE. The Dark Ages began when Greek civilization collapsed after a war with the Phoenicians in the eighth century BCE. Early Greek culture came back to life after the Dark Ages and did well for hundreds of years, until Greece was conquered by the Romans in 215 BCE. Ancient Greek culture had died out completely by 30 BCE.

Arctic Habitat: North American Eskimo Culture

Eskimo (Aleut) lived in the Arctic regions of North America. The Eskimo migrated over the land bridge that connected North America and Asia during the Ice Age (10,000 years ago). Eskimo lifestyle did not change until after the white man made contact with them in the seventeenth century. The northern habitat the Eskimo lived in was very harsh. The temperatures were (and still are) very cold most of the year. In winter, there was very little or no sunlight at all because the sun never rose above the horizon. The Eskimo led a nomadic lifestyle. They kept moving around in search of food. They lived in small groups that consisted of several families. During the winter months, they built *igloos*, shelters made from earth and stone. In summertime they lived in tents made with animal skins. The famous "ice" igloos were used as shelters by men when they were away on hunting expeditions. Either type of igloo made for warm shelter in the Arctic habitat. Eskimo ate a diet mostly of meat because the Arctic ground is too hard and too cold for most plants to grow. The very short growing season of summer provided berries in the fall. Eskimo hunted food on land and in the sea. They hunted for most of their food in summer and stored it for winter. They made sleds of wood and bone to travel across the ice. They also made boats of wood and bone with sealskin for hunting and transportation. Work was divided between men and women. Men were hunters and shelter builders. Women prepared food and made clothing from animal skins.

The Eskimo depended on animals for most of their needs. No part of an animal was wasted. Blubber from whales and other marine mammals was used as fuel for lamps, which were used for light, cooking, and even for heating. Bones from the animals they hunted were used to make tools, weapons, and boats. The religion of the Eskimo was based on folklore that explained the ways of nature and the world of the supernatural. Eskimo culture included totem worship as part of their religion. Some vestiges of Eskimo culture can still be seen today though the original complexity has been lost because of population decimation from European diseases.

Mission 8: Cultures Evolve on Planet Z

How probable is it that non-intelligent life will evolve into intelligent life that functions as a technological civilization? What are the contributing factors that decide if biologic evolution can result in an intelligent species *capable* of developing into a techno- logical society? These questions and others have been asked repeatedly by scientists over the past several decades. However, inadequacies in our knowledge of animal behavior and a lack of fossil evidence have prevented us from achieving a true understanding of evolution until quite recently. A breakthrough in our comprehension of animal behavior and a plethora of paleontological findings have changed the opinions of many scientists. The overall view now is that, given enough time, despite varied environmental circum- stances, cultural evolution is a natural consequence of biologic evolution.

Scientists hold a variety of opinions as to what aspects of evolutionary changes were responsible for the evolution of culture among humans. Overall, scientists believe that traits that have a positive survival value will tend to be produced by evolutionary pressures. Some of these traits include intelligence, complicated group interactions, and the ability to manipulate tools. To evolve a culture on Planet Z, it is useful to have a basic understanding about how culture evolved on Earth, which can be used as a model for Planet Z.

Human cultural evolution is often divided into "ages," such as the Bronze Age, Iron Age, and the Enlightenment. For the sake of simplicity, we have grouped important discoveries and skills into four general ages.

1. The first age lasted from the rise of early humans, about 3 million years ago, to the advent of agriculture, about 8500 BCE. These cultures consisted of loose, nomadic, hunter/gatherer societies that could make simple tools (tools not involving shaping or crafting materials) out of natural substances. They moved around the globe, hunted in cooperative groups, made artificial shelters, and learned to start fires (about 70,000 years ago). Signs of religion and art began to show up about 60,000 years ago in the traces of ritual burials in Europe and the Middle East. Cave paintings and sculpture appeared about 30,000 years ago. The first needle appeared about 19,000 years ago and, soon after that, pottery and the bow and arrow.

2. The second age moves from the beginning of a village-based agricultural system (about 8500 BCE) to the advent of city life (between 3500 BCE and 3000 BCE). These village dwellers lived in rich river valleys (of the Nile, the Tigris-Euphrates, the Indus, and the Huang He) with plentiful resources. They domesticated sheep and dogs, and raised corn, gourds, wheat, and barley. They invented the loom, the plow, sailboats, cold-hammered copper, simple pictographic writing, the wheel, and the waterwheel in the short span of time between 9000 BCE and 3000 BCE. Villages began to grow into cities between 3500 BCE and 1700 BCE.

3. The third age is marked by the smelting of bronze (about 3000 BCE) and the industrial revolution (about 1700 CE). City dwellers, supported by farmers and often slaves, had the leisure time to enrich their lives. Beautiful and complex works of art, huge structures (the pyramids, the Great Sphinx of Gizeh, and Stonehenge), religion, horseback riding, sailing, the smelting of iron, and the first complete alphabet (the Syrian alphabet) were some highlights of this age.

4. The fourth age progressed rapidly from the invention of steam power in 1698 to the electronic age of the 1990s: 1876, Bell's telephone; 1895, Marconi's wireless radio; 1919, the splitting of the atom; 1926, Baird's television; 1935, nylon; 1928, penicillin; 1948, the transistor; 1957, first satellite launched; 1961, first man in space; 1976, first microcomputer on a chip. Today, amazing types of technologies are available all over the world, including the ability to scan multiple radio signals in a search for signs of extraterrestrial intelligence.

Mission 9: Extraterrestrial Communication

SETI stands for the Search for Extraterrestrial Intelligence. The SETI *Academy* discussed in this book is fictional, except as it is embodied in classrooms around the country and around the world that choose to accept the SETI Institute's challenge to learn about the search for extraterrestrial intelligence. The SETI *Institute*, however, is real. Jill Tarter and all the other SETI scientists that are introduced through these instructional materials are actual working scientists. Tom Pierson is the executive director of the SETI Institute.

The SETI Institute is the home for projects related to the search for intelligent life beyond Earth. The Institute's goal is to further high-quality research into all the various fields related to factors influencing the existence, nature, and activities of life in the universe, including astronomy and the planetary sciences, chemical evolution of life, biologic evolution, and cultural evolution. The Institute also has a primary goal to conduct and promote public information and education related to the search for extraterrestrial intelligence.

The following is an excerpt from a 1977 NASA report entitled "The Search for Extraterrestrial Intelligence," edited by Philip Morrison and John Billingham.

The present climate of belief makes it timely to consider a search for extraterrestrial life, but is such a search feasible? It is certainly out of the question at our present level of technology or, indeed, at any level we can foresee, to mount an interstellar search by spaceship. On the other hand, we believe it is feasible to begin a search for signals radiated by other civilizations having technologies at least as advanced as ours. We can expect, with considerable confidence, that such signals will consist of electromagnetic waves; no other known particle approaches the photon in ease of generation, direction, and detection. It has long been argued that signals of extraterrestrial origins will most likely be detected in the so-called microwave window: wavelengths from about .5 to 30 cm. Natural noise sources rise to great height on either side of this window, making it the quietest part of the spectrum for everyone in the Galaxy.

Existing radio telescopes are capable of receiving signals from our interstellar neighbors, if of high power or if beamed at us by similar telescopes used as transmitters. The large antenna at Arecibo could detect its counterpart thousands of light years away. Indeed, it could detect transmissions from nearby stars less powerful but similar to our own television and radar. We propose a search for signals in the microwave part of the radio spectrum, but not at this time the sending of signals.

Mission 10: Decoding an Extraterrestrial Message

As of yet, no extraterrestrial messages have been intercepted, but the SETI team is looking for a microwave signal from an extraterrestrial civilization. The five-page message used in mission 10 was designed by Dr. Cary Sneider of the Lawrence Hall of Science. It tells a story in sequential pictures. The point is to see the image as a group of planets orbiting a star. Once this is seen, a story of migration because of impending destruction can be followed, and students should see where the message originates.

Page 261 begins sample discussions of the kinds of ideas that students frequently come up with.

Teacher: Let's look at the first picture. What do you think it means?

Team 1: It's an atom.

Team 2: We think it is the solar system.

Team 3: It can't be the solar system because its got just six planets. We think its where aliens live.

Team 2: Maybe they didn't know about the other planets. We still think it's the solar system.

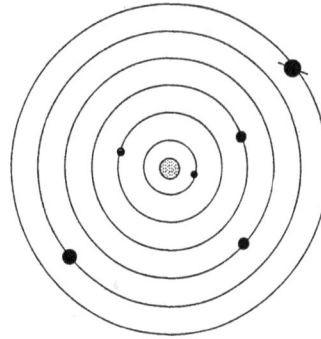

Teacher: Now look at the second picture. What do you think it means?

Team 2: We still think it's the solar system because the sixth planet has a ring, like Saturn. Maybe the triangle says they once went to Mars.

Team 3: Lots of planets have rings. We still think that's where they live—the aliens. We live on the third planet, and they're telling us that they live on the fourth planet in *their* system.

Team 4: Maybe they're telling us that they are intelligent, because they know what triangles are.

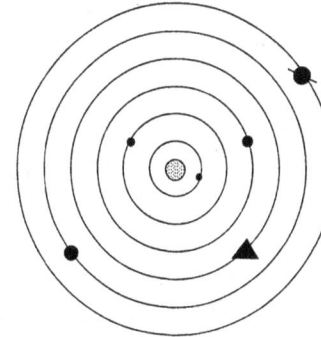

Teacher: What do you think the third picture means?

Team 2: We think they left something special on Mars, and they think people from the other planets will come and visit.

Team 5: No, it's probably just that they're trading with people on other planets in their solar system.

Team 6: Notice that two of the other planets have triangles. Maybe those two are habitable.

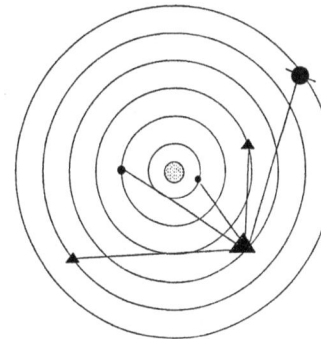

Teacher: How about the fourth picture?

Team 7: It's funny that there are no more lines. Maybe they don't travel between planets anymore. But there are still those other triangles.

Team 8: Colonies. Those two smaller triangles might mean that they have colonies on the other planets.

Team 2: If it is our solar system, then maybe they're saying they know there's life on Earth as well as Mars and Jupiter.

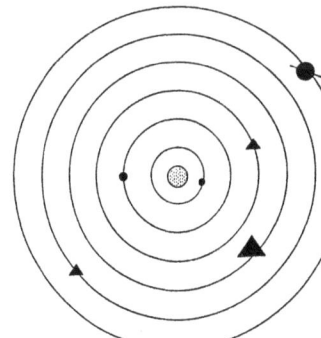

Teacher: What are your ideas about the last picture?

Team 9: We think it is a picture of a galaxy, but we can't figure out the rest of it.

Team 5: It must be our system of planets and theirs. See, the one at the top has nine planets and the one at the bottom has just six.

Team 7: Oh, yeah! In our system, the one next to Saturn is really big, like Jupiter.

Team 3: And in our system the third planet has a triangle—that's Earth!

Team 1: If it is our galaxy, maybe the lines show where we are and where they are. We're almost neighbors!

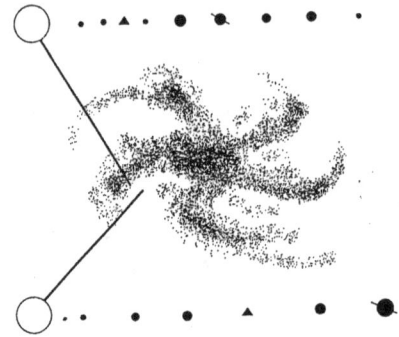

Mission 11: What Do We Say, and How Do We Say It?

The *Pioneer 10* (1971), *Pioneer 11* (1972), *Voyager 1* (1977), and *Voyager 2* (1977) spacecraft were launched bearing different modes of Earth communication. The primary mission of the probes was to study the outer planets. Since they will eventually leave our solar system and travel on to the stars, it is possible that somewhere, some distant, advanced, technological civilization might intercept one of them and thereby learn something about Earth as described and portrayed on the plaques and recordings on or in these spacecraft. Such engraved plaques can remain recognizable for perhaps billions of years.

The same message is on *Pioneer 10* and *Pioneer 11*. It was designed, created, and approved by NASA over a three-week period. This message was engraved on gold anodized, aluminum plates and attached to the two *Pioneer* spacecraft. The *Pioneer* message consists of several components that indicate various concepts. Most prominent is a representation of a naked man and a naked woman drawn to scale in front of a diagram of the spacecraft. Also included on the plate are a map that shows Earth's position in our solar system and a pulsar map, which could indicate to whoever retrieves the probe the length of time the spacecraft had been traveling and where it originated. The *Pioneer* messages were humankind's first attempt to communicate with other civilizations. Both *Pioneer 10* and *Pioneer 11* have propelled themselves beyond Pluto and are en route to interstellar space as intended.

The *Voyager* (1977) spacecraft were the next probes to travel through our solar system toward outer space, bearing a different type of message. This message was in the form of a 12-inch, copper phonograph record complete with a stylus and diagrammatic instructions on how to use it. The kinds of musical recordings included were quite varied, ranging from Bach's "Brandenberg Concerto" (no. 2) to Russian, Chinese, Japanese, African, and other types of music. In addition to music, there were recordings of greetings in many languages, sounds of the Earth, and pictures of people, animals, places, and things discovered or created on Earth. For a complete list of the information that was included in the *Voyager* recording, see "The Voyager Message" in mission 11 (page 218). The Drake Equation—$N = R_* \cdot f_p \cdot n_e \cdot f_l \cdot f_i \cdot f_c \cdot L$—estimates the number of civilizations that probably exist beyond our solar system that are technologically able and willing to communicate. As indicated in the paragraphs above, humankind has made two conscious attempts to send messages by probe to other worlds, in addition to all the years of radio and television waves that have been emanating from technological civilizations on Earth for more than 50 years. It is possible that, right now, other civilizations are sending electromagnetic waves into the cosmos as well. Such waves may be of such a low intensity that today's Earth technologies are not capable of detecting them.

Currently, the emphasis on making contact with extraterrestrial civilizations is limited to "listening" for electromagnetic signals that fall in the microwave range of frequencies with radio telescopes. There are, of course, possible misconceptions in assumptions made about the type of signal being sent and in being too anthropocentric. However, the microwave region is the most cost-effective place to begin efforts at listening to, or "eavesdropping" on, other worlds. For us, *transmitting* a signal would involve a host of costly problems. Primarily, we don't know where to send a transmission. Trying to send a probe would be a very ineffective method of attempting to communicate, as the nearest possible location is so far away that the travel time, given our current ability (probe speed), would take many human lifetimes and impractical amounts of fuel.

Mission 12: Detection: What Could Happen?

The question of how humans would respond if evidence of an extraterrestrial signal is detected is the main concept of this mission. Scientists affiliated with SETI, and behavioral scientists, have been exploring this question for a number of years. Although the available data is scant, the overall belief among North Americans is one of acceptance of the existence of extraterrestrial life-forms. Possible reactions have been sorted by behavioral scientists into the following categories:

Gender: Gender is a primary characteristic, which carries with it certain physical and social attributes that might influence human response to the detection of an extraterrestrial signal.

Religion: Church affiliation and worldview are characteristics influenced by an individual's religious affiliation or non-affiliation. In the United States, there are a multitude of different religions. An announcement about evidence of an extraterrestrial signal might be viewed as either supportive of or threatening to an individual's beliefs.

Race, Ethnicity, Place of Origin: People define themselves by social memberships such as these. There are many social groups within each culture, and most people belong to several different social groups. It is difficult to ascertain which group affiliation might most affect an individual's response to the detection of extraterrestrial signals.

Education: In societies with institutions of formal education, the level and quality of education vary greatly. These differences can result in additional variations in individual perceptions of new ideas and circumstances. Although the fastest response to an announcement of an extraterrestrial discovery would be made by the media, many schools and their supporting institutions would move quickly to bring information about the discovery into the classroom.

The discovery of an extraterrestrial civilization would ultimately become part of the knowledge base of the first generation of children to learn about it in schools. Overall, at a personal level for each individual, such a discovery would likely cause shifts in their philosophy of life.

Resources

Resources for SETI Academy Cadets

For SETI Academy cadets to develop an understanding of what it means to be a civilized, intelligent being who can send messages great distances, they will need to study traits and behaviors that they take for granted. Some resources that may be of help in their investigations appear below. No doubt, you will find other resources in your local libraries, stores, and media centers as you explore and as more resources become available.

Amato, Carol. *Astronomy*. New York: Smithmark, 1992.
A part of the Breakthroughs in Science series, this book provides a simple history of astronomy from the perspective of a variety of cultures from ancient times to the present. (An additional volume in the series, *The Earth*, is a history of geology from ancient times.)

Benton, Michael. *The Story of Life on Earth*. New York: Warwick Press, 1986.
Michael Benton's book traces the origins and development of life on Earth. It focuses on the use of evidence from ancient rocks to determine the age of Earth, how continents are moving, and what life-forms have existed. It also includes useful diagrams of the arrangement of the continents during key eras.

Branley, Franklyn M. *The Moon Seems to Change*. New York: HarperCollins, 1960.
An easy-to-understand, scientific explanation of the phases of the moon.

Burton, Virginia. *Life Story*. Boston: Houghton Mifflin, 1962.
Although this classic is often used with young children, its five-act-play format, with a prologue and an epilogue, introduces life in the Milky Way Galaxy in a smoothly told story. It can be used to support information in the SETI video image show (see *The Evolution of a Planetary System* and *How Might Life Evolve on Other Worlds?*), as a springboard for discussion of questions about the evolution of Earth and its life, as the basis for a student play, or just as enjoyable literature.

Cole, Joanna. *Evolution: The Story of How Life Developed on Earth*. New York: Harper & Row, 1987.
This book explains in simple language how fossils from rock layers are used to determine the age of living things. It provides clear examples of adaptations that allowed some living things to survive while others became extinct.

———. *Human Body: How We Evolved*. New York: Morrow, 1987.
This book, excellent for reading aloud, traces human development from primates to the present. It describes changes in teeth, eyes, brains, bone structure, and skin and the part they play in the development of human cultures. Joanna Cole leaves us to wonder about the future of physical and cultural evolution. A good springboard for discussion of these issues.

Darling, David. *Other Worlds: Is There Life Out There?* Minn.: Dillon Press, 1985.
One of the Discovering Our Universe series, this book explores the question that SETI Academy cadets will investigate: Is there life on other planets? The author answers common questions and describes the search for life on other planets in our solar system. He concludes by giving evidence that suggests the possibility of life in other stellar systems and the means by which we might detect it.

Dickinson, Terence. *The Universe and Beyond*. Charlotte, Vt.: Camden House, 1992.
    This book contains excellent artwork of cosmic objects and a well-written chapter about the search for extraterrestrial intelligence. Makes a good, visually stimulating springboard for discussion about astronomy.

Fraden, Dennis. *Astronomy*. Chicago: Children's Press, 1986.
    If students or teachers desire an historic overview of the highlights of astronomy, including what puzzles currently engage astronomers, this volume is excellent. Don't be put off by the "textbook" look of this volume. It is full of interesting facts and engaging questions.

Gallant, Roy. *How Life Began: Creation Versus Evolution*. New York: Four Winds Press, 1975.
    This noted author of science books for children has collected explanations from a number of cultures as they try to answer the questions, How did the world begin? and How did life arise? This is a one-stop source for an historical treatment of the connections between science, belief systems, cultural history, and literature. Explanations of myths from these cultures will help students understand their belief systems.

Gonick, Larry. *The Cartoon History of the Universe*. 7 vols. New York: Doubleday, 1990.
    A tongue-in-cheek cartoon history that appeals to the young adolescent mind, this paperback volume is filled with facts. This is the kind of book that gets lost in a desk because the borrower won't give it up.

Krupp, E. C. *Beyond the Blue Horizon: Myths and Legends of the Sun, Moons, Stars and Planets*. New York: Oxford University Press, 1991.
    An excellent source of legends to incorporate into literature activities.

Lasky, Kathryn. *Traces of Life*. New York: Morrow, 1989.
    This book begins with a 24-hour clock of the history of life that places the arrival of humans in the last 75 seconds. The author describes the work of real paleoanthropologists, such as Donald Johanson and Raymond Dart, and the thrill of making discoveries and piecing together the puzzle of what it means to be human. Very readable. Good career models are found here.

Leakey, Richard. *Human Origins*. New York: Dutton, 1982.
    From the fossils he and others have uncovered, Richard Leakey weaves together pieces of the story of 1 million years of human history.

Merriman, Nick. *Eyewitness Books—Early Humans*. New York: Knopf, 1989.
    Discover the world of the first people, from cave dwellers to men and women of the Iron Age.

Minelli, Giuseppe. *The Evolution of Life*. New York: Facts on File, 1986.
    Another picturesque history of the formation of our planetary system and the development of life on Earth.

Peters, David. *From the Beginning: The Story of Human Evolution*. New York: Morrow Junior Books, 1991.
    This guide to evolution uses a few well chosen animals, both living and extinct, to show the many characteristics we all have in common and bring home the idea that we

are not only related to one another, but also to a common past. The writing and pictures display a sense of involvement and fun that appeals to young readers while it engages them in a complex idea.

Rand McNally, ed. *Children's Atlas of Earth Through Time*. Chicago: Rand McNally, 1990.
This is a fine resource book for upper-elementary students. It clearly describes the formation of the universe starting with the "Big Bang" and including the development of the Milky Way Galaxy and our solar system. It goes on to outline the evolution of Earth and its life through geologic eras and periods using specific life-forms as examples.

————. *Children's Atlas of the Universe*. Chicago: Rand McNally, 1990.
This atlas provides comprehensive descriptions of what is known about the universe at an upper-elementary reading level. It begins with descriptions of Earth's rocky crust, atmosphere, and life, and moves on through descriptions of Earth's moon and all the planets and other known objects in the universe.

Sattler, Helen. *Hominids: A Look Back at Our Ancestors*. New York: Morrow, 1988.
This book, loaded with pictures, artifacts, and maps, discusses how hominid ancestors may have lived, according to evidence gathered from fossil remains.

Saville, David. *The Evolution of the World*. Winnipeg, Manitoba: Hyperion Books, 1991.
In 12 pages of text and revolving pictures, children can experience the major events in Earth's evolutionary history.

Schwartz, David. *How Much Is a Million?* New York: Lothrop, Lee & Shepard, 1985.
The immense dimensions of our solar system and the universe pose a real problem for students to imagine. This book, combined with a number of "millions" activities from mathematics sources, will help students visualize these large numbers.

Thackray, John. *The Age of the Earth*. New York: Cambridge University Press, 1986.
A good resource for grades 5-6 about geologic time and the evolution of Earth.

Williams, Brian, and Brenda Williams. *The Random House Book of 1001 Questions and Answers About Planet Earth*. New York: Random House, 1990.
A good resource for grades 5-6 about Earth's astronomical, geologic, and cultural history.

Teacher Resources

Books and Articles

Gallant, Roy. *Before the Sun Dies: The Story of Evolution*. New York: Macmillan, 1989.
Although this is considered a children's book, it is a complete, well-written volume on the evolution of our solar system, Earth, and life. It concludes with speculation about the possible evolution of life elsewhere as well as the prospects for, and impediments to, finding it.

Garrett, Wilbur. "Where Did We Come From?" *National Geographic*, October 1988, 434-35.
As an introduction to the issue's focus, this two-page article tells how members of a variety of cultures would have answered the title question. "The Peopling of the Earth," and other articles that follow, include maps of excavation sites and human migration patterns, extensive photographs of fossils and artifacts, carvings from the Ice Age, and cave paintings from Lascaux. The quality of the lead article is superb.

Goldsmith, Donald, and Tobias Owen. *The Search for Life in the Universe.* Reading, Mass.: Addison-Wesley, 1980.

This is a complete reference explaining many of the scientific concepts that make a search for extraterrestrial life plausible. This is the adult version upon which the missions of the *SETI Academy Planet Project* are based.

Leakey, Richard, and Alan Walker. "Homo Erectus Unearthed." *National Geographic*, November 1985, 624-29.

The discovery of a shattered skull led Richard Leakey and his partner Kamoya to the skeletal remains of a 12-year-old boy. Students might be interested in reading about this find of a young *Homo erectus* with a remarkably modern skeleton.

McDonough, Thomas. *The Search for Extraterrestrial Intelligence: Listening for Life in the Cosmos.* New York: John Wiley, 1987.

Thomas McDonough has written a history of the search for extraterrestrial beings, including the hoaxes, the connections with science fiction, the many discoveries, and the people that have made the search a reality. The book is written in a humorous and accessible style.

Sobel, Dava. "Is Anybody Out There?" *Life*, September 1992, 60-64.

This *Life* magazine article begins with a quote by Jill Tarter's eight-year-old daughter that sets into perspective what her mother and other SETI scientists do every day and why they do it. Nice graphics and pictures of Jill Tarter and Frank Drake. Following the article is a one-page opinion by Arthur C. Clarke entitled "Why Is It Important?" that discusses the human need to know if we are really alone.

Weaver, Kenneth. "The Search for Our Ancestors." *National Geographic*, November 1985, 560-623.

Besides the excellent photographs and drawings, there are three fold-out pages of hominid skeletons, skulls, and full-body reconstructions. The skulls would provide a good context for mission 4, "Cranial Changes."

Resource Centers

SETI teacher resource guides, posters, and videos will be available from the following sources, as they are produced. For information write to:

SETI Institute
2035 Landings Drive
Mountain View, CA 94043

For additional NASA teacher materials, including available videos and information about educational programs, contact the following or the NASA Teacher Resource Center nearest you:

Ames Research Center
Mail Stop T025
Moffett Field, CA 94035
(415) 604-3574

Jet Propulsion Laboratory, through its Public Education Office, sponsors educator conferences and provides materials on planetary missions. To be added to their mailing list, write to:

Richard Alvidrez, Manager
Public Education Office
Jet Propulsion Laboratory
4800 Oak Grove Drive
Pasadena, CA 91109-8099

The Astronomical Society of the Pacific produces an excellent, free, quarterly newsletter for teachers of students grades 3-12 that supplies clear, nontechnical articles on developments in astronomy, practical lessons for the classroom, and lists of books and audiovisual resources. To be added to their mailing list, write to:

Astronomical Society of the Pacific
Teachers' Newsletter, Dept. N
390 Ashton Avenue
San Francisco, CA 94112

Films, Videos, Laser Discs, and Computer Software

The following is a short list of the types of audiovisual materials that can support this book. Consult local audiovisual sources or the NASA Teacher Resource Center in your area for others.

Mysteries of Mankind. Gary Steer/Sley Visuals Pty, Ltd. 60 min., Stamford, Conn.: Vestron Video, 1988. Videocassette.
This video for grades 6-12 shows how footprints, stone tools, and fossilized skeletons dated 1 million years or more are used by scientific artists to construct possible models of early humans. Long, but excellent. Show only portions of the video or show it in segments.

Powers of Ten. Charles and Ray Eames/Pyramid, 8 min. Santa Monica, Calif.: Pyramid, 1989. Videocassette.
From a picnic on the ground to the outer reaches of space by "Powers of Ten," this video for grades K-12 graphically supports the large numbers involved in solar sizes and distances.

Reading Rainbow. "Space Case." Lancit Media Productions, 30 min. Lincoln, Nebr.: The Library, 1985. Videocassette.
Beyond enticing students in grades K-6 to read, this series uses field trips to put the featured book into context. On this program, the field trips are to the Lick Observatory and to the site of a radio telescope at Arecibo, Puerto Rico. In addition, LeVar Burton dedicates the show to all aliens who might be listening as he shows pictures of the geology and intelligent beings found on Earth. In *The Rise of Intelligence and Culture*, use this program to clarify how SETI scientists are using their radio telescope to detect possible signals from other civilizations. Students might enjoy debating how effective LeVar Burton's message might be and how they might change it. Call 800-952-8819 for more information.

Black-Line Masters

The following pages contain black-line masters that can be reproduced for overhead projection.

www.ingramcontent.com/pod-product-compliance
Lightning Source LLC
Chambersburg PA
CBHW080811280326
41926CB00091B/4200